ROBERT LOUIS STEVENSON AND THE COLONIAL IMAGINATION

To Frieda Manes and The Writing Group

Robert Louis Stevenson and the Colonial Imagination

ANN C. COLLEY

ASHGATE

Published by
Ashgate Publishing Limited
Gower House
Croft Road
Aldershot
Hampshire GU11 3HR
England

Ashgate Publishing Company
Suite 420
101 Cherry Street
Burlington, VT 05401-4405
USA

Ashgate website: http//www.ashgate.com

British Library Cataloguing in Publication Data
Colley, Ann C.
    Robert Louis Stevenson and the colonial imagination
    1.Stevenson, Robert Louis, 1850-1894 - Criticism and interpretation 2.Stevenson, Robert Louis, 1850-1894 - Political and social views 3.Stevenson, Robert Louis, 1850-1894 - Knowledge - Oceania 4.Missionaries in literature 5.Imperialism in literature 6.Colonies in literature 7.Oceania - In literature
    I.Title
    828.8'09

Library of Congress Cataloguing in Publication Data
Colley, Ann C.
    Robert Louis Stevenson and the colonial imagination / Ann C. Colley.
      p. cm.
    Includes bibliographical references and index.
    ISBN 0-7546-3506-6 (alk. paper)
    1. Stevenson, Robert Louis, 1850-1894--Criticism and interpretation. 2. Stevenson, Robert Louis, 1850-1894--Political and social views. 3. Stevenson, Robert Louis, 1850-1894--Knowledge--Oceania. 4. Missionaries in literature. 5. Imperialism in literature. 6. Oceania--In literature. 7. Colonies in literature. I. Title.

PR5497.R63 2004
828'.809--dc22   2003025575

ISBN 0 7546 3506 6

Printed and bound in Great Britain by TJ International Ltd, Padstow, Cornwall

Contents

List of Illustrations   vii
Acknowledgements   ix

Introduction   1

1   Stevenson and the South Sea Missionaries   11

2   Stevenson's Pyjamas   49

3   Colonies of Memory   73

4   Lighting Up the Darkness   99

5   Stevenson's Political Imagination   135

6   The Juvenile Missionary Magazines and *A Child's Garden of Verses*   179

Bibliography   203
Index   211

List of Illustrations

i   Introduction. 'Polynesia Shewing Mission Fields, 1885'   x

1.1   'Map of New Guinea.' Rev. James Chalmers. *Pioneer Life and Work
        in New Guinea* (London: Religious Tract Society, 1895), 18   16

1.2   'Apia Sunday School, 1893.' LMS Archives: Photograph.
        [Central figure is Mr. Chambers, the USA Commissioner in Apia;
        the missionary is Miss A. E. Large]. Reproduced from London
        Missionary Society/Council for World Mission Archives   27

1.3   'Natives and Author at Murua, New Guinea.' Photograph, from
        Rev. George Brown. *An Autobiography* (London: Hodder, 1908)   32

2.1   'Barefooted Stevenson wearing a *lava-lava*. Fanny is seated next to him,'
        1888. Photograph. Courtesy of the Writers' Museum, Edinburgh   56

2.2   Robert Louis Stevenson. Self-portrait on board the yacht *Casco*,
        presented to his old nurse 'Cummy' on her birthday in the year 1892.
        Oil. Beinecke Rare Book and Manuscript Library, Yale University   57

2.3   Photograph of Vailima Staff. Courtesy of the Writers' Museum,
        Edinburgh   59

2.4   Isobel Strong. 'Samoan, White, Half-Caste.' Beinecke Rare Book and
        Manuscript Library, Yale University   61

2.5   'Talolo Vailima.' Photograph. Beinecke Rare Book and Manuscript
        Library, Yale University   63

2.6   Lloyd Osbourne as Marquesan Warrior, 1888. Photograph. Courtesy of
        the Writers' Museum, Edinburgh   65

2.7   Lloyd Osbourne as Marquesan Warrior, 1888. Photograph. Courtesy of
        the Writers' Museum, Edinburgh   66

2.8   'Herman Swank.' Photograph, from Walter E. Traprock [George Shepard
        Chappell], *The Cruise of the Kawa: Wanderings in the South Seas*
        (New York: G. P. Putnam's Sons, 1921), facing 52.   67

3.1   'The Museum of the London Missionary Society.' Illustration from
        Illustrated London News (25 June 1859)   79

3.2   Henry Anelay, 'The Reverend John Williams on Board Ship with
        Native Implements, in the South Sea Islands.' Watercolor. Rex Nan
        Kivell Collection NK 187. By permission National Library of Australia   83

3.3   'Ferrante Imperato's Cabinet of Curiosities. Naples, 1599.' Illustration
       from Oliver Impey and Arthur MacGregor eds. *The Origins of Museums,*
       the Cabinet of Curiosities in Sixteenth- and Seventeenth-Century Europe
       (Oxford: Clarendon Press, 1987). Plate 4. Reprinted by permission of
       Oxford University Press   85

3.4   Wallis McKay, 'Niga and His Creed.' Illustration from Charles
       Warren Stoddard. *Summer Cruising in the South Seas* (London: Chatto
       and Windus, 1881), frontispiece   86

4.1   'Vaipuhiahi from the Harbour.' Pencil Sketch by Robert Louis Stevenson.
       Courtesy of the Huntington Library, San Marino, California   108

4.2   'Great Dance in Apemama Speak House.' Photograph. Courtesy of the
       Writers' Museum, Edinburgh   113

4.3   'Mrs. Stevenson Being Carried Ashore — Apiang.' Photograph
       . Courtesy of the Writers' Museum, Edinburgh   119

4.4   'Joe Strong Taking out his False Teeth.' Photograph. Courtesy of the
       Writers' Museum, Edinburgh   120

4.5   'Samoan Playing Cricket.' Photograph. Courtesy of the Writers' Museum,
       Edinburgh   120

4.6   'Headquarters of Wightman Bros. — Butaritari.' Photograph. Courtesy
       of the Writers' Museum, Edinburgh   121

4.7   '"Equator Town" by Moonlight.' Photograph. Courtesy of the Writers'
       Museum, Edinburgh   121

4.8   'Fanny, Stevenson, Nan Tok, and Nei Takauti. Butaritari, 1889.'
       Photograph. Courtesy of the Writers' Museum, Edinburgh   122

4.9   'Two Dancing Girls from Little Makin — Gilbert Islands.' Photograph.
       Courtesy of the Writers' Museum, Edinburgh   125

4.10   Isobel Strong. 'Drawing of Margaret Stevenson's Room at Vailima
       [showing camera].' Drawing. Courtesy of the Writers' Museum,
       Edinburgh   128

Acknowledgements

I should like to thank the library staff of the Beinecke Rare Book and Manuscript Library, Yale University, the Huntington Library in San Marino, California, the Yale Divinity School Library, the British Library, the National Library of Scotland, and the Royal Geographical Society in London. I am grateful for the kind attention given to me by the librarians in charge of the London Missionary Society Archives at the School of Oriental and African Studies, University of London. I am also indebted to Jack Judson of the Magic Lantern Castle Museum who made his extensive collection of books, magic lantern slides, and equipment available to me and to Barbara Lawson, Curator of the Redpath Museum at McGill University, who showed me the missionary collection. I am especially appreciative of the time Elaine Greig, Curator of the Writers' Museum, Edinburgh, spent when she patiently and happily went through the Stevensons' scrapbooks with me and talked about the photographs. Her prompt and encouraging remarks continue to be helpful. I am also thankful for Grant Skennerton's Help.

In order to travel and spend time at these libraries I was sponsored by grants from the United University Professions (UUP) and from the State University of New York (SUNY) Research Foundation. Through the support of the Research Foundation's Interim Director, Ted Turkle, I was able to spend my sabbatical in Britain where I did much of my research. An additional grant from the American Philosophical Society (APS) allowed me to extend my sabbatical months in London. I also wish to thank Marjorie L. Lord, the Inter-library loan librarian at Buffalo State College, as well as Kaylene Waite and Stephen S. Mangione of Instructional Resources at the College.

As the book progressed I was fortunate to share my work with Carrie Tirado Bramen, Rosemary G. Feal, Regina Grol, Carolyn W. Korsmeyer, and Claire Kahane, all members of the Writing Group. I also benefited from sensitive readings given by John Maynard and Jenni Calder, both of whom helped me see beyond the boundaries of my understanding. I am grateful to Richard Dury and Richard Ambrosini who organized the First Biennial Stevenson Conference in Gargnano, Italy where they brought together a community of people interested in Stevenson studies, all of whom, in various ways, contributed to my work and offered encouragement. Finally I should like to thank Irving J. Massey for his meticulous reading of the text. His is a voice that is never far away.

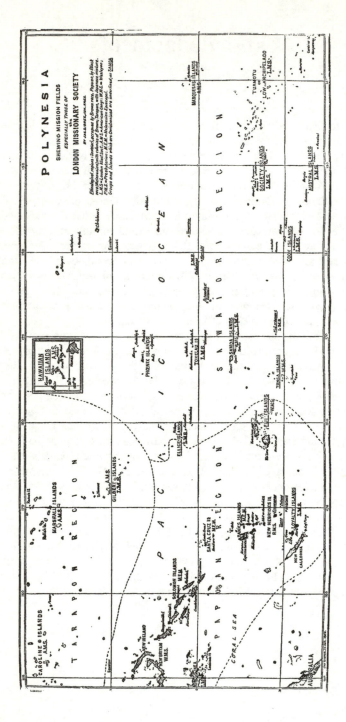

'Polynesia, Shewing Mission Fields, 1885.'

Introduction

Adventures in the Archives

A strike at the British Library in 1999 radically altered the direction of this book. I had embarked on what I thought was to be a study of Robert Louis Stevenson and nineteenth-century anthropological thought when, one morning, I found my entrance to the reading rooms blocked by picketers. Polite notices announced that the British Library was to be closed until further notice. For several days I called the library hotline or walked along the noisy Euston Road with the vague hope that my anxiety would resolve the dispute.

As the days went by and the picket line grew, I decided an interim solution to my problem was to investigate a place I had originally planned to visit only at the end of my stay, believing it to be of marginal interest: the Archives of the London Missionary Society (LMS) at the School of Oriental and African Studies (SOAS). Once there I never left. Indeed, when the British Library strike was settled a few weeks later, I paid little attention, for after I had started sifting through the diaries, letters, publications, and miscellany of the missionaries who were in the South Seas during the time Stevenson was there, I soon realized that here was a context that was as yet not fully explored. These materials were really more germane to an understanding of Stevenson's life and work in the Pacific than were the books by armchair anthropologists reposing in the British Library. By discovering his indebtedness to the missionary world, I gained a fuller sense of Stevenson's struggles with personal and cultural identity. Here was a new and important approach to Stevenson's work.

In London, when I did choose to break away from the LMS archives, I moved temporarily to places like the photographic archives of the Royal Geographical Society where, in the basement, I searched through dusty files; I also climbed stairs leading to the remains of the library in what was once the Museum of Mankind, and into attics of magic lantern collectors to look at nineteenth-century slide images of the South Seas. In addition, I spent time in Edinburgh at the Writers' Museum and at the National Library of Scotland. Back in the United States, I continued my exploration not only in standard venues like the Huntington Library, the Beinecke Rare Book and Manuscript Room, and the Yale Divinity School Library but also at the Magic Lantern Castle Museum in Texas. This museum (complete with drawbridge) was converted from a nightclub that lay next to a busy highway. Inside the museum, the owner has constructed a luxury windowless apartment for researchers where, for fear of losing his collection, he locks one in for the night and then departs, securing after him an electronic metal fence. Imagine my apprehension when, in the middle of the night, I noticed the alarm system spelling out a message, MOTION IN OUTER OFFICE. I never discovered what was moving.

The Significance of the Missionary Culture

These various archival adventures allowed me to assemble scattered information so that I could begin to grasp the nature and the relevance of the missionary culture that surrounded Stevenson during the last six years of his life (1888-1894). My research uncovered hitherto unscouted routes by which to explore Stevenson's experiences while he was a traveler, cruising among the islands, and then while he was a resident colonial in Samoa. I soon realized the importance of his occasionally critical and difficult interactions with his missionary friends, who were also ethnologists, explorers, historians, politicians, and linguists. For Stevenson, these dialogues opened up ways of discerning his milieu; and for me, they illuminated his reactions to the complexities of the island cultures as well as to the tensions inherent within colonial rule.

The missionary culture of the South Seas provides a framework by which to consider what, for Stevenson, constitutes the nature of remembrance, alienation, images, language, and power. It allows one to ponder such seemingly disparate matters as the practice of collecting curios and the vagaries of an individual's memory. It also permits one to investigate, in detail, the intensity of Stevenson's political involvement in the South Seas. The context also adds to our view of the generous reach of Stevenson's imagination. The book opens with images of the South Seas available to Stevenson in his childhood and closes with his recollections of childhood in *A Child's Garden of Verses*. The way he deals with each reveals a mind that could exceed the boundaries and demands of the colonial pattern and burst through its limits to take another's part and to join the larger community of humanity.

Stevenson in the South Seas

When Stevenson first entered the Pacific in 1888, he had not come directly from Scotland, but indirectly via Bournemouth (England), Saranac Lake (New York), and San Francisco. 1887 was the year of his second trip to the American continent, and this time he had arrived a celebrity. The success of *Treasure Island* (1883), *Kidnapped* (1886), and *Strange Case of Dr. Jekyll and Mr. Hyde* (1886) had won him the public's eager attention and had added to his reputation as a travel writer (*An Inland Voyage, Travels with a Donkey in the Cévennes*, and *The Silverado Squatters*) and an essayist (*Virginbus Puerisque, Familiar Studies, Memories and Portraits*). He had left behind the rains and chills of Bournemouth and traveled across the Atlantic to the dry, cold air of the Adirondack Mountains. In coming to

Saranac Lake, famous for its sanitaria, he hoped to find a place that would provide a palliative to his chronic ill health and prevent the hemorrhages that periodically bound him motionless to a bed.

While at Saranac Lake Stevenson received an invitation from Samuel S. McClure to write a series of travel articles on the South Seas for a syndicate of newspapers. The request was too tempting to ignore, especially since Stevenson and his wife Fanny[1] had been thinking for a while about a trip through the Pacific islands. In a way, McClure's commission was a dream come true, for as a young lad, Stevenson had indulged in reveries about the islands and had written the first installment of an adventure story set in the South Seas. Also, he loved the sea (he had sailed in the rough northern waters with his father on inspection tours of the lighthouses engineered by the Stevenson family), and believed its air good for his health. A few months later, on 28 June 1888, after poring over A. G. Findlay's *Directory for the Navigation of the South Pacific Ocean* and musing over visions of cascading tropical streams, Stevenson, with Fanny, his stepson Lloyd Osbourne, and his mother, Margaret Stevenson, sailed from San Francisco out into the Pacific. For the next six months, on board the yacht *Casco*, they visited the Marquesas, navigated past the valley described by Herman Melville in *Typee*, spent time in Fakarava, and went on to Tahiti where it was discovered that the mainmast of the *Casco* was dangerously weakened by dry-rot. Stevenson fell seriously ill, so Fanny moved him from Papeete Bay to the less populated Tautira, where they stayed for almost two months. When the boat was repaired, they sailed from Tautira on Christmas Day and arrived in Honolulu in January, 1889.

Much taken with the pleasures, the novelty, the excitement, as well as the dangers, of cruising, Stevenson planned another journey, this time on the yacht *Equator*. On board were Stevenson, his wife, his stepson, and Joe Strong (the husband of his stepdaughter Belle). Stevenson's mother had returned to Scotland to spend time with an ailing sister. For several months, from June to December, 1889, they sailed through the Gilbert Islands, spent time in Butaritari and Apemama, and eventually reached the Samoan Islands. It was while they were in Samoa that Stevenson first considered remaining in the South Seas and settling on the island of Upolu. Stevenson was gradually coming to realize that if he were going to survive, he would have to remain where the climate was the least harmful to his damaged lungs. Although he periodically thought about visiting Britain, he was never able to leave the South Seas. Sickness, family responsibilities, and eventually a lack of will intervened and thwarted his intentions. Before making this permanent move, however, Stevenson, who had fallen ill and needed to get out of Sydney, decided to take a third voyage to help him recover. As a result, on 11 April 1890 he with Fanny and Lloyd boarded the steamer the *Janet Nicoll*. During this voyage he revisited some of the islands he had seen on previous trips and continued north into the Marshall Islands; he then turned south, passed by the New Hebrides, and disembarked at the French colony of New Caledonia. The ship also briefly visited Noumea.

Throughout these travels he met beachcombers, traders, plantation owners, islanders, slaves, chiefs, missionaries, naval officers, and colonial officials, all of whom, from their own perspectives, introduced him to island life and forced him to realize that he had stepped out of a familiar context and entered territories for which he had no ready overarching or facile metaphor. His commentary appearing in McClure's newspapers reveals his assiduous notetaking and illustrates his attempts to make sense of what he was seeing. When he was to combine these articles with his journal notes to assemble his semi-anthropological study of the region, *In the South Seas*, he left behind a record of a person who was dedicated to his task, yet struggling to come to grips with his encounters and to render them as truthfully and as completely as possible. After Stevenson had built his home, Vailima, near Apia, the main port on the Samoan island of Upolu, and had become a resident, he continued to study Pacific culture. He also became entangled in the intricacies of colonial politics — a natural development, since he was living near Apia, which had the largest population of whites and was the location not only for the headquarters of the London Missionary Society, agents of foreign and political interests, but also for the offices of the three competing colonial powers: Germany, Britain, and the United States.

These experiences, obviously, could not help but affect the course of his fiction. He continued to write extensively, often romantically and lovingly about Scotland, and to revisit its highlands and lowlands through his work on *Catriona* (*David Balfour*), *The Master of Ballantrae*, and *Weir of Hermiston*. But Stevenson also launched upon what has now come to be known as his South Seas or Pacific fiction. In these texts he took as his subject the white man's presence in the Pacific and depicted, as forthrightly as he was able, the encounters between colonials and islanders and the ensuing frictions among the various groups populating the beach. These texts plus his study of Samoa's contentious and difficult past (*A Footnote to History*, 1892) reveal just how schooled he was by these disturbing realities. Consequently, as many have documented, Stevenson periodically broke away from the glorified narratives of boys' adventure stories and the pervasive imperial myth of Robinson Crusoe, to write ballads based upon Samoan legends and to compose tales, fables, and short novels that drew upon his immediate experiences as a colonial. He laid bare the contradictions, the ambiguities, and the complications (as well as the humor) attending the overlapping of cultures and the imposing of one assumption upon another. The missionaries played a major role in this drama.

Stevenson and Empire

When Stevenson sailed through the islands and finally landed in Upolu, he arrived, whether he intended to or not, as a representative of the British Empire, and, therefore, as a person of consequence. Like a visiting foreign dignitary, he was constantly courted by chiefs or officials and offered special privileges: in Hawaii, he dined with royalty, and in Apemama, he lived in accommodations especially constructed for him by the High Chief Tembinoka. Such was the aura of importance given to him as a distinguished British subject that once, for all too brief a moment, several natives, including the King, in Butaritari believed he was Queen Victoria's son or intimate personal friend, an error of which Stevenson took a winking advantage so that he and his household might be spared the intrusion of riotous, drunken islanders.[2]

Stevenson had, in a sense, merely joined the large number of Scots who already lived in the South Seas and had cast their lot with Empire. Scottish financiers, engineers, missionaries, shipbuilders, ironsmelters, and explorers had spread throughout India, Africa, and into the Pacific.[3] As a result, when Stevenson traveled around the South Sea islands, he frequently conversed with people from home: with Mr. Robert Stewart, a Fifeshire man trading in the Marquesas; with Mr. McCallum, of Hiva-oa, who still carried his Burns with him; with Duncan Cameron, an old dissenting Highlander, long settled in Tahiti, 'but still breathing of the heather of Tiree' (*In the South Seas* 131); and with Dr. Samuel Davies, a LMS missionary, who had studied medicine in Edinburgh and with whom Stevenson had 'an age-long talk about Edinburgh folk' (*Letters* 7: 45).

Scotland and Empire were both available through these reminders of home, but, paradoxically, Scotland was even more valuable as a point of reference that helped him understand his new surroundings. As Julia Reid and others have remarked, Stevenson often relied on his Scottish past to gain access to the South Seas. Scotland offered parallels by which, for instance, he could better understand the structure of island society (through its clan system) and its political dilemmas.[4] Scotland had, after all, been a victim of English policies as some areas of the South Seas had been subjected to foreign rule. Furthermore, Stevenson recognized a similarity between the 'savage' South Sea islanders and the 'barbaric' Highlanders exploited and harmed by fellow Scots (lowlanders) who, as Jenni Calder points out, 'regarded them as primitive savages speaking a barbaric language' and 'holding back the progress of civilsation'. That circumstance placed Stevenson in the odd position of thinking of himself both as a victim and as an intrusive colonial. Calder explains: 'Stevenson as a Lowlander is, vis-à-vis the Highlands, an "intrusive colonial", but as a Scot is a victim of English cultural imperialism.'[5] Such an ambiguous situation is probably responsible for many of the tensions and incongruities one runs across when considering his reactions to his new surroundings.

Wherever Stevenson traveled, he could not avoid reminders of the British Empire and of his own place in it. Portraits of Queen Victoria pasted inside islanders' dwellings, and photographs of her affixed to saloon walls, to the forecabin in the *Casco*, or projected through magic lantern slides onto a dark island night were rarely far from view. The monarch was a person, as Margaret Stevenson remarked, with whom most islanders were familiar, and who, when they saw her image, cried out, 'Victoreea!' (Balfour 95-96).[6] When Stevenson moved to Samoa (and displayed a British flag from the roof of Vailima), he drew yet closer to the powerful symbols of Empire. He was constantly in sight of the British trading vessels and warships that populated the port of Apia. Officers from these men-of-war visited the Stevensons, frequently supplied medical advice, and arranged entertainments, even circuses, for the whites and for the islanders. Moreover, Stevenson rubbed shoulders and exchanged words, sometimes angry ones, with British officials who represented the Crown. And, of course, he maintained close contact with the LMS missionaries who, in spite of their growing autonomy, were, in their own way, still agents of Empire. When one of Stevenson's missionary friends lectured before the Royal Geographical Society, he described his native preachers in New Guinea as 'true Britons to the backbone', who 'swear by Queen Victoria and her officers.' The Reverend James Chalmers added, 'often have I seen uncouth savages listen with staring eyes and open mouth when "Victoria's" greatness and goodness have been told' (195).

The question that all this raises is to what degree Stevenson was really 'Victoria's son' (no matter how convincing he appeared to be in Butaritari!). Recently critics have wanted to release him from such a parentage and have emphasized his antagonism to imperialist doctrines and to colonial intervention.[7] Indeed, as several chapters in this books will discuss, Stevenson did rebel against certain elements of imperialistic ideology, wrote stories that undermined the ethos of colonial intervention, questioned various notions of racial superiority, despised the common ignorance that regarded races 'in a lump' (*In the South Seas* 60), and was quite willing to consider the behavior of his own culture as being more barbaric than what he encountered during his travels. However, much as he rebelled, Stevenson seems still, in some respects, to be Victoria's son. Looking closely at Stevenson's reactions to the missionary culture and the Samoan political environment, one has to recognize, or, perhaps, reluctantly admit to oneself, that there are significant moments when he supports the colonial imperative and values its presence, indeed finds solace in it as well as hope for an island's future. One would rather stay with the last scenes of Stevenson's life when he openly opposed or resisted the ruling foreign interests by defending Mataafa, the deposed Chief, and helped his warriors who had been thrown in jail by bringing food and negotiating their release. However, it would not be honest to confine oneself to such examples.

Stevenson and Particularity

The value of engaging the later part of Stevenson's biography is that it forces the careful reader to struggle with the tensions of actually living within the site of Empire and, therefore, to deal with its contradictions. A study of Stevenson's relations with the missionary culture helps one to realize this dilemma and to immerse oneself in the dialogues that occupied Stevenson and helped to direct the multi-voiced South Seas fiction. One must not look for a system or a universal, but, instead, for the shifting tones of the particular experiences, as one voice or circumstance replaces another.

The ensuing tensions, however, do not compromise Stevenson's integrity. I suggest that, in addition to being a corrective to or a revision of our understanding of him, the paradoxes and incongruities are more aptly a reminder that it is not always appropriate to march out such routine terms as 'imperialism' to frame a discussion of Stevenson's life and work. Such terminology weighs down the nuance and topples the delicate and shifting freight of life and thought. To impose a concept like 'imperialism' on Stevenson's work tends to exclude, and, consequently, to exile or discard what does not fit into its space. We lose too much and we invent where perhaps nothing exists. Reading about Stevenson's life and thinking, especially about his interactions with the missionaries, confirms how necessary it is to be suspicious of ideologically weighted language. It is better to engage the individual encounter and continuously renegotiate, as did Stevenson, the impact of the particular episodes as they occur. I find that I agree with Jonathan Lamb, Vanessa Smith, and Nicholas Thomas, who, as editors of *Explorations and Exchange: A South Sea Anthology 1680-1900*, identify with a number of scholars 'who have become increasingly attendant to the particular rather than the universal aspects of colonial encounter.' They are suspicious of generalizations that obliterate 'the specificity of each enterprise' (xvi).

When Stevenson went to the South Seas, he not only moved away from familiar metaphors; he also moved into a region of thought that encouraged him to discard generalities and to honor, instead, the moment separated from its surroundings. He realized, as Irving Massey observes, that 'every experience equips itself with a space around it' (282). This is why he could move with such facility from one person or concern to another, and work, as he did, on multiple projects. He felt no need to tie everything together; he accepted non-closure, inconsistency, and the transitory. He also accepted the relativity of social practice: nakedness in Scotland might be one thing; in Samoa it is another. Neither state is responsible for or reflects upon the other. Only in this way could he survive the ambiguities and the perplexities of his new life. Imperialism, therefore, is not a very useful term to describe the character of Stevenson's experiences in the South Seas, even though he is the child of Empire.

Stevenson once told a friend that in the South Seas exclusiveness was impossible; it was necessary to embrace multiplicity (*Letters* 6: 381). I believe we should heed his thought. For Stevenson (and, I should hope for us, when reading him) it is the particular, not the framing term, that counts. He is not interested in developing a policy or a hierarchy of thought; rather, he is committed to recording a series of horizontal experiences or what Benedict Anderson in his *Imagined Communities* terms 'a succession of plurals' (32). It is this simultaneity that creates meaning, not a ruling system. As a result, Stevenson's *In the South Seas* starts to resemble what Clifford Geertz (following Gilbert Ryle) calls 'thick description' (6,

21, 23) amassing detail after detail and, in the end, refusing to impose either a structure or an ideology. The culture that emerges is not a system but an assembly of events, of dialogues, and finally of particulars.

In the writing of this book, I have, in a sense, taken my cue from the anthropologist or the fieldworker who travels to a strange area and attempts to make sense of what she finds. As a result, instead of imposing a system, I have chosen to record the multiplicity of details that sometimes reveals an underlying pattern but, what is more important, continually places one in the very dilemmas that make Stevenson and his South Sea writing intriguing. Each of the following chapters honors this fraternity of particulars. The first chapter, 'Robert Louis Stevenson and the South Sea Missionaries' gives a history of the missionaries in the Pacific and concentrates on Stevenson's criticism of, yet ultimate support for, their work and how these attitudes help shape his South Sea fiction. The next three chapters, 'Stevenson's Pyjamas', 'Colonies of Memory', and 'Lighting up the Darkness', focus on other aspects of Stevenson's interactions with the missionary culture. These various exchanges articulate Stevenson's struggles with personal and cultural identity in the South Seas, and provide a means through which to comprehend what, in Stevenson's mind, constitutes the nature of memory, alienation, and class. In addition these chapters suggest new ways of thinking about the style and the subject matter of his writing. 'Lighting up the Darkness' also touches upon his interest in photography, panoramas, and magic lantern shows, revealing Stevenson's sensitivity to the ways light plays upon darkness to create meaning. The fifth chapter, 'Stevenson's Political Imagination', explores the nature of Stevenson's commitment to political issues and his thoughts about power and nationhood. Once more returning to the presence of the South Sea missionaries, the chapter also examines Stevenson's protracted conflicts with one of his missionary acquaintances who became entangled in Samoan politics. The final chapter, 'The Juvenile Missionary Magazines and *A Child's Garden of Verses*', dwells upon Stevenson's recollections of his childhood not only to suggest an unacknowledged source for the collection of poems (the juvenile missionary magazines) but also to illuminate the generous reach of his imagination that exceeds the formulae of the missionary culture and the boundaries of the colonial construct. This assemblage of topics discloses Stevenson's fluctuating adjustment to the novel and as yet unassimilated conditions of his life in the South Seas.

Notes

1. Stevenson had met Fanny Matilda Vandegrift when in July, 1876 he had gone to an artist colony in France. At that time Fanny was estranged from, but still married to, Samuel Osbourne. They lived in California. She had three children: Hervey who died at the age of four (in 1876), Isobel (Osbourne), and Lloyd (Osbourne). Fanny was ten years Stevenson's senior. Eventually in August, 1879 Stevenson set sail from England and followed Fanny to California. His account of this trip became *The Amateur Emigrant*. After her divorce, they married on 19 May 1880. Stevenson was close to and supported Fanny's remaining two children, Isobel (sometimes referred to as Belle), now a young adult, and Lloyd a few years younger than she. All of them shared his life in the South Seas and lived with him in Samoa. For a while Isobel was married to Joe Strong, a painter and photographer, and lived in Hawaii. She had a son Austin. After Isobel's divorce from Strong, Stevenson became Austin's official guardian.

2. Stevenson describes the situation that elicited the drama. He explains that the day after a drunken brawl had threatened their safety, one of his acquaintances, Mrs. Ricks the only white woman on the island and the wife of the American consular agent, told the King of Butaritari, who was himself suffering from a bad hangover, that 'I was an intimate personal friend of Queen Victoria's; that immediately on my return I should make her a report upon Butaritari; and that if my house should have been again invaded by natives, a man-of-war would be despatched to make reprisals.' Stevenson continues, by saying that the sick monarch 'had conceived the notion (he said) that I was a man of some importance, but not dreamed it was as bad as this; and the missionary house [where Stevenson was staying] was *tapu*'d under a fine of fifty dollars' (*In the South Seas* 181). Later, others on the island believed him to be Victoria's son.

3. For a discussion of Scotland and empire, see Martin Green. *Dreams of Adventure, Deeds of Empire*. New York: Basic Books, Inc. 1979; and Linda Colley's review 'We Are All Scots Here' of Michael Fry's *The Scottish Empire* in *London Review of Books*. Volume 24, No. 24. 12 December 2002. 14-15.

4. For examples of the parallels that Stevenson saw between Scotland and the South Seas, see his discussion of the Marquesas in *In the South Seas*:

    > It was perhaps yet more important that I had enjoyed in my youth some knowledge of our Scots folk of the Highlands and the Islands. Not much beyond a century had passed since these were in the same convulsive and transitionary state as the Marquesas of to-day. In both cases an alien authority enforced, the clans disarmed, the chiefs deposed, new customs introduced, and chiefly that fashion of regarding money as the means and object of existence. The commercial age, in each, succeeding at a bound to an age of war abroad and patriarchal communism at home. In one the cherished practice of tattooing, in the other a cherished costume, proscribed. In each a main luxury cut off: beef, driven under cloud of night from Lowland pastures, denied to the meat-loving Highlanders; long-pig, pirated from the next village, to the man-eating Kanaka. The grumbling, the secret ferment, the fears, and resentments, the alarms and sudden councils of Marquesan chiefs, reminded me continually of the days of Lovat and Struan. (12)

5. I am grateful to Jenni Calder for these remarks she made in a letter to me, dated April, 2003.
6. Another example of this recognition occurs in *The Beach of Falesá* when, Uma, the native woman, recognizes the picture of Queen Victoria, calls her 'Victoreea' and exclaims 'he big chief' (Menikoff 162).
7. A sampling of this approach can be found in Elleke Boehmer. *Colonial and Postcolonial Literature: Migrant Metaphors*. New York: Oxford UP. 1995. Patrick Brantlinger. *Rule of Darkness: British Literature and Imperialism, 1830-1914*. Ithaca: Cornell UP. 1988. Linda Dryden. *Joseph Conrad and the Imperial Romance*. Houndmills: Macmillan Press Ltd. 2000. Rosalyn Jolly, Ed. *South Sea Tales*. Oxford: Oxford UP. 1996. Wendy R. Katz. *Rider Haggard and the Fiction of Empire: A Critical Study of British Imperial Fiction*. New York: Cambridge UP. 1987. Katherine Bailey Linehan. 'Taking up with Kanakas: Stevenson's Complex Social Criticism in "The Beach of Falesá".' *English Literature in Transition, 1889-1920*. Volume 33, No. 4. 1990. 407-22, and in Andrea White. *Joseph Conrad and the Adventure Tradition: Constructing and Deconstructing the Imperial Subject*. Cambridge: Cambridge UP. 1993.

Chapter One

Stevenson and the South Sea Missionaries

Introduction

When Stevenson was an infant, the *Juvenile Missionary Magazine of the United Presbyterian Church* (Edinburgh, 1851) announced a magic lantern exhibit featuring a series of 'Dissolving Views of Scenes in the South Seas' to be held every evening at 8 o'clock in the Elysian Rooms. The purpose was to illustrate the missionary operations through brightly lit images that took the young audience into the interior of a New Caledonian Chief's House, where the children might view 'heathen Customs', and let their eyes wander through scenes displaying 'the first fruits of fifteen years' Missionary labour on the islands of Tahiti' ('South Sea Island Evangelised' 144). The running commentary would have stressed the successes and struggles of the enterprise as well as the mandate to save one's pennies so that even a young person could contribute to the noblest work on earth.

Nearly forty years later, between 1888 and 1894, Stevenson was to translate and qualify these didactic dissolving views through the medium of his own travels in the Pacific islands — experiences that were often framed by the missionary presence. Even though his perception of island culture was no longer subject to the missionary magazine patter, it was still dependent upon his interactions with the missionaries and their institutions. As we shall see, the missionaries constituted one of the most enduring and significant entities in the Pacific and were important to Stevenson in his orientation to his new surroundings. And, as we shall subsequently discover, although Stevenson knew that these missionaries had contributed to the destruction of island cultures, he also understood that in the context of the late 1800s, when Pacific communities were increasingly threatened by other foreign invasions, the missionary and his culture had paradoxically become a buffer against these new incursions, helping to protect the integrity of the island life. The shaping of his imagination and the composing of his South Sea stories are indebted to such paradoxes as well as to the complexities and ambiguities attending the missionaries' policies. Much of the tension within Stevenson's South Sea discourse is obligated to this reality.

Missionaries in the South Seas

Stevenson came to the islands almost a hundred years after the first missionaries had set foot on their shores. Among the first groups to establish stations was the London Missionary Society (LMS), composed largely of Congregationalists and Presbyterians. In 1795, encouraged by the region's pleasant climate and provoked by vivid, if not startling, reports of the area's depravity and barbarous customs, a group of individuals founded the LMS and made plans to enter a territory that in their minds was ripe for salvation.[1] They were eager to reach a place where infanticide and cannibalism supposedly thrived among the worship of heathen idols. After raising significant amounts of money, they gathered twenty-nine missionaries who set sail from England aboard the *Duff* on 10 August 1779. Although there were a few clerics, the majority of the passengers were the 'godly mechanics' selected not only for their religious zeal but also for their practical skills. The *Duff* arrived in Tahiti in March, 1797, the place that seemed, through the various explorers' accounts, to be the most tantalizing and ready for conversion. After leaving the bulk of the missionaries there, the ship moved on and deposited the rest of the passengers elsewhere, for instance, on the Marquesas, where the Society hoped to spread its influence.

Immediately the vulnerability of the missionary endeavor became obvious. There were communication difficulties, for these pioneers had trouble learning the various languages. The few vocabulary aids given them by a survivor of the mutiny of the *Bounty* had proved impossible to master; consequently, they found themselves relying on the linguistic skills of beachcombers who, after deserting a trading vessel or surviving a wreck, were scraping together a living on the island and mingling intimately with the natives. From the Society's perspective, these outcasts were not the most moral or desirable of intermediaries. There were also problems with disease, conflicts among themselves and with the natives, and, eventually, crises in faith. Hardship and circumstance compromised their evangelism and conspired to bring an end to their efforts.

In 1817, what is known as the second generation of LMS missionaries left England and came back to the South Seas to try once more. Among these were William Ellis and John Williams, two giants in the missionary field who succeeded in staking claims, acquiring land, and convincing various chiefs, such as Pomare II of Tahiti, to destroy their heathen idols and hurl them from their native thrones (Ellis 1: 257). Through their tireless labors, they set up stations throughout the Pacific: in the Cook Islands, Tonga, the Marquesas, the New Hebrides, and the Society Islands.[2] Ellis believed it was important to bring the written word, so he traveled with a printing press and set up a series of what Vanessa Smith refers to as 'literary-textual encounters' that spread the word, through translated, printed texts, and excited the converts, especially those with authority, for literacy enhanced their power. The missionaries taught people to read. News of success, very much exaggerated in the missionary magazines that boasted of mass and instantaneous conversions, made Ellis and Williams celebrities in Britain. In 1834, on a furlough,

Williams was lionized in England and in Scotland. Their books describing their experiences in the South Seas were popular: Ellis's *Polynesian Researches* (1829) and Williams's *Missionary Enterprises* (1837) were known to a large community that eagerly supported the spread of Christianity by donating money to build ships that would allow both Ellis and Williams to travel from one heathen Pacific island to another. Williams was particularly ambitious. His desire was to reach as many places as he could, so he spent much of his energy in training native converts to become preachers whom he would assign and send to various places — a practice that was to continue throughout the LMS history in the Pacific: by the second half of the nineteenth century, native pastors were numerous. In 1830, in *The Messenger of Peace*, Williams set off for Samoa. Soon Upolu (the island upon which Stevenson was to settle) was to become a headquarters for his consolidated efforts. The spread of the missionary enterprise continued.

Williams would in any case, perhaps, have been remembered, but his dramatic martyrdom on 20 November 1839 — a necessary ingredient in missionary history — secured his place. Pictorial and verbal representations of his death in Erromango (in the New Hebrides) abound. Images of his being pursued and clubbed by angry natives as he attempted to reach the safety of his boat are part of the mythology that surrounds him. His martyrdom reinforced both the nobility and the importance of the missionary effort, and certainly kept the spirit of Williams alive: one morning in 1890, while the *Janet Nicoll* steamed by Erromango, Stevenson and his wife stared at the spot where Williams had been killed by the natives.

By the time Stevenson was cruising the islands on his three voyages, visiting Hawaii, and eventually taking up his residence in Samoa, the missionaries were, of course, an entrenched presence and were more than ever intricately woven into the political, institutional, and social fabric of the various islands. This circumstance often placed them in the position of being peacemakers among warring native factions and had made them particularly visible in Hawaii where, since 1820, the American Missionary Society had worked its way into the coterie of the royal family and its privileges.[3] Stevenson frequently benefited from conversing with these missionaries, for they were a splendid source of information. Many of them had studiously explored the history of the region, had learned the languages, collected tales and songs, and had, in some cases, subordinated their religious interests to their ethnographic research. Neil Gunson, in his history of the missionaries, suggests that this shift in emphasis was a sign that the old, overbearing attitude of the pioneering generation, initially convinced of its own superiority, had, through years of contact, softened and evolved into a more humane and sympathetic relationship with the culture they had invaded. He also proposes that this research sometimes offered the disillusioned missionary a means 'to escape from the reality of failure' (211). Contrary to the confident phrases in the missionary publications, there frequently lurked doubts that their labors were futile, and, that, as Stevenson observed, the work could be 'one long dull disappointment, varied by acute revulsions' (*Letters* 8: 325).

Rivalries and Frictions: The Religious Sects

Through his travels Stevenson became aware of the fickleness of Pacific people's commitment to the new religion. He understood that the conversions the missionaries claimed in their publications were not necessarily absolute. As Barry Menikoff points out, 'Stevenson recognized what many white missionaries refused to see, that the adoption of Christianity by the native islanders had little effect on their beliefs and superstitions' (79). Stevenson realized that the lingering faith in the old deities and beliefs still played a role in the inhabitants' lives so that native manners and what people referred to as 'superstitions' persisted under Christian forms. Fully understanding this reality, he liked to compare this duality to 'the theological Highlander [who] sneaks from under the eye of the Free Church [of Scotland] divine to lay an offering by a sacred well'. He was intrigued and heartened by the fact that in Tautira the chief's sister, although 'very religious [and] a great church-goer', privately worshipped a shark (*In the South Seas* 141).

      Stevenson's experiences also made him more aware of the fluidity with which islanders switched denominational allegiances. For instance, in the Marquesas, Stevenson learned about a chief of Tai-o-hae who had first been a convert to the Protestant mission but had died an avid supporter of Catholicism and the French. And when, on that same voyage, he moved on to the Paumotus archipelago, Stevenson was amused to observe that the supposed division between the Catholics (present in the region since 1827) and the Mormons (they had begun evangelizing in 1844) was not set in stone. Although both denominations 'fronted each other proudly with a false air of permanence', their membership flowed in a perpetual flux: 'The Mormon attends mass with devotion; the Catholic sits attentive at a Mormon sermon, and to-morrow each may have transferred allegiance.' One of Stevenson's informants told him: '*Pour moi les Mormons ici un petit Catholiques*' (*In the South Seas* 130-31). Later in Papeete Bay and Tautira (the land where decades before Pomare had handed over his idols to the LMS missionaries), Stevenson's mother recorded meeting natives who referred to the 'Roman Protestant Church'. During her stay on the island, she herself participated in this *mélange* with her willingness to participate in various church services, a practice she probably would not have allowed herself in Edinburgh:[4] On the one hand, she went to the Protestant Church where, to her delight, she experienced 'a real mission congregation' (*From Saranac to the Marquesas and Beyond* 201); but she also talked with the Mormons of Papeete Bay; she visited the Roman Catholic Church, and, from her room, she keenly watched the Marist priest, Père Bruno, reading the breviary on his veranda.

      Not all the places the Stevensons visited, however, were in such flux or had populations that were able to coexist in such benign proximity. In Ellis's and Williams's time there had been attempts to cooperate with other denominations and, for instance, work out congenial arrangements with the Wesleyans, but as time passed, fear that other sects might intrude upon and infiltrate a missionary society's territory often led to fierce competition. This rivalry among the different religious groups became, in fact, such a decisive part of Pacific history that a French historian characterized the period between 1797 and 1870 as '*la guerre des missions*' (Koskinen 108).

The competition among sects began in earnest during Williams's years when the antagonism between the LMS and the Catholics became intense and gave birth to stories of the evils and tricks of 'Popery' (among other things, they were said to hand out tobacco) that continued to enliven many a Sunday school meeting or missionary report. Moreover, this rivalry had led to the enduring impression that Catholics consciously intruded upon Protestant areas and stole the converts. In reaction, years after the passing of the second generation of missionaries, Protestants still spoke of preparing counter-measures to defeat Catholic aggression. LMS-trained native preachers before being assigned a position on an outstation, let us say in New Guinea, would sometimes anxiously ask not only if there were 'tailed or big-eared people' in the Torres Straits but also if there were any 'Romanists'.[5] Eventually rivalries spread to include all sects so that anxious amities as well as uneasy truces among conflicting missions continued to chart the South Seas. On the few occasions when the Protestant missionary societies did cooperate, they spent their time negotiating the apportionment of districts, for instance, in the New Hebrides, where they were able, subsequently, to work without any controversy.

By the time Stevenson arrived, the Catholics, Protestants, Congregationalists, representatives of The Free Church of Scotland, United Presbyterians, Wesleyans, members of the Church of England, Mormons, and Baptists had diligently mapped the islands according to what territories each missionary society possessed or dominated. In *The Martyrs of Polynesia* (1885), a book celebrating protestant missionaries who had met violent deaths, the LMS missionary the Reverend A. W. Murray provided a map of these mission fields. According to his information, the Marshall Islands and the Marquesas belonged to the American Congregational Society; the Gilberts, the Ellice, and the Society Islands to the London Missionary Society, and Samoa was split between the Wesleyans and the London Missionary Society. He ignored those places embracing Popery. Moreover, around the same period a LMS missionary who pioneered in New Guinea was careful to create maps that marked what regions of that virtually unexplored land were the property of the Roman Catholics, the Germans, the Anglican Missions, and, of course, the LMS. (In 1871, the directors of the LMS had decided to extend their territory to include parts of New Guinea.)

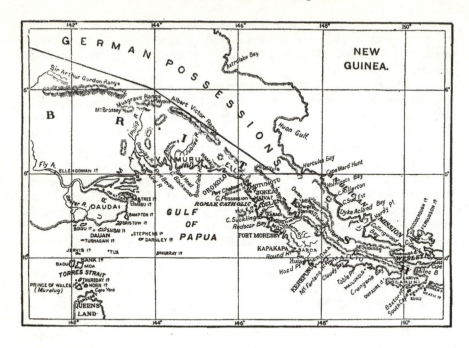

1.1   'Map of New Guinea.' Rev. James Chalmers. *Pioneer Life and Work in New Guinea*

Other publications marked a mission's territory by noting the number of converts on each island. For instance, in 1830, agents of the London Missionary Society claimed that in Samoa there were 26,493 followers of the LMS; 4,794 Wesleyans; 2,852 Catholics, and a few who professed to be Mormons. By taking censuses and charting their claims, the various missionary societies imposed the grid of their influence or orientation on the landscape, reshaping the internal contours of the islands and transforming the native social and belief system. The contours of the islands and transforming the native social and belief system. The earliest maps these societies had made initially reflected the territories of chiefs under whose protection they functioned, but in the latter part of the nineteenth century, these maps revealed the more autonomous and authoritative nature of a missionary culture less dependent on the goodwill of the native leadership and more beholden to the home office. No wonder that each society had its own Foreign Secretary.

As Stevenson was to learn, the presence of another sect was unsettling, even, as in the case of the LMS, when it had a significant number of converts. A few years before Stevenson's arrival, for instance, a missionary on the Hervey Islands, wrote to the LMS headquarters that he was 'worried about Wesleyans or Mormon friends who are … diligently attacking our position' (LMS Archives, Correspondence). During Stevenson's time, the presence of the Wesleyans continued to be a distinct irritant, especially in Samoa. In an 1893 report of the Samoan District Committee, the missionaries complained that the Wesleyans were winning converts by permitting Samoan dances and other objectionable practices that the Society had banned. In Apia (the main port on the Island of Upolu in Samoa and the headquarters for the LMS), there were also rumors that the Wesleyans had just sanctioned the revival of tattooing — another LMS missionary taboo. What was also threatening to the LMS was, paradoxically, the increase of the white population in Apia. Naval officers, foreign businessmen, and officials brought other religious beliefs with them that could potentially challenge the ascendancy of the LMS and its affiliation with the congregationalists and presbyterians. The LMS missionaries were anxious about the British officials and naval officers who were members of the Church of England; they also took note of the German resident officials, sailors, and traders who were either Lutherans or, as the Reverend James Whitmee put it, 'preferred our Roman Catholic rival' (LMS Archives, Box 42). In spite of this competitive atmosphere, though, the LMS headquarters chose, in its public relations, to propagate the idea of cooperation, and published righteous claims in the March, 1890 issue of *The Chronicle* that 'the mission work of the Pacific, so far as the Protestant churches are concerned, is so arranged that the one does not interfere with the other' ('Mission Work in the Pacific' 77).

Rivalries and Frictions: Traders and Beachcombers

The competition among the missionaries for territory and followers was not the only source of friction; there was also a thriving antagonism between the missionaries and the white traders and beachcombers, two groups of whites often coupled by those who saw them as a threat to the Societies' autonomy. These two sets of Europeans, as the editors of *Exploration and Exchange* point out, 'represented a split, rather than a unified European identity', a circumstance and a contradiction that was 'apparent to the islanders among whom they resided'

(Lamb 119). The beachcomber, the trader, and the missionary were all battling for influence over their surroundings and the endorsement of the native leadership. They rarely worked to help each other, except on those increasingly few occasions when the beachcombers and traders functioned as interpreters and go-betweens for the missionaries. It is interesting to note that when Stevenson prepared his address (delivered by his mother because he was ill) to be read before .the Women's Missionary Association and members of the General Assembly of the Presbyterian Church of New South Wales, at Sydney (18 March 1893), he chastised the missionary culture for holding on to its prejudice against the traders and for overlooking the reservoirs of 'moral power' and wisdom that these people had. Stevenson was well aware that among the traders there were unsavory, unethical characters, but he also knew that some were quite respectable and could be put to good use by the missions:

> Many of these despised traders are in themselves fairly decent and more than fairly decent persons. They dwell besides, permanently amidst the native population, whereas the missionary in some cases, and perhaps too often, only there upon a flying visit. The trader is therefore, at once by experience and by influence, the superior of the missionary. He is a person marked out to be made use of by the intelligent missionary. Sometimes a very doubtful character, sometimes a very decent old gentleman, he will almost invariably be made the better by some intelligent and kindly attention for which he is often burning; and he will almost invariably be made the worse by neglect or insult …. the mission and the traders have to be made more or less in unison. (Balfour 2: 230-31)

The main contention was the missionaries' belief that traders were an immoral lot and that beachcombers were even more dissolute — an image not helped by the fact that there were records of slave traders ('blackbirders') who had taken advantage of people's trust in the missionary. They had disguised their vessels to look like missionary ships and dressed the officers up as clerics so as to mislead those they were about to kidnap.[6] As the years passed, the missionaries, in their reports and publications, contributed to the stereotype of the trader as a wild, irresponsible liar, cheat, and womanizer. Although the more domesticated figure of the resident trader eventually replaced this harsh portrait, a certain distrust of the trader and, especially, the beachcomber clung to the missionary's idiom so that during Stevenson's time one could still find missionaries complaining about the beachcomber's destructive influence upon both the natives and the other white residents.

Needless to say, the antagonism was mutual. Traders, particularly, resented the missionaries for interfering with their business and compromising their profits. They were displeased with the missionaries for encouraging the natives to pursue their own initiatives, and they were indignant and exasperated when the missionaries tried to prevent them from exploiting the natives through unscrupulous trading. In January, 1891 a LMS missionary, the Reverend G. A. Harris, found himself in dire trouble because of this conflict. In a letter to the LMS Foreign Secretary, Harris pleaded for help:

> My position just now is very difficult & critical one. In consequence of my sympathies with the natives in all their troubles & difficulties, I am of course regarded with much disfavour by many of the white traders here [Mangaia] & at Rarotonga. In fact, it suits the policy of these Europeans to circulate slanderous & lying reports concerning myself & my doings.

Harris continued his letter by worrying about the future of the Hervey Islanders:

> Without a true friend or two standing by these Hervey Islanders, they will speedily go to the wall & be almost crushed by the force of the outside world. And if it be impossible to prevent the overflowing tide from reaching them, it may nevertheless be possible to *stem* it for a season or hinder the immediate results of its overwhelming force. (LMS Archives, Box 40)

LMS Missionary Life in Samoa

By the time Stevenson was committed to his life in the South Seas and residing at his home Vailima in Samoa, the London Missionary Society was an extraordinarily strong presence. Their headquarters were in Apia, so many of Stevenson's friends and acquaintances were from the Mission House. Through them and through less intimate relationships with Wesleyan missionaries and Marist priests, he learned, even more particularly, about the ins and outs of missionary life, its institutions, and its impact upon the islanders. Thanks to the Reverend W. E. Clarke, a person who was to become one of his closest companions, Stevenson also became familiar with the procedure of visiting outstations in order to check on the native pastors in charge of a mission community and to examine their pupils. At the end of December, 1889, for instance, Stevenson went with Clarke on a *malaga* (an outing) to Fangaloa, a dozen miles to the east of Apia, to visit a LMS missionary school. In his manuscript journal of the four- or five-day visit, Stevenson offers a slightly irreverent, yet affectionate, account of a suffering Clarke laboring through the school's examinations and proceedings:

> I turned into the school house, a native house in shape, with a native roof — only the walls of stone, where the competing scholars sat on their hams crossfeeted on the floor, and poor Mr. Clarke, at the pulpit, toiled over the fruits of the competition. The divinity paper would have broken any class in England. When was Sodom destroyed? 1898 to a

minute, on the authority of Dr. Turner (a man troubled by no womanish doubts) in his (otherwise) excellent handbook of scripture history.[7] Compare the religious and secular year of the Hebrews? Even Sampson scholars find this tough, but one lady solved the problem creditably and having answered all the rest carried off full marks, 10. I looked with curiosity when the slates were returned to see the appearance of this fair divine and behold it was a big, winning, Hebe [Greek goddess of youth] who had already made herself conspicuous by the boldness of her singing and (shall I say) the gallantry of her behaviour at the gift-giving. (Talatasi) It must be borne in mind that the Bible is all their literature. (Beinecke ms. 6556)

On another occasion, in January, 1890, Stevenson spent a week with the Reverend James Edward Newell, a LMS missionary and Senior Tutor, at the Malua Training Institution in Samoa, to the west of Apia.[8] Like other LMS training colleges in the South Seas, this one was dedicated to training future native pastors, for whom there was an increasing demand. The Malua Institution was run by two white missionaries and one native pastor. In September, 1890, there were, according to *The Chronicle of the London Missionary Society*, '149 students, including [their] 56 wives, all in residence, and in various stages of training'. Their activities were as follows: 'Four days in the week are entirely devoted to mission work [religious study and practice in preaching]; one day to technical education; the sixth day to the plantations, which cover 500 acres' on which 'each student is supposed to rear 100 bananas and 100 cocoa-nut trees'. The supply furnished the establishment with food. In a, perhaps, surprising afterthought, the person who wrote the article added that 'Native customs are encouraged, European tabooed, and English is taught' ('Round About Apia' 279). The institute's graduates would be assigned posts and go out as native pastors representing the LMS Society, but as 'natives', not as Europeans, and settle in established as well as newly-founded or isolated missions. The women would teach Sunday School and do the housekeeping. The idea was that a native was closer to the islanders' experience and could make the appropriate connections between an island's culture and the religious teaching. Periodically, just as Clarke did when he went to Fangaloa, the white missionaries visited these outstations, then sent reports back to the LMS Foreign Secretary in London. Sometimes these reports indicated that the native pastors were troublesome because of a severity born from being too literal minded, probably a consequence of their training.[9]

Teaching institutions were an important part of the missionary effort, so that throughout the South Seas the missionaries founded and supervised training colleges, schools for boys, for girls and 'promising young women', and schools for half-caste children. The LMS missionaries in Samoa were particularly keen to establish a half-caste school. In a note written to the LMS Foreign Secretary on 21 April 1889, Clarke declared: 'The race struggle has now begun in Samoa in grim earnest; and the higher civilization is bound to dominate. My firm conviction, frequently expressed is that the future hopes for the native race be in its half caste populations. Already they are an influential community' (LMS Archives, Box 40). His opinion was supported by the Reverend G. Pratt, who thought it wrong to abandon a half-caste population which was of increasing importance in the community. The missionaries were eager to have an educated population, and, by means of their schools, to insure their authority over those who might become powerful in the future.

The missionaries whom Stevenson knew were not only committed to far-reaching educational opportunities for the islanders but also were dedicated to serving the European or white community, so in Apia, for example, there were church services for the Europeans, a school for children of foreigners, a coffee house, social club and library for white residents and visiting sailors (Miss Large of the LMS ran such an establishment); they also opened their grounds for tennis games.

Stevenson's Critical Attitude

The South Seas missionaries were by no means deaf to criticisms about either their efforts or their very existence. They had heard travelers ask, 'What right has an English or French missionary to say to a whole race, "You shall not dance, you shall not sing, you shall not smoke, under the possible penalty of eternal damnation in the next world"?' (The Earl and the Doctor 160), and they had listened to others fault them for their supercilious, patronizing attitude. Such a demeanor, according to their critics, was 'harmful to the native races' (St. Johnston 16) and destroyed 'the elements of manliness and cheerfulness' by introducing 'a hopeless apathy' and an obsequious affect (*The Quarterly Review* 120).[10] This kind of hostile commentary was common and contributed to a lingering disapproval or suspicion about missionary efforts that Stevenson had absorbed, and that he carried with him as he traveled around Polynesia and investigated their good or destructive influence. The troublesome topic played, quite regularly, in his consciousness. In fact, if one looks at early drafts of his *In the South Seas*, one discovers that he initially planned to have a separate chapter on the missions. His lively interest in the subject also emerges in his wife's oft-quoted letter (21 May 1889) to Sidney Colvin in which she complains bitterly about the kinds of South Seas materials that fascinated him, yet do not, in her mind, contribute to producing a profitable book. Among those items is his attention to questions concerning the validity of the missionary presence:

> He has taken into his Scotch Stevenson head, that a stern duty lies before him, and that his book must be a sort of scientific and historical impersonal thing, comparing the different languages (of which he knows nothing, really) and the different peoples, the object being to settle the question as to whether they are of common Malay origin or not. Also to compare the Protestant and Catholic Missions, etc. In fact to bring to the

> front all the prejudices, and all the mistakes and all the ignorance
> concerning the subject he can get together .... Suppose Herman Melville
> had given us his theories as to the Polynesian language and the probable
> good or evil results of the missionary influence instead of *Omoo* and
> *Typee.* (*Letters* 6: 303-304)

Stevenson, however, was not to be deterred by such opposition, for he understood that the missionary, whatever his or her religious affiliation, was a prominent and integral part of the regions he was now trying hard to comprehend. Furthermore, he could not ignore what in addition to being so noticeable in the present had already been a factor in his own past. Even though he had, in his early twenties, openly rebelled against his parents' theological views and declared himself an agnostic — an almost mortal blow to his father —, he never did completely rid himself of a religious orientation, nor did he erase his memory of his family's devotion to missionary causes both domestic and foreign. Stevenson's allegiance to his upbringing in the Church of Scotland was never to replicate the zeal of his childhood when he would avidly listen to his nurse's stories about the Covenanters; rather, it was to keep a respectable, ironic distance, but not one that cut off access to belief. Such a course allowed him the privilege of being both critical and pious. At times, as an adult, Stevenson could write fluently and sincerely to his depressed father about the value of religion; he could tell a young friend that 'I do believe with my heart and soul in a God, and a righteous God' (*Letters* 7: 74); or, later, in a sad letter to the deposed Mataafa, the defeated chief of Samoa, Stevenson could genuinely resort to a vocabulary from his youth: 'My heart is sad by reason of my love for you. The power of God is great. The righteous and the wise are in his hand with all their works. Farewell in the love of Jesus' (*Letters* 8: 356). But, at other moments, he could express his displeasure with prettified religion and 'petty religion that takes the name and attributes of God for an election ticket' (*Letters* 7: 74). Again, on other occasions, this time in a letter to George Meredith about his intermittent practice of assembling his staff for prayers on Sunday nights, Stevenson could speak of his mixed feelings about the exercise:

> We have prayers on Sunday night — I am a perfect pariah in the island
> not to have them oftener, but the spirit is unwilling and the flesh proud,
> and I cannot go it more. It is strange to see the long line of the brown
> fold crouched along the wall with lanterns at intervals before them in
> the big shadowy hall, with an oak cabinet at one end of it, and a group
> of Rodin's [sculpture] ... presiding over all from the top — and to hear
> the long rambling Samoan hymn rolling up. (*Letters* 8: 163)

Whatever the ambiguity, the impulse to use religion as a reference was almost continuous. No wonder, then, that Stevenson easily became involved in the debates, leaning sometimes to support and sometimes to disapproval, about the value of the missionary project.

The 'Sharper Criticism'

When Stevenson first went to Honolulu, and before he ever went to Samoa, he wrote a short piece to accompany 'A Samoan Scrapbook', a collection of his son-in-law's photographs featuring the Hawaiian Embassy to Samoa; it included scenes of a group of Sunday School children and a view of the annual convocation of the Samoan church. His essay opens with remarks about the missionary culture in the islands that illustrate just how pressing the subject was: 'In all South Sea talk, the question of the missionary leads. Nowhere else have Christian missions enjoyed a greater measure of immediate success, or suffered, and perhaps deserved, a sharper criticism.' As the essay unfolds, Stevenson, although often kind to the missions, does participate in this 'sharper criticism' and faults them for a tendency to believe, too readily, that conversion can be absolute, and to ignore the fact that 'incongruous superstitions still live on' among the natives (Beinecke ms. 6825); he had already made similar remarks concerning conversion and belief when he had been in the Marquesas and the Paumotus.

Throughout his life in the South Seas, even when he was on good terms with the Mission House in Apia, Stevenson periodically expressed displeasure with missionary attitudes or practices, and registered his impatience with their parochialism and naiveté. In November, 1893, for instance, Stevenson became embroiled in a public dispute and 'crossed swords' with the Reverend John William Hills, a LMS missionary, over a proposal to build a hospital for diseased prostitutes in Apia (*Letters* 8: 217).[11] Being the major port in Samoa, Apia attracted the prostitute trade.

The argument with Hills, the LMS, and the Wesleyan Missionary Society was not whether there should be a hospital or not or whether there should be a Contagious Disease Act: about these matters they were in agreement; but Stevenson rejected the approach of people like Hills, who argued from the impractical perspective of a stern righteousness that naively dreamed of and demanded universal chastity, and who accused those like Stevenson, who supported the petition to conduct monthly examinations of the prostitutes and keep them locked up in a hospital until they were cured, of trying to make indulgence in vice easy and safe. Annoyed with Hills, Stevenson exclaimed: 'he is an enemy to the vice of fornication so uncompromising that he had rather the whole race should be diseased, and perish as the Hawaiians are perishing, and the Marquesans have already perished, of general sterility [from syphilis], than that he should seem in any way to hold a candle to that sin'. Stevenson, vitriolic and impatient, added, 'In this disease he [Hills] recognizes the Scourge of God against transgression; perhaps views it with something of a sneaking favour, as an ally, ugly but vigorous, on his own side.' In a letter he intended to publish in a local newspaper, Stevenson summarized the differences between them: 'He thinks of the vicious who receive the direct shot, I of the children who suffer by ricochet: he of the sins, I of the punishment and the dread impartiality of devastation. Or to resume a little closer: I am concerned with the Sixth Commandment and the desire to let men live; he with the Seventh and his hope to make men pure' (*Letters* 8: 222-23).

At other moments the overbearing and self-righteous nature of the larger missionary culture aggravated Stevenson. It was what ultimately prevented his taking his final voyage around the islands on the *Morning Star*, a missionary ship on which, as Lloyd, his stepson, put it, they all would have been subjected to the rule of 'no smoking [Stevenson was a chain smoker], not a drink, no profanity; church, nightly prayer-meetings, and an enforced intimacy with the most uncongenial of people' (Osbourne 93-94). Stevenson had little patience with those missionaries intent upon repressing the innocent pleasures of life. And although he claimed to be repentant when he broke the missionary rules, he also had some difficulty with the Sabbatarians who insisted that the Sabbath should remain inviolate under any and all circumstances, and protested if the consuls arranged a fête on the sacred day. One Sunday in Apia (August, 1894), when Stevenson joined a paper chase arranged by the German Plantation Company (and had a thrilling time), he returned to confront the displeasure of his missionary friends, who were already having problems with his so-called Bohemianism and some of his political views, and had to apologize.

Stevenson felt that a number of the missionary taboos were out-dated and silly. He grew especially impatient with the restrictions concerning native dances. Missionaries of many denominations outlawed public displays of the *Siva* (the Samoan National Dance) because of its supposedly lewd or obscene content and, in addition, threatened to excommunicate those church members who attended such performances. Stevenson was full of admiration for Clarke when the missionary made the decision to be present at one such celebratory display in November, 1890. So impressed was Stevenson with his friend's willingness to go against such a restriction that he wrote and offered his help if any difficulty followed. The tone of the letter's opening paragraph reveals the seriousness of what we might now consider to be a trivial matter: 'My dear Clarke, I was unable to speak with you when I was down after the feast. After what you had previously told me about the *Siva* I was more than astonished to see you present' (*Letters* 7: 38-39).

All of these annoyances reflected Stevenson's vexation with a pervasive narrow-mindedness that he feared the missionary culture fostered. Stevenson was attracted to Clarke because he was willing, on occasion, to see beyond the rules. He wished more people who went into the ministry had, like Clarke, 'the inestimable advantage of having grown up a layman [not a son of a parson or a missionary]. Pity they all can't get that!' (*Letters* 7: 307). He also appreciated the fact that, from time to time, Clarke rebelled against missionary work and threatened to resign (see *Letters* 8: 79). Stevenson had little respect for those who lost themselves in the trivia of doctrine. In a letter to a friend who had written to him about a small doctrinal matter, he begged her to rid herself of such minor concerns and remember that 'we are the cranks of a huge machine'. He went on to explain 'That churches may sustain us, I am the last to deny, though one of the last to feel ... but a church is not the universe and can never be the house of the Great God' (*Letters* 7: 74).

From Stevenson's point of view, the lack of this larger perspective could discourage the play of mind and, instead, encourage a parochialism within missionary circles that not only created unnecessary competition but also a thoughtless regurgitation of doctrine. He deplored the rush to create pious followers who imitate — swallow 'tinfoil formulas' (*Letters* 7: 111). Early in his travels he complained about the sisters in the girls' school in Tai-o-hae who have 'too much concern to make the natives pious' (yet don't succeed),[12] and later (January, 1890), in a draft of a speech to the Samoan students at the Malua Institution, he exhorted the young men and women to learn religion, but not to memorize it. His remarks actually complemented what many of his white missionary friends in Samoa already worried about: the unnecessary bigotry and indiscriminate understanding of their native followers who exercised the Society's rules and teachings without knowing how to distinguish what is essential or not.[13] In his talk, Stevenson makes a distinction between parroting and knowing:

> I was in an island not very far from here, where they are trying to teach them French .... They read as parrots speak. Now we may not be quite so stupid as these Marquesans, and yet we may be no better at all.
>
> We may learn a great deal about religion, yet not learn religion. We may know a thousand texts, and get no sense from them, as a blind man may have a thousand lanterns and yet see no better. (Balfour 2: 223)

Stevenson also questioned whether the missionary societies, in their haste to obtain pre-eminent authority, had not, in their past, sometimes destroyed or detrimentally revolutionized an island culture. With this in mind, in July, 1894, Stevenson shot off a letter to Adelaide Boodle, a young friend from his Bournemouth days, who had just decided to become a missionary, and pleaded with her to remember that '*you cannot change ancestral feelings of right and wrong without what is practically soul murder*' (*Letters* 8: 325). That sentiment parallels a similar expression of despair from the fifth chapter of *In the South Seas* when Stevenson bitterly suggests that missionaries, though they would never have thought of bombarding a village, 'even in order to convert an archipelago', had in their history wrought 'a change of habit' that 'is bloodier than a bombardment' (34).

Stevenson's Support of the Missionary Effort

Although Stevenson repeatedly acknowledged that the missionary effort 'did have its gross blots' (*In the South Seas* 64), ultimately he never failed to defend or support it. He contributed to campaigns for new missionary buildings, clubs, and institutes for foreigners and half castes; he chaired special missionary events; he attended English services in Apia; he expressed interest in the various societies' teaching institutions (including Miss Large's LMS Sunday School); he addressed various South Seas missionary organizations; he gave Bible classes to young half castes, and even agreed to teach Sunday School. When Stevenson engaged in these efforts, particularly those in which he attempted to teach classes to young students, there were, of course, few pious platitudes concerning bringing light to darkness; instead, there was often a pleasant, ironic familiarity that either showed through his delight in the pupils who sang hymns and were dressed in their Sunday best [Stevenson always loved children] or informed his comments concerning his difficulties in teaching religion to a group of children who gazed at him 'with goggle eyes without a spark of intelligence in them'. When, for instance, he visited Miss Large's Sunday School, and despaired that he was getting no response, he offered sixpence to any boy who would ask a question. It was not until he offered half a crown that he received the question, 'Who made God?' Unable to answer the query, Stevenson was both defeated and beguiled. According to one amused witness, that half-crown effectively ended his career as a missionary (*Letters* 7: 385n). Later, in April, 1894, as an experiment and under pressure, Stevenson did agree to take an official role with the LMS Sunday School in Apia and replace W. L. Chambers, the retiring American Land Commissioner (LMS Archives, Box 40, Folder 43). In a letter he told Colvin that he was joining the 'Sunday School racket' (Moors 32).

Several critics have suggested that Stevenson only cooperated in these activities out of loyalty to his mother who, all her life, was a supporter of the missionary movement. In the South Seas, when the Stevensons traveled around the Marquesas, Paumotus, and Tahiti, Margaret Stevenson made a point (often going by herself) of visiting the Protestant missionary chapels. She gave a set of communion vessels to one — after she saw they were using 'two black-beer bottles' for the ritual, and took pleasure in meeting members of the congregation. Once settled in Samoa, she attached herself to the LMS Mission House and gladly participated in Sunday School prize-giving ceremonies. Furthermore, when she periodically returned to Scotland, she frequented missionary meetings and, at a ladies' conference, once read a paper entitled 'Glimpses of Mission Works in the South Seas' (28 May 1890). Although her letters to her sister reveal that she, like her son, was capable of seeing the humor in some of her interactions with missionaries and their followers (such as the time an overly zealous convert almost dragged her back to her house), she was not as critical as Stevenson. She was, therefore, not self-conscious about using a well-rehearsed phrase like 'these brothers and sisters so recently rescued from heathendom' (*From Saranac to the Marquesas and Beyond* 194), and she was happy to hear the daughter of a chieftain speak at length about being raised by English missionaries (178).

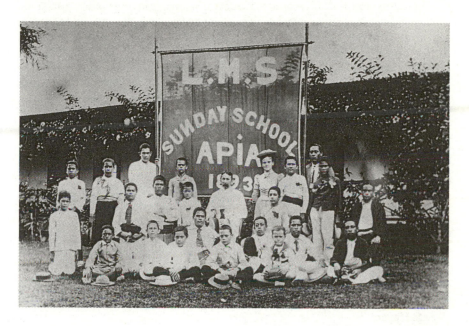

1.2   'Apia Sunday School, 1893.' [Central figure is Mr. Chambers, the USA Commissioner in Apia; the missionary is Miss A. E. Large.]

Obviously Margaret Stevenson's residence in the South Seas did encourage her son's attentiveness to his mother's preferences: Clarke and another of Stevenson's friends, H. J. Moors, for instance, remark that the frequency of Stevenson's attendance at church was predicated on her presence. Both commentators are probably correct. However, if one reads Stevenson's talks on missionary matters and goes through his entire correspondence, one finds more at play than his merely acting out the part of the child of the Covenanter who is loyal to his parents and who is devoted to the evangelical and his 'ugly beauties and grotesque heroism' (*Letters* 7: 111). One also finds a sincere appreciation for the missionary, and a distaste for the ignorance and malice of prejudices against the figure. One even notices a disapproval of his own initial biases against missionary societies — preconceptions that were at first 'reduced, and then at last annihilated' the longer he lived in the South Seas (Balfour 229). Stevenson warned his readers that 'those that have a taste for hearing missions, Protestant or Catholic, decried, must seek their pleasure elsewhere than in my pages' (*In the South Seas* 64). The consequence is that even though Stevenson liked to refer to himself as a friendly onlooker or dispassionate critic of the Societies, and, as we have seen above, admitted that they had their faults, he was ultimately a defender of their enterprise. At times he referred to missionaries as the 'best and most useful whites in the Pacific' (*In the South Seas* 64) or spoke of them as 'our foremost torch-bearers of civilisation' (*Letters* 8: 183), a comment that shows that Stevenson was not always averse to adopting the familiar vocabulary of imperialism.

A Safe Haven

There are several reasons why Stevenson was willing to give such hyperbolic praise. Compared to most other whites — particularly a significant number of the colonial officials and politicians Stevenson met in Samoa and, to some extent, the traders and especially the plantation owners — the missionaries tended, more than other colonial entities, to have the islanders' interests at heart. The harmful policies of the missionary pioneers had been largely abandoned, to be supplanted by the detrimental and self-serving interests of foreign powers. Stevenson found himself surrounded by missionaries who were among the more enlightened, who were now eager to preserve the remaining native traditions, and who demonstrated some regard for native opinions. Early in his travels, Stevenson was impressed with the celibate Catholic priests for their ability (because of their not being influenced by wives still tied to Western culture) to fall into the native way of life and more readily to see their surroundings through the native viewpoint (*In the South Seas* 64). He thought it a feather in the missionary cap that the charm of native manners had survived in spite of the new conditions set by the missionaries in the past.

After he turned from being a tourist to a resident and began to witness the machinations of the various political powers, Stevenson complimented the missionaries for their willingness to institute change gradually, to meet the natives half way, and not simply impose an order from the outside. In his 18 March 1893 address to the Women's Missionary Association, Stevenson praised those missionaries who 'are inclined to spare so far as it is possible native opinions and set native habits of morality; to seek rather the point of agreement than the points of difference; to proceed rather by confirmation and extension than by iconoclasm.' Recalling their history, Stevenson continued: 'When the missionaries — the earlier missionaries – "broke the tabus" in the South Sea Islands, they chose the path of destruction, not of utilisation, and I am pleased to think that these days are over, that no missionary will go among a primitive people with the idea of mere revolution, that he will rather develop that which is good, or is capable of being made good, in the inherent idea of the race' (Balfour 2: 229-30).

As the above quotation suggests, Stevenson also admired the missionaries for their commitment to advance what was commendable in a race and bring it 'forward' (2: 229) — perhaps an uncomfortable endorsement for those who prefer to think of Stevenson as consistently exempting himself from the paternalism of his colonial surroundings and in the South Seas writing fiction that subverted the tenets of imperialism. Like all of us, Stevenson was partially a product of his class, time, and circumstances. One should realize, though, that in approving the missionaries' campaign to advance 'the race' and bring in civilization, Stevenson had in mind the reality of the growing threat of outsiders, especially Europeans, and the need to strengthen opposition to their increasing influence. As we shall see in a later chapter on Stevenson's political activities, he was worried about the growing leverage of the Germans and the multiplication of foreign businesses and opportunists. A selection from his January, 1890 address to the pupils at the Malua Institution gives one an appreciation for Stevenson's sense of this impending crisis:

> Again there is another danger: the loss of your land to foreigners. It is good to make laws, and good to keep them; but let us remember that a law in itself is but a form of words ....
>
> It will be very difficult to keep this law about the land, unless you help. Yet another way. Trouble comes upon your people; and it is a trouble, like death, that must come and for which you must be prepared. The world is very full of men, many often starving; in these crowded lands, men have learned to work desperately hard; with all their hard work, they are still too many of them in their own place; they flow like water out of a full bucket, and they come, they must come, they have begun to come to your islands. Then the fight will befall, it has begun already; it is a true fight, although swords are not drawn nor guns fired, your men's lives and men's deaths are on the issue. (2: 225)

He especially wanted the native preachers, trained and helped by the LMS, to become the guides and teachers of the next generation so that the islanders would not be trampled upon by outsiders and risk losing control over their land. Simply to be pious was not sufficient. These future native preachers needed to be taught not only to heal the sick and visit prisoners but also to *prevent* disease and trouble so that the 'whole race does not [symbolically and literally] fall sick and die'. One way to preserve their culture was for them to convince their parishioners to be 'more industrious, to make a little money, and to save a little money' so that they could hold on to their land and resist the foreign plantations (2: 225-26).

By exhorting the young people sitting cross-legged before him at the Malua Institutions to take such a role and to become the parents of their country, Stevenson was twisting the parlance of imperialism that referred to natives as children — spinning the language on itself — and turning an all too familiar cliché on its head so as to defeat the deadly consequences of colonial rule. Illogical as it may sound, Stevenson paradoxically looked upon the missionary culture as a refuge for what moral goodness or vitality remained after various foreign intrusions. He saw the Mission Stations and Institutions as centers where islanders could find and develop strengths within themselves to oppose forces that were detrimental to their future. Stevenson was obviously not so much concerned with saving souls as he was with salvaging a nation about to be pulled apart, ravaged by foreign interests and internal strife; he was intent upon proposing practical means by which to counteract that possibility. Since he was neither an official, a trader, nor a missionary, and lived up the hill from Apia — physically separated from the colonial offices, he felt that he was in a strong position to act as an impartial facilitator. The missionaries, he thought, could be a significant part of the solution. In fact, Stevenson once wrote to Henry Clay Ide, the American Land Commissioner in Samoa, concerning the futility of finding effective white political leaders, and declared that 'We want men who will work as the missionaries work' (*Letters* 7: 194).

Missionaries as Heroes

Stevenson's approval of the missionary presence was not only a reflection of its usefulness but also of his unmistakable attraction to individual missionaries. Their extraordinary lives captured his imagination and even, at times, blinded him to the faults he associated with the missionary culture.

Father Dordillon, whom Stevenson met on the first voyage, fascinated him because of his public severity (he once sent a white man to jail for desecrating a Saint's day) which either alternated or mingled incongruously with a gentle, private softness. The admixture reminded Stevenson of 'some divine in the old school of Scotland' and momentarily recaptured images of curates from Stevenson's youth (*In the South Seas* 63). Stevenson also admired Father Dordillon for his tenacious grip on life, and for exploring new interests when he was no longer capable of pursuing his ministry. (Perhaps Stevenson recognized his own resiliance in the face of illness.) During Dordillon's last years, when he was frail and eventually bed-ridden, he had transformed his rigorous and harsh life first into the tending of a garden and, later, when that was no longer possible, into the cutting out of paper flowers.

On the second voyage Stevenson met Robert Maka, a native preacher from Hawaii, who was living in Butaritari, one of the Gilbert Islands. (The Stevensons stayed in his house.) In Stevenson's mind Maka was 'the best specimen of the Christian hero', for he alone had 'stood to his duty' when he had saved two lives at the risk of his own ('he had bearded a tyrant in his hour of blood') and had persevered under extreme difficulties when faced with a cannibal king who, in the end, fell under the missionary's influence (*In the South Seas* 65, 162). This native preacher had trod right out of the Sunday School adventure books presented for good attendance. And, like Dordillon, he had migrated to the South Seas out of Stevenson's past. The sight of Maka walking in his 'tall hat, black frock-coat, black trousers; under his arm the hymn book and the Bible; in his face, a reverent gravity .... myself following with singular and moving thoughts' took Stevenson home — this time to a green Lothian glen, where, 'Sunday by Sunday', he had accompanied his maternal grandfather (a minister in the Church of Scotland) back to his lodgings. But later, in his typically ironic mode, Stevenson admitted that while listening to one of Maka's tedious sermons, he had had to fight a sleep that 'breathed' on his joints and eyelids and 'hummed' in his ears. His struggles to stay awake amused an equally bored member of the congregation who 'gloated with a fixed, truculent eye upon the stages' of his agony (172-73). Heroism and nostalgia are more often than not mortal.

Brown and Chalmers

Once in Samoa, Stevenson, as I have mentioned, became close friends with Clarke, a steady, reasonable, and comforting presence. In addition, however, Stevenson briefly came to know two remarkable missionaries who woke up his adventurous imagination and never risked putting Stevenson to sleep as Maka had done. The Reverend George Brown (a Wesleyan) and the Reverend James Chalmers (LMS) — Chalmers also went by his native name, 'Tamate' — were pioneers who worked in uncharted and difficult circumstances and territories.[14] Almost single-handedly they faced great hardships; suffered from sickness and fever; treated ghastly wounds; survived wild seas; explored and mapped unknown rivers; and periodically were in danger of losing their lives, yet remained intrepid and always self-reliant.

In his autobiography, Brown often boasted how in perilous circumstances, he had to act alone:

> My crew, as usual, were very frightened, and as they positively refused
> to land, I hoped that a white man who was in our party would land with
> me; but he also refused, and so real appeared to be the danger to them
> all that they would not even anchor the launch whilst I went on shore. I
> went up alone. (Brown 106)

He also relished his confrontations with natives who brandished spears decorated
with human leg and arm bones, and the moments when 'suddenly some twenty or
thirty men, painted with ochre and lime as for war, and armed with spears and
tomahawks, rushed out from the back of the house' and made toward him (190).

1.3   'Natives and Author at Murua, New Guinea.'

Obviously Stevenson, who found terror quite palatable — he once told a
friend that terror was 'one of the chief joys of living' (*Letters* 7: 374) — and who
never let go of his fascination with cannibalism, was entranced by these stories and
is said to have wanted to write Brown's biography. Furthermore, he admired
Brown's scandalous and courageous behavior when, in April, 1878, the missionary,
angered by the cannibalization of four of his native teachers in New Britain, had
ignored missionary etiquette and organized (and led) an expedition of local traders
against the murderers — an example, in Stevenson's mind, of how missionary and

trader could cooperate to the benefit of all. In a letter to his mother, Stevenson wrote that he had met 'the man who fought a battle with cannibals at New Britain, and was so squalled over by Exeter Hall' (*Letters* 7: 6). Here was an episode in a Henty or Ballantyne novel come to life.[15]

If Brown was a first cousin to the boys' adventure hero, then Chalmers was a stepson of the mythic hero. He was larger than life and as 'big as a house, and far bigger than any church' (*Letters* 7: 186) — literally much taller than Brown whom Stevenson depicted as a 'small, slight fellow'. In contrast, Chalmers was 'a big stout, wildish-looking man, iron grey, with big bold black eyes, and a deep straight furrow down each cheek' (*Letters* 7: 6). Stevenson's high regard for the missionary is suffused with an ardor rarely, if at all, extended to others. As he admitted to his mother, 'I have a *cultus* for Tamate; he is a man nobody can see, and not love .... I am highly *mitonari* [in favor of church membership or feeling religious] now ...' (*Letters* 7: 15).[16] Following his first meeting with Chalmers on board a steamer between Sydney and Samoa, a flurry of letters burst forth declaring his admiration. On 5 November 1892, Stevenson wrote to Chalmers, 'I shall never cease to rejoice I had the good fortune to meet you' (*Letters* 7: 36). Days later, disappointed that he could not see Chalmers before the missionary left for New Guinea, Stevenson confessed his veneration:

> I am a man now past forty: Scotch at that: and not used to big expressions in friendship — and used on the other hand to be very much ashamed of them. Now, when I break my word to you, I may say so much: I count it a privilege and a benefit to have met you, I count it loss not to meet with you again.
>
> 'Just now', I make haste to add. If death spare us, and the juncture of life permit, I mean to see you, and that soon. If things oppose, accept the expression of my love and gratitude: my love for yourself, my gratitude for your example and kindness .... But O, Tamate, if I had met you when I was a boy and a bachelor, how different my life would have been. (*Letters* 7: 47-48)

Does this mean Stevenson would have sooner given up what efforts he had made to please his family (like getting admitted to the Scottish Bar), and have early on thrown all to the winds in order eagerly to follow in the footsteps of the adventurer and seek uncharted lands? Probably so. His words, though, do not imply he wished he had become a missionary.

Stevenson had been thrilled when Chalmers had selected him to introduce his lecture to the white community in Apia (18 September, 1890). Prompted by his enthusiasm, Stevenson had given in to the moment and closed his opening remarks in good missionary form: 'I believe we shall all be stimulated to greater courage in taking up the cross that all heroic souls have taken — the cross of light and progress' (Lovett 354). When Stevenson listened to that lecture and later read Chalmers' *Pioneer Life and Work in New Guinea*, he heard him describe native guides who wore armlets made from the jawbones of a man they had killed and eaten, and acts of wild bravado.

Chalmers was a good raconteur; however, a harsh streak cuts across Chalmers' narratives to expose a person who is authoritarian, if not tyrannical. One incident from *Pioneer Life and Work in New Guinea* concerning a confrontation with a chief is revealing:

> A chief came to the house one morning, and was very troublesome, saying, 'You are useless as a chief, having no arms; whenever you go, you are unarmed.' I told them I was a man of peace, had come to preach peace, but if necessary should defend myself. I brought out two bottles — one containing sulphuric acid and the other muriatic acid. I poured a little of each on the ground close by him; the fumes went into his face. Frightened, he started and ran .... A fortnight afterwards the chief returned, wishing to make friends. (156-57)

No words of his, though, are more damning than those concerning an 1875 visit he made from Rarotonga to a missionary outstation run by native pastors:

> I, the English missionary, will not allow the native pastors to think and act for themselves. I compel them to do what I say or think may be right. I dare them to think they are aught else than my servants. I insist on the entire submission of deacons and church members to my infallibility. They must ever remember they are mine, not Christ's & my will must be done. The same extends to the church and judges, they must do as I say in all matters great and small. This is not overdrawn. The white missionary am king supreme & unless kings, queens and judges submit to me I am mortally offended & the anathemas of my sacred office are hurled against these proud rebellious ones, they are at once ex-communicated & only readmitted to favor & church privileges when they return bending lowly in my presence and throw themselves prostrate on the ground at my feet. (LMS Archives, ms.163)

Admittedly, between 1875 and 1890 such pompous and willful attitudes relaxed and, in general, missionaries became more enlightened; however, echoes of this earlier imperious, aggressive tone continued to reverberate in Chalmers' later narratives, and, in turn, it must be confessed, attracted, if not enchanted, Stevenson. As we have already seen through his admiration for the more severe aspects of Dordillon's, Maka's, and Brown's characters (as well as of his own tyrannical fictional characters), Stevenson was often drawn to a commanding, imperative presence. His blood also raced with a certain rush of pleasure at the thought of living, as did Chalmers, on the edge of violence and disaster: Stevenson was thrilled when the yachts he charted either dangerously leaned into the tumultuous seas or, through the dark night, precariously maneuvered through reefs and treacherous archipelagos. Indeed, as others have recognized, Chalmers, with his swashbuckling stories and Scotch brogue, was 'a man after Stevenson's own heart' (Moors 67). He satisfied a desire for adventure and, I might suggest, authority, that was thwarted by the restrictions imposed by Stevenson's profession, his family circumstances, and, obviously, his chronic sickness. Chalmers was able to go places where few whites had gone, carry out daring deeds, and exert an influence that Stevenson could not. In the missionary's presence, he could live vicariously and see standing before him a 'hero; the only one I ever met ...'. Stevenson declared to his stepson, 'as heroes are my daily bread, I batten on him like beef and ale: he feeds me' (*Letters* 7: 36). Because of his own death in 1894, Stevenson was never to know that Chalmers was to join a select company of Christian martyrs and loom even larger as a hero in the popular mind. In April, 1901, Chalmers was murdered in New Guinea, and, as the story is told, cannibalized.

Chalmers and Brown might have served as heroes in a place that was sorely in need of them, but more important, as far as Stevenson was concerned, was their brash unconventionality, which resonated with his own Bohemian impulses and, in addition, supported many of his quarrels with the missionary culture. Neither Brown nor Chalmers conformed to the meek missionary stereotype nor was bound tightly to the Missionary Societies' rules. Both were rowdy, 'splendid men with no humbug' (*Letters* 7: 6) — qualities that charmed their faults away, even though Stevenson was not always blind to them. They turned their backs on narrow restrictions and openly drank and smoked before colleagues who sat there shocked amidst a 'sanctified air, that is delicious to behold' (*Letters* 7: 9). Stevenson first met them in the smoking room of the ship; later he took immense pleasure when Chalmers smoked a pipe with him on the veranda at Vailima. They also willingly acknowledged and debated the errors and merits of their work. Neither wholeheartedly conformed to the moral, upright, and obedient protagonists of either the Sunday School pages or the popular boys' adventure stories. In addition, what made them even more appealing was their extensive travel in the Pacific. Brown and Chalmers had been more places than most, knew more than most whites, had practical experience dealing with all types of colonials and islanders, and, consequently, were, in Stevenson's eyes, eminently better qualified to take public office (even though missionaries were not in the running) than many of the ill-informed foreigners sent to take official positions. Thinking about the possibility of a single protectorate in Samoa, Stevenson once fantasized that someone like 'the missionary Brown', would be preferable as a ruling white official to anyone else (*Letters* 8: 240).

Missionaries and the South Seas Fiction

Given the way the missionaries and their culture occupied Stevenson's consciousness, it is not surprising that their fictional counterparts populated his South Seas tales. Stevenson often relied upon a missionary's interactions with the natives, chiefs, traders, officials, residents, and beachcombers to illuminate the character of island life and to advance the movement of his narratives. The most remarkable and widely-read of these stories is *The Beach of Falesá*. This narrative is told through the eyes of Wiltshire, an English trader, who comes to an island that has a history of missionary presence to set up business in the copra trade. He meets savage opposition from a white competitor, Case, who is determined to destroy him and enjoy the monopoly of the trade: Case has already murdered or intimidated those who have preceded Wiltshire. As the story develops, Case places one obstacle after another in Wiltshire's way, including arranging a false marriage between Wiltshire and Uma, a native woman who has been tabooed both for being an outsider (she is kinless and comes from another island), and a person unlucky in love (she has been rejected by a minor chief from another island). Because she is tabooed, no one will come near her or Wiltshire. The new trader's survival ultimately depends upon his own resolve and gumption to destroy the terrifying woods in which Case has hung wind machines and fake images to scare the superstitious natives. Wiltshire's determination to rid the island of Case's vicious presence, however, is aided by Tarleton, a white Protestant missionary, who arrives on the island to visit a missionary outstation. In the end Wiltshire conquers Case (stabs and kills him) and exiles the worst of the dissolute whites; surrenders his dreams about returning to England, and settles down to enjoy his domestic life as well as his trade — although he worries about the future of his half-caste children.

In the telling of his tale, Stevenson enlists the rivalries and frictions attending and sometimes sullying an island's missionary culture. To begin with he draws on the conflict between the traders and the missionaries — a hostility, as I have pointed out in the first part of the chapter, that Stevenson thought counterproductive and unnecessary. When Wiltshire, the trader, first sets eyes on Tarleton, the white missionary, he is full of suspicion because of the missionaries' pervasively negative criticism of his kind. Wiltshire declares that he does not 'like the lot, no trader does; they look down upon us and make no concealment; and besides they're partly kanakaised, and suck up with natives instead of with other white men like them' (Menikoff 148). He is well aware that the missionary generally despised his sort because of their loose morals, the inferiority of their class, and their business practices that cheated the natives whom the missionaries tried to protect. Wiltshire's opening words to Tarleton are: 'I want to tell you first that I don't hold with missions ... and that I think you and the likes of you do a sight of harm, filling up the natives with old wives' tales and bumptiousness.' A moment later, he adds, 'I'm no missionary nor missionary lover; I'm no kanaka nor favourer of Kanakas: I'm just a trader, I'm just a common, low, god-damned white man and British subject, the sort you would like to wipe your boots on' (Menikoff 149). Eventually, as Stevenson would wish, when Tarleton talks at length with Wiltshire, the two cooperate and the problems with Case and his degenerate followers get resolved.

Stevenson also builds his story around the conflicts among the various missionary societies — conflicts that, as I have said, were pervasive. When Wiltshire makes his way through the island, he soon learns there are murderous or destructive factions among the various sects. Among others, there are 'Papists' or 'Popeys', and it is amusing to find Stevenson speaking of Father Galuchet or 'Father Galoshes' as a good natured soul but so grizzled and dirty that 'you could have written with him on a piece of paper' — a remark that replicates Stevenson's commentary on the kindness, yet filthiness, of the priests he had met in the Marquesas and Tahiti. There are also 'Hard-shell Baptis'', a weak native preacher, and a self-declared immoral cleric dressed in a big paper collar. Each partly is at the mercy of the other and each maps the island according to his interests. Because of the importance of these factions, Wiltshire finds himself asking Uma, his native wife, if she were a 'Popey'. She adamantly replies, 'No good, popey' and asks Wiltshire to attend the Protestant service. Wiltshire, who through his occasional remarks, reveals that in his distant past he has had some perfunctory religious instruction, probably through the Church of England, declines, but walks by the Protestant chapel and looks in; Stevenson's description of the natives at worship recalls his mother's account of her visit to a church in the Marquesas.

Some of the text's most grisly (and, perhaps, humorous) moments magnify the nastiness of this competition. The rivalry among the groups, for instance, structures the interpolated story of one of Wiltshire's predecessors (Johnny Adams), who was poisoned by Case and who, when he was dying, begged to have the attendance of a priest: 'Get the priest, don't let me die here like a dog' (132). Father Galuchet was summoned, but Papa (Captain Randall), the violent, base drunk who unofficially ruled the trading business and was an adamant Baptist, refused to let the priest in. Galuchet hammered on the door and cried out that there was a soul to save. Later, when the man had been buried, word came back to Papa that 'Galoshes' was praying on the man's grave. Case, who is telling the story to Wiltshire, describes the confrontation:

> Papa was pretty full, and got a club, and lit out straight for the place; and there was Galoshes on his knees, and a lot of natives looking on. You wouldn't think papa cared that much about anything, unless it was liquor; but he and the priest stuck to it two hours, slanging each other in native; and every time Galoshes tried to kneel down, papa went for him with the club. There never were such larks in Falesá. The end of it was that Captain Randall [Papa] knocked over with some kind of a fit or stroke, and the priest got in his goods after all. But he was the angriest priest you ever heard of; and complained to the chiefs about the outrage, as he called it. That was no account, for our chiefs are protestant here; and anyway he had been making trouble about the drum for morning school, and they were glad to give him a wipe. (133)

Because Stevenson was determined to write narratives that depicted the realities of these complex, and, as one sees in the above passage, often political, relationships, he naturally not only included the missionary as a character in these texts but also expressed his concerns about their policies and attitudes. The consequence is that details and incidents in 'Something In It', 'The Isle of Voices', *The Beach of Falesá*, and *The Ebb-Tide* reflect Stevenson's criticism of the missionary culture. Several of the stories register what I have already pointed out to be Stevenson's impatience with the missionaries' unwillingness to acknowledge the validity of indigenous beliefs and superstitions. In these texts, trapped in the confines of his own religious orientation, the missionary cannot get it into his stubborn head that there is 'something in' the taboos practiced by the islanders and that these should be taken seriously rather than demeaned and supplanted by the missionary's own set of Christian prohibitions. Those familiar with the fable 'Something In It' know the fate of the missionary who ignored the natives' warning that if he touched the house of yellow reeds tied with black sinnet, he would instantly become the prey of Akaänga, a cannibalistic mythic figure. At first the missionary scoffed at their belief as well as their caution, and declared 'There is nothing in it', but by the end of the fable, after the missionary has barely escaped with his life, he knows better and is forced to admit, 'I seem to have been misinformed upon some points .... Perhaps there is not much in it, as I supposed; but there is something in it after all. Let me be glad of that' (Jolly 255-57). Note, however, the cautious syntax of the evangelical's assent; he is not completely converted.

Stevenson's annoyance with the missionaries' tendency to deny both the power and the persistence of native superstitions also shapes his characterization of the white missionary in 'The Isle of Voices', a story about a native who, through the magic of a warlock, travels to and gets trapped (and will be cannibalized if he is not rescued) on an archipelago where disembodied voices haunt the woods and the beach. The missionary in the tale dismisses the validity of such a possibility. Because he finds Polynesian superstitions to be incomprehensible, he condemns himself to the fringes of island life — he only comes in at the end of the story and is consulted by the islanders as a last resort. Consequently, after he has listened to the rescued native's narrative of his troubles on the enchanted island, he carelessly rejects the account as 'extraordinary rigmarole' and asks for a donation to the missionary funds — a humorous dig at the missionary societies and their persistent soliciting for donations in their magazines and through their personal appeals to Stevenson.

In his South Sea tales Stevenson also registers his irritation with a more general narrow-mindedness demonstrated by the missionary society's insistence on superficial codes of behavior. In *The Ebb-Tide* (partially written with Lloyd Osbourne) Stevenson uses a moment in one of his character's tirades to lash out at missionary culture and accuse its representatives of going 'the wrong way to work'. He enumerates the pettinesses of the missionaries' regulations, such as their requirement that natives, once converted, cover their nakedness and wear the missionary mother-hubbard frocks. He also faults the missionaries for relying too heavily on the ornaments of religion: 'they are too parsonish, too much of the old wife, and even the old apple-wife. *Clothes, clothes*, are their idea; but clothes are not Christianity, any more than they are the sun in heaven, or could take the place of it! They think a parsonage with roses, and church bells, and nice old women bobbing in the lanes, are part and parcel of religion' (Jolly 203-204).

The Villain and the Vulnerable Hero in the South Sea Tales

Although this character's criticisms reflect Stevenson's own, the evangelical figure, Attwater, who speaks these damning words, is by no means, as those who have read *The Ebb-Tide* understand, a person to be trusted. Attwater is, indeed, one of the most disturbing characters in what is one of Stevenson's most gruesome portrayals' of island life, especially as experienced by whites who have become the victims of their own weaknesses and their own colonial imperatives.

The Ebb-Tide is the story of three down-and-out whites of various classes (and ways of speaking) who are at the end of their tether.[17] By chance and some scheming they take charge of the *Farallone*, a schooner that has been infected by smallpox and carries, they think, a cargo of champagne. The three beachcombers plan to steal the *Farallone*, sell its cargo, and escape to a more lucrative life. However, shortly after they sail, two of the three break into the champagne, become hopelessly drunk, and nearly wreck the vessel. Eventually, they learn that the cargo is bogus — it consists mostly of bottled water — and they search for a place to land. Suddenly into view comes an island that is not charted, but, desperate, they bring the *Farallone* to shore. Once they disembark, they find themselves in a region that has fallen victim to an epidemic of smallpox that has depopulated the island, and in the clutches of Attwater, a tall, physically imposing individual. Attwater is a man who had come to the South Seas partially because of his interest in the missions, but who has since become a trader in pearls, and an official as well. He is a hybrid of the worst elements delineating a destructive colonial presence; he is missionary, trader, beachcomber, and official rolled into one violent, disruptive, and unpredictable entity. He, like the schooner, is a microcosm of imperialist society. At the end of the novel, Attwater has murdered one of the beachcombers (who, in turn, had schemed to murder Attwater by throwing acid in his face); converted another who, daily on his knees, grimly parodies the worst of an evangelical zeal based on piety and terror; and more or less seduces the last of the three, Robert Herrick, who succumbs to the fact that Attwater, like him, is a university man, and from a class superior to that of his companions.

What is Stevenson implying about missionary culture in his depiction of this towering Attwater? When one thinks back to Stevenson's fascination with people like the missionary Chalmers, who ruled their territories as autocrats, who were larger than life, physically strong, and self-willed, there is a temptation to find a correspondence between these heroes and Attwater. Robert I. Hillier has suggested that Attwater reflects Stevenson's attraction to heroism. He finds a correspondence between Brown's absolute power in Tonga or Chalmers' tyrannical nature ('My tyranny is well-liked by the natives' [Lovett 241]), and the role of Attwater. He even proposes that 'Stevenson placed himself in a relationship somewhat like that of Herrick to Attwater at the end of the novel' (136). But, of course, this is overstating and even misrepresenting the case. As Hillier admits, one can go too far in promoting the parallels. I would rather suggest that Attwater exaggerates the very worst tendencies of people like Brown and Chalmers, and, indeed of the whole missionary enterprise that had readily violated an island's traditions by attempting too radically and completely to graft itself upon its culture and social system. In so doing, missionaries became part and parcel of the worst of the larger colonial enterprise — all of which Stevenson deplored in spite of his sense that a good missionary or a good white official could also be of help.

Attwater has none of the 'ugly beauties' Stevenson could associate with the evangelical Church of Scotland martyrs he had read about as a child and who continued to prowl around his imagination (*Letters* 7:111).[18] He has only their ugliness. He is Chalmers and Brown taken to a distorted and dangerous extreme. Rather than being the hero, Attwater with his silken brutalities is very much the villain, and, of course, as others have recognized, a precursor of Joseph Conrad's Kurtz.[19] In fact, the hidden heroes of the piece are the natives, the hands on the schooner, who every Sunday quietly gather with Bible in hand. Strange to say given the portrayal of Attwater, thanks to their missionary training, they are the only moral people in the book. Furthermore, their missionary training has allowed them some sense of solidarity, a trait necessary for survival when on board a vessel (symbolically a state) run by destructive and incompetent white leaders. The scene reflects the basic paradox: the missionary culture that can be so destructive can also serve as a refuge. In spite of its latent paternalism, Stevenson's description of the scene is moving and, for the reader, a relief:

> Upon the Sunday each brought forth his separate Bible — for they were
> all men of alien speech even to each other, and Sally Day communicated
> with his master in English only, each read or made believe to read his
> chapter, Uncle Ned with spectacles on his nose; and they would all join
> together in the singing of missionary hymns. It was thus a cutting
> reproof to compare the islanders and the whites aboard the *Farallone*.
> Shame ran in Herrick's blood to remember what employment he was on,
> and to see these poor souls — and even Sally Day, the child of
> cannibals, in all likelihood a cannibal himself — so faithful to what they
> knew of good. (Jolly 168)

The ironies and ambiguities complicating this scene reverberate in other South Sea tales in which Stevenson cannot help but show a certain respect and affection for the missionaries — in spite of their limitations and their parochial tendencies. For instance, in 'Something in It', as Jolly notices, one has to recognize that the missionary, for all his blindness to his own shortcomings, is also partly to be admired. He is a kind of resolute hero. He actually saves himself through his stubborn loyalty to the missionary culture's regulations or taboos. In this parable, because the missionary is a 'blue-ribbon man' and refuses to break his pledge by imbibing the kava offered by the spirits — this is the kava that would have stunned him and led to his death — and bolstered by his strong conviction of being in the right, he proves to be too much for the mythical Akaänga who, exasperated, releases the missionary from his clutches beneath the sea and sends him back alive. Similarly, in 'The Isle of Voices', the missionary, for all his shortcomings, proves in some sense to be in the right. His recommendation that the natives, who are worried the warlock will continue to pursue them, should ward off this and other evil spirits by giving dollars to the lepers and to the missionary fund, works: 'Keola and Lehua took his advice, and gave many dollars .... And no doubt the advice must have been good, for from that day to this Kalamake [the warlock] has never more been heard of' (Jolly 122). In the framework of the story, the missionary's counsel seems silly and trivial, but in the context of the ending, it is strangely correct. As in 'Something in It', the missionary and his idiosyncrasies ironically become part of the solution.

The missionary figures in these two tales are obviously more comic than heroic. It is not until one looks at Tarleton, the white missionary in *The Beach of Falesá*, that one sees Stevenson creating a character who is more than simply an emblem of the failings and the blots of the missionary culture — although there are still the occasional foibles and shortcomings to ridicule: for instance, Wiltshire makes fun of Tarleton's tendency to go on too long while praying. In contrast to his counterparts in the other stories, Tarleton receives both the narrator's [Wiltshire's] and Stevenson's qualified approval. He might have none of the physical, swashbuckling bravado of either a Brown or a Chalmers, but he does have an immense knowledge of the island culture, an evenness of temperament, and a certain aplomb and authority to carry him through the most difficult situations — brave behavior in a complex, fractious society. At times his bearing and movements almost shadow the train of a hero's grandeur, especially in Wiltshire's eyes. For instance, when Wiltshire describes Tarleton's entrances and exits, it is as if — in spite of his prejudices — he is gazing at someone who is extraordinary, if not almost magnificent. Watching the missionary boat approach the shores of Falesá, the trader enviously observes Tarleton, dressed smartly in white clothes, commanding a white vessel shooting for the mouth of the river, and when Tarleton leaves, Wiltshire again catches sight of the boat, with its four-and-twenty paddles, and admires how, accompanied by the voices of the singing oarsmen, they flash through the water. The spectacle carries a hint of the epic or the operatic and, as in any heroic narrative, the scene's luminosity vividly contrasts with the frightening darkness of Case's folly and the putrid dinginess of Captain Randall's filthy body.

These semi-heroic associations continue once Tarleton steps on to the island and, like a *deus ex machina*, starts to mend wrongs. At Wiltshire's prompting he sets Uma and Wiltshire's false marriage straight (although, one has to remember that marriage would not have been an issue for them in the first place if the missionaries had not insisted on changing the islands' mores). Then, in a lengthy monologue, Tarleton helps Wiltshire understand Case's viciousness, the history and terrible fate of his predecessors, the weaknesses of the native preacher, and the sly character of an island chief; he also provides the names of those he could enlist to help him. His knowledge is so wide-ranging as to hint at the omniscience of the heroic mind. Later, Tarleton intercedes to bring an end to the ostracism of Uma and Wiltshire by demanding that both the Catholic priest and the native Protestant preacher visit Uma's home and so set an example to others. With this deed, Tarleton rises above the rivalries dividing the religious sects and momentarily unites them to help heal a wounded island. Eventually Tarleton shows up at another crucial moment, when Wiltshire has stabbed and killed Case. Followed by a string of kanakas, singing to keep their courage up, and with Mea, a native who has befriended both him and the trader, the missionary walks through the dark night of the forest to find and rescue Wiltshire. Wearing his white pith helmet, he steps out of the darkness in time to bury Case and carry out a wounded Wiltshire. He continues his healing vocation when he then sets Wiltshire's injured leg (but, as Wiltshire points out, it was a missionary splice, so he limps to this day). Although qualified by Wiltshire's occasional cutting remarks and asides, the portrait is positive and affectionate. Like the trader, one wants to start cooking dinner for Tarleton, and would like to have him as an ally.

Throughout, Stevenson has emphasized Tarleton's benevolence. The missionary exhibits none of the harsh, authoritarian demeanor of a Chalmers or a Brown when dealing with the islanders (even his stern lecture to the fallen native pastor is only a distant, benign echo of Chalmers' 1875 horrific report to the LMS quoted above concerning disobedient native pastors). Tarleton is 'anxious to do well for the natives' (Menikoff 154), and has their best interests at heart. Stevenson asks the reader to like him for this genuine impulse. The reader, like Uma and eventually Wiltshire, the narrator, cannot help but be drawn toward him: 'He was the best missionary I ever struck' (186) — a compliment that recalls Stevenson's praise of his intimate friend Clarke, who was supposedly the model for Tarleton. As part of his concern for the islanders, Tarleton demands that Wiltshire pledge to treat the natives fairly, but the trader, being who he is, will only obey as long as he is on Falesá and subject to the missionary's omniscient eye; once he moves to another island, he breaks his promise and begins to fiddle with the account books. In the end, therefore, Tarleton is not almighty; we have seen Stevenson's reminder that the missionary's word is always subject to the conditions of its surroundings.

In this respect a portion of *A Beach of Falesá* is given over to Tarleton's difficulties with the native pastor, Namu, who, during the missionary's absence, has easily fallen under the influence of Case and has participated in the burying alive of one of Case's enemies. When Tarleton speaks of the terrible incident and the native pastor's complicity in it, he cannot fully comprehend why someone he had helped to educate would offer up a prayer at the hateful scene. Tarleton's puzzlement registers his weaknesses and his vulnerabilities. To his credit, in Stevenson's eyes, Tarleton does recognize that he has been deceived and now realizes that a person in whom he had great confidence and thought fully reliable is not. Even after Namu has repented in front of Tarleton for his lapse, the missionary is fully aware that later, when Namu refuses to visit the tabooed Uma, he is still under Case's spell and that 'the dog has returned to his vomit' (Menikoff 157). But, as Menikoff suggests, Tarleton does not fully understand either Namu's shrewdness or his innocence, nor his susceptibility to superstition (79). In spite of such blind spots, however, the missionary admits to his own perplexities and realizes that he is not infallible. He cannot really answer his own questions, except to say that his life appears to be a mockery — a reaction that recalls Clarke's periodic disillusionment with the missionary effort:

> I felt myself in a very difficult position. Perhaps it was my duty to have denounced Namu and had him deposed; perhaps I think so now; but at the time, it seemed less clear. He had a great influence, it might prove greater than mine. The natives are prone to superstition; perhaps by stirring them up, I might but ingrain and spread these dangerous fancies. And Namu besides, apart from this novel and accursed influence, was a good pastor, an able man, and spiritually minded. Where should I look for better? how was I to find as good? At that moment with Namu's failure fresh in my view, the work of my life appeared a mockery; hope was dead in me .... (155)

To make matters worse, Tarleton discovers that he too is not exempt from Case's trickery. He suffers the embarrassment of being made a fool of in front of the natives by Case who, using a common conjuring trick, snatches a dollar bill from the missionary's head and holds it in the air for all to see. With one snap of the wrist, Tarleton's reputation, for the moment, is compromised in front of his congregation. Tarleton recognizes that his training is not adequate for such situations: 'I wished I had learned legerdemain instead of Hebrew, that I might have paid the fellow out with his own coin. But there I was, I could not stand there silent, and the best that I could find to say was weak' (156).

Conclusion

Such frailties and flaws are part of any attempt to deal with the intricacies of the island culture in which the various languages of the beachcomber, the trader, the missionary, the traveler, the resident, the native, the official, and the chief criss-crossed and gave voice to a virtual babel of attitudes and approaches to their surroundings and themselves. The complexity of Tarleton's responses toward his work, himself, and others (white and native), as well as their complicated reactions to him, are what fascinated Stevenson and kept the realism within the pages of *The Beach of Falesá* outside the margins of the earlier adventure novels and far away from the simple magic lantern slides of South Sea missionary houses, chapels, martyrs, and heathen idols being shown in the Elysian Rooms when he was a child. No slide show, not even a dissolving presentation in which one picture blended into another, could represent the multiple perspectives and ambiguities of Stevenson's Pacific fiction, which is solidly set in the contemporary world rather than in some mythic, martyred past and is, as Jolly remarks, dedicated to 'diverse forms of encounter and exchange' among 'the members of various island societies' (xxxiii). These narratives were also remote from the self-confident leaves of the Sunday School books that rarely admitted qualification or acknowledged both the virtues and the injustices or abuses on all sides.

Stevenson's depiction of the missionaries not only brings his readers closer to this complex reality but also provides a doorway through which readers can enter and explore the passages of Stevenson's imagination in his last years. In the following chapters, the missionary and his culture serve as a conduit to Stevenson's responses to memory, to appearance and reality, to the imagery of darkness and light, as well as to the world of real politics. Just as the missionary culture in the South Seas opens ways of comprehending the complexities of the island cultures so too does it help reveal the intricate ways in which Stevenson, as a traveler and resident white colonial, negotiated his reactions to his new surroundings as they replaced the assumptions and mythology he had left behind when he sailed across the Pacific ocean and settled in Samoa.[20]

Notes

1. The LMS founders were influenced in their thinking about this new territory through accounts written by explorers like La Pérouse, Bougainville, and Captain Cook whose murder in Hawaii particularly captured people's imagination. For histories of the London Missionary Society, see John Davies. *The History of the Tahitian Mission, 1799-1830.* Ed. C. W. Newbury. Cambridge: Hakluyt Society. Cambridge UP, 1961; Neil Gunson. *Messengers of Grace: Evangelical Missionaries in the South Seas 1797-1860.* Melbourne: Oxford UP, 1978; Norman Lewis. *The Missionaries.* New York: Holt, 1988; and Richard Lovett. *The History of the London Missionary Society, 1795-1859.* 2 Volumes. London: Frowde, 1899.

2. The children watching the magic lantern slides in the Elysian Rooms would have stared in wonder at pictures of these 'grotesque' figures. The missionaries made sure that many of these discarded or confiscated idols were sent back to England and, there, put on display in missionary museums, exhibits, and slide shows. In the missionary parlance, of course, these specimens represented the barbarous nature of heathenism.

3. Obviously, not all the missionaries were representatives of Protestant sects. When Stevenson was on board the *Casco* cruising in the Marquesas and the Paumotos, he met Catholic priests (like Father Siméon Delmas, Father Dordillon, and Father Orens), lay brothers (like Brother Michel), and sisters (teachers at the Catholic missionary schools) who guided him, led him to places where there had once been human sacrifices, served as interpreters, told him something of the history of the community, the beliefs and traditions of the inhabitants, and invited him to visit their pupils and attend their services. Later, when he settled in Samoa, Stevenson continued to enjoy a cordial relationship with the Marist priests on Upolu.

4. On the voyage of the *Casco*, Stevenson actually seems to have had more difficulty than his mother when being confronted by the chaos of religions. She seems to have slipped from one group to an other with far more ease than he. Stevenson, on the other hand, interrupts his account of the phenomenon with asides in which he admits to feeling uncomfortable when confronted with an image of the Virgin Mary or the relics treasured by Father Orens. See *In the South Seas* 46, 91.

5. The LMS missionary the Reverend James Chalmers recorded these questions when he went to examine and prepare students from the Malua Institution whom he was going to place in New Guinea. See Richard Lovett. 362-63.

6. The negative image of the beachcomber was also propagated by the Sunday School adventure books. In *The Cruise of the Dainty or Rovings in the Pacific* [1880], William Henry Giles Kingston describes the beachcomber, appropriately named Sam Pest:

> He [Sam Pest] was, I found, a regular beachcomber — a name generally given to the vagabond white men who are scattered about in numbers among the islands of the Pacific, to the great detriment of the natives, as by the bad example they set than they interfere much with the proceedings of the missionaries. (93)

7. Dr. George Turner was a LMS missionary who in 1861 published *Nineteen Years in Polynesia* and in 1884 his *Samoa a Hundred Years Ago and Long Before.*

8. James Edward Newell was also an authority on Samoan law and habits. Many of his

handwritten notes on Samoan customs are in the LMS Archives, SOAS, U of London. Newell gave an address in Samoan at Stevenson's funeral.

9. In Samoa, during the Reverend Clarke's time, the white missionaries wanted to amend the rule that any church member present at the *Siva*, the supposedly licentious night dance, would be automatically excommunicated. The white missionaries preferred to purge the dances of any sexual elements. They were, however, opposed by the native pastors who, when they discussed the matter, insisted on keeping the original rule and banning the night dances altogether. Later, Stevenson remarked in a letter to Sidney Colvin (November, 1890), 'the native pastors (to everyone's surprise) have moved themselves in the matter of the native dances, desiring the restriction to be removed [the ban on watching the *Siva*] or rather to be made dependent on the character of the dance' (*Letters* 7: 43).

    Another instance of the native pastors causing trouble by being too literal was recorded by Fanny Stevenson in her *The Cruise of the 'Janet Nichol': Mrs. Robert Louis Stevenson's Diary of a South Sea Cruise*.

    > The Samoan native missionaries told their people that for certain crimes it was allowable to kill the offender. Such a case occurred, and the guilty person, who richly deserved his fate, was put to death. Then the native missionaries said that the taking of life called for capital punishment. Fortunately, at this junctive, a white missionary from Samoa appeared on the missionary ship, and it was arranged that the avenger be exiled for an indefinite period. (178)

10. *The Chronicle of the London Missionary Society* (February, 1895) began an article on Stevenson by first noting that, 'Hostile criticism of missions is common enough on the part of travellers and irresponsible persons' (27).

11. John William Hills (1864-1932) was an LMS missionary in Samoa. From 1887 to 1890 he worked in Apia. He founded and ran a training school of Samoan boys in Leulumoega, west of Apia. Hills liked Stevenson, but did find it 'difficult to be quite at ease with him, for I could not but think of his vitriolic attack on my friend Dr Hyde [the Protestant clergyman who viciously attacked Father Damien and to whom Stevenson addressed a letter defending the work of Damien and damning Hyde's unchristian attitude]' (*Letters* 8: n.217).

12. In his *In the South Seas*, Stevenson mentions that the boys and girls who attended the Catholic schools in the Marquesas did not go voluntarily. Stevenson refers to the French government's 'miserable system' of requiring young children to leave home and be under the supervision of the priests and sisters:

    > The youth, from six to fifteen, are taken from their homes by Government, centralised at Hatiheu, where they are supported by a weekly tax of food; and with the exception of one month in every year, surrendered wholly to the priests. (45)

Stevenson notes that very few, barely a handful, ever returned to visit the school once they had been allowed to leave.

13. In *In the South Seas*, Stevenson writes:

> It might be supposed that native missionaries would prove more indulgent, but the reverse is found to be the case. The new broom sweeps clean; and the white missionary of to-day is often embarrassed by the bigotry of his native coadjutor. What else should we expect? On some islands, sorcery, polygamy, human sacrifice, and tobacco-smoking have been prohibited, the dress of the native has been modified, and himself warned in strong terms against rival sects of Christianity; all by the same man, at the same period of time, and with the like authority. But what criterion is the convert to distinguish the essential from the unessential? He swallows the nostrum whole; there has been no play of mind, no instruction, and, except for some brute utility in the prohibitions, no advance. (65)

14. The Reverend George Brown (1835-1917), English Wesleyan Methodist missionary and explorer, worked in the South Seas for nearly fifty years. He was in Savaii (one of the Samoan islands) from 1860-1874 and founded the Mission in New Britain. He was there from 1875 to 1881. From 1887 to 1908 he was the General Secretary for Foreign Missions. During that time he acted as Special Commissioner for Tonga 1888 to 1890. Brown was a magnificent photographer. The Royal Geographical Society has many of his photographs.

    The Reverend James Chalmers (1840-1901) was a Scottish missionary and explorer. After working in Rarotonga (Hervey Islands) from 1867-1876, he went to New Guinea and spent most of the rest of his life exploring and setting up new missionary posts. In April, 1901 he and a fellow missionary were murdered at Dopima in the Gulf of Papua.

15. George Alfred Henty was one the most popular writers of Boys' adventure fiction in the late nineteenth century. Among his many books are: *By Sheer Pluck: A Tale of the Ashanti War*; *For Name and Fame: or, Through Afghan Passes*; *The Dash for Khartoum: A Tale of the Nile Expedition*, and *Condemned as a Nihilist: A Story of Escape from Siberia*. R. M. Ballantyne, of course, wrote *The Coral Island*, supposedly a model for *Treasure Island*.

16. According to Marie Clothilde Balfour, who edited Margaret Stevenson's letters from the South Seas, *mitonari/mitonaree* means church membership.

17. In his introduction to his edition of *The Beach of Falseá*, Barry Menikoff remarks that in the telling of the story, Stevenson places emphasis on the authentic expression and idiosyncracies of each character's speech. Indeed, he rightly suggests that 'language is Stevenson's central theme. For it is language that defines the self, and just as Wiltshire struggles to find his own identity through language, so the profane and scurrilous language helps to define the world of Falesá' (57).

18. In a letter to his young friend Adelaide Boodle, Stevenson remarks on his 'old Presbyterian spirit' and reminds her that he is 'a child of the Covenanter — whom I do not love, but they are mine after all, my fathers and my mothers — and they had their merits too, and their ugly beauties, and grotesque heroisms, that I love them for, the while I laugh at them' (*Letters* 7: 111).

19. Alan Sandison in his 'Robert Louis Stevenson: A Modernist in the South Seas', reminds one that contemporary critics faulted Stevenson in *The Ebb-Tide* for breaking with convention and dispensing with a hero altogether. See Alan Sandison. 45-51. For instances of the comparisons between Stevenson and Conrad, see Linda Dryden. *Joseph*

Conrad and the Imperial Romance. Handmills: Macmillan, 2000, and Andrea White. *Joseph Conrad and the Adventure Tradition: Constructing and Deconstructing the Imperial Subject*. Cambridge: Cambridge UP, 1993.

20. In her article, 'Robert Louis Stevenson and Samoan History: Crossing the Roman Wall', Roslyn Jolly comments that 'Stevenson saw the European "invasion" of the Pacific as an expansion of the frontiers of Roman civilisation, which he identified with modernity and the west. As his biographer, Graham Balfour wrote, Rome represented to Stevenson, "a whole system of law and empire". The culture of the Pacific region fascinated him because it had developed outside that system, and it invited the traveller to step outside it too' ('Robert Louis Stevenson and Samoan History: Crossing the Roman Wall.' 113-20).

Chapter Two

Stevenson's Pyjamas

Introduction

Buried among Robert Louis Stevenson's miscellaneous papers at the Beinecke Rare Book and Manuscript Library (Yale) is a seemingly insignificant tailor's bill made out to 'R. L. Stevenson, Samoa' from Chorley, the tailor in Sydney (Australia). The bill lists such items as '1 pair of white serge tros.', '1 pair of Bedford Cord riding tros.', and '3 pairs of pyjamas'. Although at first this list of outfits seems trivial, it serves to remind one that the whole business of what to wear was a vital element in the life of Stevenson in the South Seas. When he sailed into the Pacific, he entered territories that had been partially mapped by missionaries who, ever since their first arrival on the islands, had tried to enforce strict rules about native clothing, a fact, we recall, that Attwater in *The Ebb-Tide* complains about when he characterizes the missionaries as thinking of little but '*Clothes, clothes*' (Jolly 203). Clothing was no minor matter for these missionaries who wanted to cover the natives' nakedness with western attire and mother-hubbard frocks that masked the curves of a body as well as the lure of its flesh. Their preoccupation with the issue obviously had little consequence for Stevenson's personal choices, but it does alert one to a subject that might otherwise slip by. It makes one more mindful of the importance of clothing in creating cultural and personal identity. It also offers an occasion to explore Stevenson's rather idiosyncratic relation to his clothes, a relationship that mirrors the paradoxes and tensions of his life as a white colonial traveler and resident. Moreover, it provides an opportunity to consider how clothing becomes an integral part of the ways in which we relate to ourselves, our surroundings, and our mortality.

Stevenson's choice of apparel was as much linked to his existence on the islands as were the words and subjects of his writing. His attention to his attire and others' commentary on it offer some sense of the fabric of Stevenson's experiences and, indirectly, of his writing. In particular, Stevenson's selection of outfits makes apparent the various roles clothes play in representing a life. As we shall see through the reactions to his and his family's garments, a person's vestments can be a means by which people tend to appraise an individual's character and morality. In addition, as we shall also discover (in the section 'Undress and the Idea of Cultural Contagion'), to the critical observer, the choice of clothing can register the extent to which individuals have been affected by their cultural surroundings and have allowed themselves to be influenced by them. Stevenson's selection of garments also reminds one that clothing is tied to authority and to one's status in society, a well-recognized fact that Stevenson did not ignore when he wanted to establish his position in Samoa.

The sections 'Dressing Up: The Vailima Livery' and 'Dressing Up: The Half-Caste Club' discuss Stevenson's efforts in this regard. Clothes, though, also have a fantasy life, allowing for roles that Stevenson and his family indulged in when they either borrowed clothes or adorned themselves in fancy dress. 'Dressing Up: Reconfiguring the Body' and 'Dressing Up for the Camera' are about their delight in putting on these garments that for a while created an illusion of their being something other than themselves, as well as about the ways in which this activity sustained and entertained them, and, in Stevenson's case, asserted his sheer will to live. This practice of dressing up, however, was not all play; it had its consequences, for it exposed the discrepancies between the wearer and his or her attire as well as the confusions of cross-cultural dressing. It also inevitably revealed the final discrepancy between one's clothes and one's body and underlined the reality that the body cannot forever be sustained by what adorns it. The last section, 'Death and the Gap', is about how this reality marked Stevenson's end.

The Context

In the nineteenth century, clothing had already been and continued to be an issue for those who visited and came to live in the South Seas. In accounts of travel among the islands and atolls, one comes across passage after passage about the dress and ornamentation of the inhabitants. And in nineteenth-century anthropological studies of the region, one runs into the obligatory chapters describing the function and materials of the islanders' garments. These pages are reminders that outsiders tend to judge an alien society through the mode of its dress or undress, and that dress seems to provide a window through which to catch a glimpse of a culture. For the travelers and the anthropologists alike dress was the code that marked the boundary between the known and the unknown.

No more obvious example of these principles exists than the attitudes and policies of the Western missionaries living in the South Seas during the eighteenth and nineteenth centuries. As I have already mentioned, these missionaries paid close attention to the attire of the natives they wished to convert and control, for they believed that the undermining of the traditional fabric of island society was a necessary prerequisite to conversion.[1] By refashioning the body's surface, they hoped to refashion the mind. In this respect it is especially interesting to read the diaries of missionaries sent to visit the more remote out-stations and note that clothing inevitably becomes the focus and the means by which to mark any progress. Their remarks show that by attempting to obliterate the 'strange dresses of the people' ('Missionary Meeting at the Samoas' 178), and by replacing the 'disgustingly' scant clothing of their converts (Turner 80) with loose gowns and 'coal-scuttle' bonnets (Cumming 13), they were attempting to prescribe a more correct character. Proper clothes were a measure of success. In 1886 the *Missionary Herald* announced: 'But to-day! Oh, the glad happy change! Men, women, and children well dressed, some of them richly dressed for this people!' ('The Fourth of July in Micronesia' 523). Another missionary magazine featured pictures of South Sea villages before and after the coming of Christianity. In the village 'Under Heathenism', natives dance barefoot, half-naked, in grass skirts, and resemble satyrs from promiscuous Roman frescoes. Adorned with feathers, bones, and teeth, the featured figures engage in what once would have been labelled 'savage' conduct: in one corner of the picture, for instance, a topless woman cruelly pulls her naked child's hair. But in the 'Same Village under Christianity', politeness, restraint, industry, and a sense of propriety are visible through the native women's loose, shapeless calico dresses, pinafores, bonnets, stockings and shoes, and through the men's Western shirts and medium-length, skirt-like wraps or kilts to cover their loin cloths (the Reverend George Turner, however, regarded the covering worn by the men of Tana as being highly indecent, as it accentuated the parts concealed).[2] These garments nullify the past and display a people now ennobled, sexless, modest, and 'in their right minds' (Marriott).

A fact not to be overlooked is that it was not only the South Sea natives who came under critical scrutiny for the manner of their dress. Western residents were also subjected to close examination. Travelers and missionaries often found themselves surrounded by the curious eyes and fingers of the natives. Out of sheer inquisitiveness, islanders frequently closely examined a visitor's attire and encouraged sailors and missionaries to undress before them.[3] The Reverend James Chalmers when exploring South-Eastern New Guinea reported that the people persuaded him to take off his boots and wanted not only to inspect but to feel his feet. He also described how they were eager to see what lay beneath his shirt and required him to exhibit his chest — a revelation followed by the crowd's giving 'one terrific shout'. Consequently on subsequent excursions into and around the island, Chalmers eagerly threw his shirt aside so he might display his chest — that is 'until an old chief, who became much attached to Mrs. Chalmers, brought in to her a present of a man's breast, saying it was the best piece, and she must have it'. After that, Rev. Chalmers admitted, 'I was a little chary, and very seldom exhibited my chest' ('Explorations in South-Eastern New Guinea' 8); nevertheless, as I have recorded in the previous chapter, in 1901, Chalmers was cannibalized in the Gulf of Papua. Whether the above episode reported by Chalmers is true or not, exaggerated or misunderstood, the incident emphasizes the role of clothes in mapping alien territory and in the uncovering of an individual's identity.

Robert Louis Stevenson and the Mode of Undress

Given the importance of clothing in representing the state of the individual and the morality of a culture, it is, perhaps, not surprising that when Stevenson traveled and lived in the South Seas, his attire was also subject to close scrutiny and was frequently the subject of observers' commentary. Indeed, it is extraordinary how many memoirs dwell on the manner of his dress. Westerners who came through or who had settled in the area felt somehow compelled to remark upon his appearance. Their reactions are interesting not only for themselves but also for what they reveal about Stevenson's relation to his milieu (his newly-tailored self) and, more significantly, for the insight they provide into the ambiguous nature of clothing: that it both protects one from what is outside and, simultaneously, reflects what surrounds one. As we shall see, clothes can be prophylactic as well as vectors of cultural contagion, for they shield one from the outside at the same time as they register what has crossed the boundary from the outside to the inside, and reveal to what extent one has been contaminated by the surrounding society.

When Stevenson and his family first landed on the shores of Samoa, they were spied by missionaries who immediately determined they were not of their ilk, for the Stevensons were obviously not abiding by the rules regarding dress that the missionaries encouraged. In his diary the Reverend J. E. Newell records how the Stevenson party burst on the Samoan world in 'the most extraordinary, unconventional' costumes — '(I would say *Bohemian*, if you would not misunderstand the term) that was ever seen' (LMS Archives, Box 6). And the Reverend W. E. Clarke had a similar reaction. When he first laid eyes on them he thought them stray members of a wandering minstrel troupe. In an article he wrote for the *London Missionary Chronicle*, Clarke records the moment:

> I met a little group of three European strangers — two men and a woman [Stevenson, Lloyd Osbourne, and Fanny]. The latter wore a print gown, large gold crescent earrings, a Gilbert-island hat of plaited straw, encircled with a wreath of small shells, a scarlet silk scarf round her neck, and a brilliant plaid shawl across her shoulders; her bare feet were encased in white canvas shoes, and across her back was slung a guitar.
>
> The younger of her two companions was dressed in a striped pyjama suit — the *undress* costume of most European traders in these seas — a slouch straw hat of native make; dark blue sun-spectacles, and over his shoulder a banjo. The other man [RLS] was dressed in a shabby suit of white flannels that had seen many better days, a white drill yachting cap with prominent peak, a cigarette in his mouth, and a photographic camera in his hand. Both the men were bare-footed. They had, evidently, just landed from the little schooner now lying placidly at anchor, and my first thought was that, probably, they were wandering players en route to New Zealand, compelled by their poverty to take the cheap conveyance of a trading vessel. ('Reminiscences of Robert Louis Stevenson')

This Bohemianism of 'undress' that offended the missionaries' sense of propriety also disturbed Western businessmen and visitors. Indeed their repeated references to the Stevensons' uncleanliness, shabbiness, and long dishevelled hair almost parallel the missionaries' scorn and disapproval of the natives they were attempting to convert and make clean, neat, correct, and sober looking.[4] The carelessness of the Stevensons' dress bothered Henry Jay Moors, the expatriate who helped Stevenson to settle in Samoa. In his memoir, Moors complains that even when Stevenson came down to Apia, he looked 'about half dressed' and was lax about his personal adornment. He continues his reminiscence by pointing out that he never saw Stevenson 'in a stiff shirt nor a stand-up collar in my life'. And he adds, 'Up at Vailima they all went about in their bare feet except when expecting guests' (Masson 225). Another Westerner, J. C. Thiersens, also remarks on Stevenson's slovenly dress and remembers that Stevenson 'did not seem to trouble much about his outward appearance, indeed he struck one as being "artistically grubby". During the week he was on board he wore the same clothes, namely, a dingy flannel shirt, an aged brown velvet coat, and his trousers and shoes had evidently seen better days' (256). Perhaps the most scathing reports on Stevenson's attire are to be found in letters written by Henry Adams after a brief visit to Vailima (16 October 1890) : 'As we [Adams and John La Farge] reached the steps a figure came out that I cannot do justice to. Imagine a man so thin and emaciated that he looked like a bundle of sticks in a bag, with a head and eyes morbidly intelligent and restless. He was costumed in very dirty striped cotton pyjamas, the baggy legs tucked into coarse knit woolen stockings, one of which was bright brown in color, the other a purplish dark tone.' Later Adams describes Stevenson and Fanny as looking like odd birds: 'He seems never to rest, but perches like a parrot .... The parrot was very dirty and ill-clothed as we saw him, being perhaps caught unawares, and the female was in rather worse trim than the male' (*Letters* 7: 2-3). Priggish Adams wished that Stevenson had spent his money buying soap rather than building a house in Samoa. It is interesting to note that Stevenson was not always unaware of the criticism. In one of her letters home during the voyage of the *Casco*, his mother, Margaret Stevenson, remarked to her sister, Jane Whyte Balfour, that Père Bruno of Tautira was going to take 'Louis as the text of his sermon' and comment not only on his cheerfulness during his severe sickness but also on the style of his dress that the priest felt should be held up as an example. Père Bruno valued the fact that Stevenson 'only wore what was useful and necessary, and never went in for anything ornamental or extravagant!!' She added, 'Louis is delighted that he has *at last* found someone who appreciates his taste in dress, and wishes he could have a copy of the sermon to send to some of his scoffing friends' (*From Saranac to the Marquesas and Beyond* 248-49).

Undress and the Idea of Cultural Contagion

As the above comments suggest, the Stevensons' vestimentary practices went against the dominant Western discourse and, worse, as far as their friends in Scotland and England were concerned, showed signs (were tangible proof) of the Stevensons' going native, a metamorphosis that even Stevenson's mother, the usually staid-looking and apparently prim Margaret Stevenson, seemed to be undergoing when from Nuka-hiva (2 August 1887) she wrote to her sister that she and Fanny had dressed 'like the natives' and were enjoying a 'strange, irresponsible, half-savage life' (*From Saranac to the Marquesas and Beyond* 85). Charles Baxter [Stevenson's Edinburgh friend] and Sidney Colvin [Stevenson's London friend] especially worried about the changes they read about and saw in the photographs that Stevenson sent home. At one point (21 March 1894) Colvin, angry with Stevenson's evident immersion in his new life, asked, do any of 'our white affairs' interest you? 'I could remark in passing that for three letters or more you have not uttered a single word about anything but your beloved blacks — or chocolates — confound them; beloved no doubt to you; to us detested, as shutting out your thoughts, or so it seems, from the main currents of human affairs ...' (*Letters* 8: n.279). These friends, from the very beginning of Stevenson's life in the islands, fretted over Stevenson's growing interest and preoccupation with South Sea cultures and feared that he was involving himself too deeply in the life and the study of the natives as well as in the political and natural history of the region. Colvin especially had no taste for Stevenson's 'Pacific work' and believed that these interests contaminated Stevenson's prose and forced him into producing dull, lackluster pieces that in their attempts to be scientific lacked anecdote and adventure, the two ingredients necessary for public success.[5] For both Baxter and Colvin, Stevenson's choice of clothing — the Gilbert-island hat, the rolled-up pants, and the garlands of flowers he wore around his head (a practice, by the way, discouraged by the missionaries and one for which a native could be fined)[6] — displayed a similar sort of contagion. They were evidence that Stevenson was becoming increasingly infected by his so-called uncivilized surroundings and that he was, by degrees, being transformed into some sort of broken-down trader and abandoning the stand-up collar society of Edinburgh. In particular Stevenson's pyjamas — a loose jacket and trousers made of striped cloth — were disturbing to his compatriots, for as Reverend Clarke pointed out, these pyjamas were the '*undress* costume of most European traders in the seas'. Such an image would have undoubtedly alarmed Colvin, especially after reading a 4 December 1888 letter from Fanny in which she proudly announces that 'a simple pajama suit of striped light flannel' is 'his only dress'. From Tahiti she also told Colvin that Stevenson was taking sea baths and living 'almost entirely in the open air as nearly without clothes as possible' and that he and Lloyd (Stevenson's stepson, Lloyd Osbourne) wore wreaths of artificial flowers on their hats (*Letters* 6: 227).

This state of undress was a sign of the erasure of boundaries between what his friends perceived as the civilized and the uncivilized. Clothes were boundary markers and were supposed to protect one from being infected by whatever lurks beyond them. To be in a mode of undress was to violate those frontiers, to lose the covering/protection and status offered by European clothing, and to bring one too close to the unsettling otherness of an alien culture. Such a condition destroyed or weakened the divisions between Stevenson and his alien surroundings. To choose loose clothing and to wear as little as possible was threatening not only because it drew close to the fashion of the natives but also because the openings it created allowed one literally and metaphorically to be infiltrated, even touched, by one's surroundings. In Stevenson's case it exposed him too directly to a way of life and sets of beliefs and experiences that had little to do with the society and rank he had left behind and which, according to popular opinion, was not only inferior but also rude, licentious, and even cannibalistic.

Clothing like Stevenson's pyjamas at least offered a minimum amount of protection from his surroundings and, for the most part, served to distinguish him from the natives, but the habit of Stevenson and his family to walk around barefooted offered absolutely none. Consequently, even though Stevenson's preference for pyjamas was somewhat disturbing to his friends, the choice of casting off his shoes was significantly more upsetting, for now there was absolutely no symbolic boundary between the vulnerable flesh and the alien land. Images of his naked feet sinking into the sand and mud and braving the rough, uneven forest floor bothered his acquaintances. In their minds going about without shoes or stockings increased the threat of cultural contagion, a possibility made worse by the Stevensons' delight in this questionable practice. One smiles to think how both fascinated and alarmed friends and family at home must have been to learn that Fanny had had to decline an invitation to a social function given by the American consul because she could only find one shoe and not the other. When she sent her apologies, she signed the note '*Cinderella*' (LMS Archives, Newell Box 6). To read the letters and pocket diaries of Stevenson's mother who was fond of commenting upon how 'Lou goes about in shirt & trousers & bare feet' (Beinecke ms. 7304. July, Monday 9, 1888) and who bragged to a friend 'no such things as shoes and stockings are ever worn by any of us at Vailima' (*Letters from Samoa* 202), and to glance at Fanny's letters explaining that 'as to shoes and stockings we all have scorned them for months except Mrs Stevenson, who often goes barefoot and never, I believe, wears stockings' (*Letters* 6: 227) is to become aware of their pleasure and pride in their choice. For some of their friends, though, this practice was too close to going native. The Stevensons' willful discarding of such protection and their adopting the habits of the Samoan natives who, according to the missionary Arthur E. Claxton, had nothing to do with either boots or stockings,[7] were for them yet further unsettling signs of Stevenson's supposed decline, his exposure to a foreign land, and his repudiation of Western culture. To his friends the sight or thought of a shoeless Stevenson destabilized what had been their familiar notion of him and reminded people what anyone (including the missionaries) knew so well: that nothing/nobody ever crosses the beaches of the South Seas unchanged. Once more the manner of dress or undress measures and monitors alteration. For others the practice also had its moral implications and added yet another dimension to people's objections. The Reverend Newell's reaction to the Stevensons' penchant for going barefoot is typical. In his notes he claims he 'never but once' saw Fanny wearing shoes and stockings. He recalls that her feet 'peeped out ... innocent of covering' (LMS Archives, Box 6) — a condition that compromised his sense of decorum since he, like many other missionaries, insisted his converts and pupils wear shoes as a mark of respect or dignity. To don a pair of shoes, no matter how misfitting or uncomfortable, was to demonstrate that one was no longer a heathen.

2.1   'Barefooted Stevenson wearing a *lava-lava*. Fanny is seated next to him,' 1888

In a sense the choice to go without shoes makes its mark in many of Stevenson's South Seas tales where he seems, for a moment, to abandon the romantic story telling and adventure traditions of his Scottish fiction in order to expose the bare and factual footprints of characters like Case, Wiltshire, Uma, and Mr. Tarleton in *The Beach of Falesá*. In such stories, as we have seen in the previous chapter, he refuses the more conventional heritage, so he can feel the heat of the sand and the sting of the island cultures' complexities with the nakedness of his bare feet. He walks through these tales unshod, more open to the rough edges of experience and to the realities of life on the beach.

Dressing Up: The Vailima Livery

But in the South Seas Stevenson was not always in pyjamas and barefoot, for there were also times when he wished to identify with the colonial powers and to show his respect for authority and European custom. His acquaintances need not have despaired as much as they seem to have done. At these moments Stevenson abandoned his loose, informal clothing, dressed up, and took his shoes along. Once, when he was invited to King Mataafa's house for a state occasion, he tried his hardest to be respectable, even though the mud got the better of his intentions.

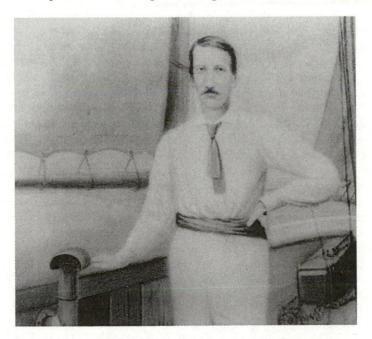

2.2   Robert Louis Stevenson. Self-portrait on board the yacht *Casco*

In a letter to Colvin (May, 1892) Stevenson describes the attempt:

> I had started barefoot; Belle [Stevenson's stepdaughter] had soon to pull
> off her gala shoes and stockings; the mud was as deep as to our knees,
> and so slippery that ... Belle and I had to take hands to support each
> other .... You are to conceive we were got up to kill, Belle in an
> embroidered white dress and white hat, I in a suit of Bedford cords hot
> from the Sydney tailors; and conceive us below ink-black to the knees
> with adhesive clay, and above steaming with heat.

Three miles later they found water to wash their feet, but before they got to the
King's house they were 'sadly muddied once more' (*Letters* 7: 299-300). But such
incidents did not hinder Stevenson's occasional desire to dress more formally and
to remind those around him of his position in society. Especially when he was
settled in Samoa and wanting to be thought of as the Laird of Vailima, ready to
display his authority, Stevenson often elected (frequently for photographs and
portraits) to don leather riding boots, proper cord riding breeches, a white shirt, and
a broad, bright red sash around his waist.

    This costume bore the marks not only of colonial authority and the rule of
the white man but also of royalty, for the red sash in the South Seas was traditionally a
badge of power. A clue to its symbolic authority is in John Williams's *A Narrative of
Missionary Enterprises* (1837). He tells how, as a missionary, he collected a red sash
and sent it to the missionary museum in England, and he describes how it was used at
the inauguration of the greatest kings. He explains that 'the most honourable
appellation which a chief could receive was, *Arii maro Ura*, King of the Red Sash'
(144). In a manner of speaking, by wearing his version of the red sash, Stevenson
appointed himself as leader of his realm. Indeed he ran his estate as a small fiefdom:
he made the laws, tried misdemeanors, and meted out the fines. And fully
understanding the power of clothes to assert this authority, he also used his servants'
outfits to control them and to define the boundaries of his property. By requiring his
staff at Vailima on formal occasions to dress in kilts (*lava-lava*) of Royal Stewart
Tartan (a tartan Stevenson carefully selected), white shirts for the men, a chemise for
the women, and striped jackets, Stevenson created what his mother referred to as the
'Vailima Livery' (*Letters from Samoa* 231) that served both as a 'badge' of the estate
and a reminder of his homeland. When the 'Vailima boys' (*Letters from Samoa* 199)
were in Apia, the closest town to Vailima, one would know where they came from
and whom they served.

    Yet Stevenson's dress code could and did go astray. As was often the case
in the South Seas, no matter how many regulations concerning clothing were laid
down, one could never be sure of their execution. Eighteenth- and nineteenth-
century explorers' and missionaries' accounts of Pacific islanders frequently
contain passages about how the natives, even when instructed in matters of fashion,
adorned their bodies with the bits and pieces of European clothing and got it all
wrong. There are numerous reports of islanders endeavoring to push their legs

2.3   Photograph of Vailima Staff

through the sleeves of coats, of natives sticking their arms through trouser legs, wearing only one boot, placing the shirt over the coat,[8] and, worse yet in these writers' opinion, mixing up the gender of the clothing, so that like the Reverend Chalmers they have to persuade a male native in the Gulf of Papua to take off the woman's dress and put on a man's shirt ('An Adventurous Journey in the Gulf of Papua' 55). Vailima was no exception to this confusion: the neat, trim, controlled appearance one sees in the photographs of Stevenson's household help was not always to be. There were times when the staff created confusion by borrowing Stevenson's or Lloyd's clothing or dressing themselves up in family discards. The costume code that Stevenson wanted to impose was not always understandable or logical to those from the island culture, so his sense of authority was frequently undermined by the disorder of their dress. On one occasion Stevenson's mother, exasperated, exclaimed that Simé (one of the staff) 'is just now wearing a dark *lava-lava* with a long flannel nightgown of Lou's on top of it; while Arick (another servant) has a pink and white striped flannel jacket over his tight red "petticoat"!' (*Letters from Samoa* 170). Later in December, 1892 Margaret Stevenson despaired at the staff's fondness for wearing any old clothes on which they could lay their hands, even 'an old red cotton tablecloth that Fanny had thrown away' (*Letters from Samoa* 57-58). For this reason, Stevenson's mother burnt her old 'widow caps' [these are the 'widow caps' that Mataafa recognized as being like those worn by Queen Victoria]; but, as she explained to her sister, 'the other day, being in a hurry, I threw one all crumpled up into my waste-paper basket. The next day ... you may fancy our laughter when one of the boys appeared proudly decorated with my cap. He evidently thinks it very fine, as he has worn it ever since, and is so pleased with his adornment that we have not had the heart to interfere' (*Letters from Samoa* 254-55).

Dressing Up: The Half-Caste Club

Stevenson's sense of the importance of dress in determining social rank also becomes evident in his dealings with the Half-Caste Club he founded and that met at Vailima until it failed after a few meetings. Following the lead of his missionary friends who, as we have seen in the previous chapter, were concerned about the role and fate of the half-castes in Samoa and who, consequently, set up special schools so that they might take a more prominent role in the leadership of the islands, Stevenson, his mother, Fanny, and Belle held weekly gatherings at which the half-castes were supposed to learn European manners and customs.[9] An essential element in their education was the requirement that they 'dress as neatly as they could'. On every meeting night Stevenson's mother and Belle criticized the women's 'appearance and deportment' (Moors 103). This attention to the half-castes' clothing is readily visible in Belle's sketches of a ball at which Europeans and Samoan half-castes were present.[10]

It is interesting to note that the half-caste woman is not allowed the plunging necklines and corseted waist of the European woman; rather, she is required to follow the missionary fashion and wear a loose dress that disguises the sexual contours of her body and demurely fastens at her neck. Her attire, therefore, makes sure that no matter how thoroughly she absorbs Western ways and no matter how much her features and skin color resemble those of a white person, she is not to be misread and mistaken for something other than herself. It guarantees that there will be no passing and that she is to carry on the missionary agenda. In other words, her dress, while in one way conforming to European standards, in another way registers the limits of her power; it is a badge of her bondage to the Europeans. Her position is tailored into her costume.

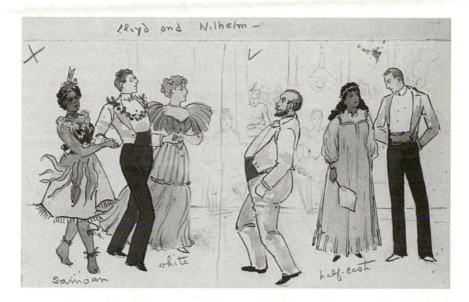

2.4   Isobel Strong. 'Samoan, White, Half-Caste'

Dressing Up: Reconfiguring the Body

As careless as Stevenson might have seemed to those who happened to see him in his shabby and informal pyjamas, his broad red sash, the Vailima livery, and the dress of his half-caste club suggest that he was perfectly well aware of the role played by dress in distinguishing those who had power from those who lacked it. Clothes were a way of establishing oneself in society, a means that becomes even more obligatory when one is stranded in a place far away from the usual associations and cut loose from familiar social patterns. But for Stevenson these items of clothing as well as the boots and the Bedford cord breeches were not only vestments of societal structure and authority, they were also expressions of a lifelong fascination with the romantic exploits of his fictional creations, like the brooding, exiled, but virile Mr. Henry in *The Master of Ballantrae*; they formed a part of his personal fiction. They expressed his own need, as a chronically ill person, to reconfigure himself, to cut a swashbuckling figure, to feel the pleasure of vigorous activity (as he did when he weeded the grounds around Vailima), and to create robust, vital subjects that, in a sense, put on leather riding boots and turned its back on the naked realities of *The Beach of Falesá*. The outfit and pose he adopted for a portrait painted on board the *Casco* (1891) and later in Vailima display his desire for this reconfiguration. They furnish his weak, skeletal body with a simularcum of strength and activity, an illusion that was somewhat successful, for his friends, when they saw him in such an outfit, thought he appeared 'chivalrous' (although incongruously so when riding Jack, his aged and less than graceful horse).[11] The riding breeches, boots, shirt, and sash were a way of projecting his desires.

In addition, costumes were part of his and his family's delight in simply dressing up. S. R. Lysaght recalled that Stevenson 'found a curious pleasure in dressing, or as children say, "in dressing up"'. He remembered that one evening at dinner Stevenson wore an Indian costume, 'an embroidered thing [obviously Lysaght did not approve] folded and crossed upon his chest' (Masson 266). His love of his black velvet and brown velveteen jackets was allied to this impulse; in the tailor's bill there are several entries for these materials. Stevenson was not alone, for the family took enormous delight in fancy-dress balls held by the German and British Naval officers and at the various consulates. Margaret Stevenson reported to her sister (18 October 1891), 'We are very much interested in a fancy-dress ball that is to come off on the 9th of November in honour of the Prince of Wales's birthday .... Fanny has designed one [a costume] for Mrs. G — [Gurrs] to wear, which will be most effective, I think; she is a very pretty Samoan girl, and the natural native dignity will help to make her a charming "Zenobia, Empress of the East"' (*Letters from Samoa* 96). This romantic, splendid, fantastic costume was far more appealing to them than the European clothes that according to Stevenson's mother, 'do vulgarise all these brown people so terribly'. Though this kind of clothing was *de rigueur* in the Stevensons' half-caste club, Mrs. Stevenson complained that, 'the ugliest style of dress in existence seems destined to overrun the world' (45). The extravagant costume evidently fit more conveniently into their exotic notions of their surroundings.

Dressing Up for the Camera

There was, however, nothing quite like dressing up for photographs. Here the fantasy of being something one is not could have its freest and, sometimes, most private play. At home in Vailima and when they traveled, the Stevensons spent considerable time on photographic projects. One of the tragedies of their travels occurred when a chest-load of photographs was thrown overboard and other packets of film were damaged as a result of a fire on board one of their chartered yachts. Eager to impress their readers and friends in Britain, they also took idealized pictures of their household staff.

2.5   'Talolo Vailima'

In a 20 January 1890 letter to Colvin, Fanny recalled one of these photographic sessions and revealed how in dressing the servant up, the mundane was once more discarded in favor of the exotic.

> The secretary who usually comes clad in an undershirt and a strip of curtain stuff is gorgeous in the photograph with all sorts of finery. The undershirt cast aside, leaves are bound round his loins, beads and particoloured leaves are twined through his hair, and round his neck he has a borrowed chief's necklace of large white teeth, to say nothing of a bead bracelet borrowed from a lady. He looks much better in these borrowed plumes than when dressed as the secretary. (Beinecke ms. 3670)

One is reminded of the time when the Reverend Newell traveled to England with Saaga (a South Pacific islander), dressed him up as a Samoan warrior, and paraded him before the congregation of the Grosvenor Street Chapel.

What is not recorded in Fanny's report or in any of the biographies is that members of Stevenson's family also participated in this 'borrowing' and arrayed themselves to be photographed in native costume, rather in the manner of Williams, the missionary, who back in England decked his own portly person with the native tiputa and mat, fixed a spear by his side, and adorned his head with the cap of many colors, worn on high days of chiefs.[12] In the Writers' Museum, Edinburgh are two 1888 photographs of Lloyd wearing a Marquesan warrior's costume, brandishing a fighting club (made out of wood, sinnet, and dog hair and decorated with tiki faces), and posing as 'Chief Moipu', as if for some ethnographic study, in a makeshift studio — a shadow indicates the use of a flash. Pieces of string attached to Lloyd's fingers hold him still. The bits and pieces of the costume are authentic, from the headdress made of pearl and tortoise shells to the anklets.[13]

Given the nature of Lloyd's pose, it is, obviously, best to treat the photographs as parodies of the many ethnographic engravings supplementing descriptions of Pacific voyages. In particular, the pictures bear a startling resemblance to one in an 1886 missionary travelogue showing a Marquesan warrior. The angle of Lloyd's head, the mock-studied seriousness of his expression, the displaying of the Samoan club, and, most of all, Lloyd's monocle add to the parodic tone and, furthermore, anticipate the satiric ethnographic photos of South Seas expeditions that apparently were later available to British and American readers. One example of this genre that came to my attention when a friend found the book in a secondhand bookshop is *The Cruise of the Kawa: Wanderings in the South Seas* by a 'Walter E. Traprock' [George Shepard Chappell] (1921). Its pages sport seventeen illustrations, each of which is more preposterous than the other and each of which pokes scathing fun at the clichés of South Seas voyages. One of these illustrations is a photograph of Herman Swank, the 'Premier painter of Polynesia', wearing 'his paloota, or wedding crown, the gift of his lovely island bride' while standing in his Western slippers and nightshirt on the beach.

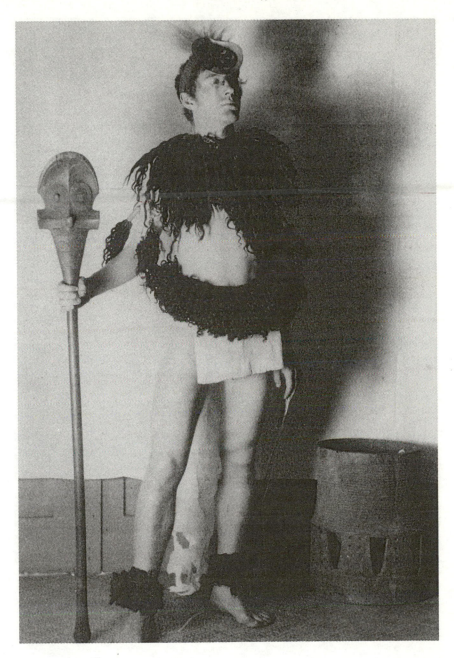

2.6   Lloyd Osbourne as Marquesan Warrior, 1888

2.7   Lloyd Osbourne as Marquesan Warrior, 1888

These photographs in *The Cruise of the Kawa* recall the missionary fashion shows in England: in the late nineteenth century and at the turn of the twentieth century it was possible to rent South Seas outfits from the London Missionary Society and use them in Sunday School pageants and plays.[14]

2.8 'Herman Swank'

These pictures are as disturbing as those taken by Westerners of South Seas chiefs dressed up in mismatching and ill-fitting European clothes, an event, by the way, that was frequently recorded in the travelogues of explorers and missionaries and one that seems to have been a facile way in which to register the authors' feelings of superiority to the natives.[15] C. F. Wood's 1875 account of his yachting cruise among the Pacific islands includes one such incident when a chief, proudly wearing a melange of souvenirs and castoffs left by Western visitors, endured having his picture taken in the sweltering heat. The chief first 'put on a warm flannel shirt of some blazing red tartan, wrapped a heavy woollen shawl of a somewhat similar pattern around his loins, on the top of this put an old Russian naval officer's coat, buckled an ancient military sword round his waist, put an Inverness cape on the top of this coat, covered his head with a wide-awake hat, and grasping a telescope in one hand and an old Tower musket in the other, went forth to be photographed' (Wood 13-14). In another incident Wood describes how a Fijian chief, Thakombau, was dressed by his ministers to be photographed on board *HMS Dido*. Instead of his usual loose flowing robes of Fijian tappa, in which he looked every inch a king, his ministers tricked him out in a close-fitting sky-blue jacket and flesh-colored tights. Wood remarks, 'I don't know where they got the idea from, but the result was a mixture of a London footman and a barrel-organ monkey' (Wood 66). Even the marginally more sensitive Stevenson was guilty of participating in such activities when he photographed the King of Butaritari and encouraged him to pose before the camera in the vicious heat while burdened by a European uniform bedizened with gold lace and melting under his cocked hat (*In the South Seas* 177).

Death and the Gap

The attempt to mimic or represent the values and codes of another culture by borrowing its clothes not only exposes the confusions resulting from the imposition of one order upon another but also, and more poignantly, reveals the inevitable gap between the wearer and his or her clothing. That is to say, the incongruities of dressing up in someone else's costume force one to realize that the body underneath and its surroundings are often at odds with its covering. The garment and the body it adorns do not exhibit a seamless continuity. Consequently, rather than seeing a native or a Westerner in these photographs, one notices someone attempting to masquerade as something other than him or herself. Individuals like Lloyd and the King and Queen of Butaritari never revealed their foreignness, their otherness, more blatantly than when they put on their guises. At least the Fijian chief, after having his picture taken in European attire, immediately took the alien garments off (something one could not do with a tattoo). It is interesting to note that accounts of such photographic sessions typically close with a description of the rapidity with which the incongruous and misfitting clothes are discarded. Wood in his *Yachting Cruise in the South Seas* mentions that after a chief had endured being photographed in uncomfortable European clothing, 'he then retired to his house, where I shortly afterwards found him, in the costume of our first parents, drinking cocoa-nuts and fanning himself' (14). Dressing up can become a dressing down.

But dressing up not only makes more noticeable the gap between the body and the dress; it also makes more real the certainty that, finally, the body can no longer be sustained, protected, or represented by what adorns it. Stevenson's loose-fitting pyjamas may have shielded him from the sun and filled out his skeletal thinness and may have momentarily disguised his physical weakness, but not for long. The body has its own rhythm and deteriorates beneath the freshly tailored material. Some of the photographs taken at Vailima, even the ones taken a few days before his death, show Stevenson wearing his riding boots, red sash, cord trousers, and dress shirt; he appears to be a figure untouchable by death. But these dress clothes mask the clock of mortality that beats beneath them. For a while they can function as a form of physical editing, but they can never completely conceal the body's vulnerability. In the end, perhaps, clothes serve not so much as a symbol of cultural contagion or of one's position in the world, but as some sort of sign that one is alive and out in the world. They represent the will to live. Margaret Stevenson wrote in a 4 December 1894 diary entry, shortly after Stevenson's death, that 'Dear Lou wanted to die *with his clothes on*' (Beinecke ms.7304). Indeed his wish was granted, for he died dressed in the illusion that clothes create and in the delusion that his life would continue.[16] Stevenson literally died with his boots on. When he collapsed at his home on 3 December 1894, Lloyd unlaced his stepfather's boots, temporarily admitting that the mirage could no longer be maintained. Soon, though, custom saw to it that once more clothes would attempt to mask mortality. Late in the night of his dying, the family, according to Lloyd, 'washed his body and dressed it in a soft white-linen shirt and black evening trousers girded with a dark-blue silk sash. A white tie, dark-blue silk socks, and patent leather shoes completed the costume.' This attire would remind the European world that Stevenson was one of them, that he had not gone native. To emphasize this point, Lloyd was quick to point out that the sash was not an unusual or improper piece of clothing: 'The sash may sound extraordinary, but it was the custom to wear sashes in Samoa' (Osbourne 147).

Lloyd's attention to the clothes in his account of Stevenson's last hours is indicative of the way individuals turn to clothes to help them respond to and define critical events. Indeed so important was the matter of dress at this moment, that one of the first reactions to the news of Stevenson's passing was that messengers were sent 'from every direction' so that one of the shops could be opened in Apia and 'dozens of bolts of black cotton cloth' brought up to Vailima. Lloyd explained that 'two yards of this wide, black cotton would suffice to make a *lavalava*, as the kilt-like Samoan garment is called; and in these and white-cotton undershirts our Vailima retainers would make a creditable appearance, and one which they would consider appropriate' (Osbourne 146-47).

Clothes marked the end as well as the beginning of Stevenson's years in the South Seas; they were the subject of both his arrival and his departure. In this context the tailor's bill from Sydney emerges as one of the more salient leftovers of Stevenson's life between 1888 and December, 1894. And Stevenson's clothes are still with us. When one goes to the Stevenson Museum at Saranac Lake, one cannot help but stare at the velvet jacket hanging in the room, or when one looks at the various cabinets in the Writers' Museum, Edinburgh, one cannot help but be drawn to those displaying his white cotton yachting cap, his boots, and his jackets. When they stand alone, without the person within them, these items, for a minute, seem to restore credibility to that life; they carry on and make more real what has gone, no longer as a mask for, but as an emblem of, a person.

Notes

1. See, for instance, Edmond 111.
2. See Gunson 200.
3. Sutton speaks of this principle in *Strangers in Paradise*. In Wilson's *A Missionary Voyage to the Southern Pacific Ocean, 1796-1798*, there is an account of another episode:

   > They [the missionaries and the ship's captain] were received by young king (Otoo) and his wife Tetua, both carried on men's shoulders; each took the captain by the hand, and in dumb silence surveyed him attentively, looking in his face and minutely examining every part of his dress. The queen opened Mr. Cover's shirt at the breast and sleeves, and seemed astonished at so clear a sight of the blue veins. (62)

4. In *Nineteen Years in Polynesia: Missionary Life, Travels, and Researches in the Islands of the Pacific*, Turner writes about changes in dress since the landing of the missionaries in Samoa:

   > Soon after the arrival of the missionaries, a marked change took place. With few exceptions, the men cut their hair short, abandoned the short and narrow leaf apron and, when they appeared at public worship, dressed, if possible, in a regatta or white shirt, and a piece of calico round the loins. Coats, waistcoats, trousers, neckerchiefs, and straw hats came into use. The women, too, commenced wearing loose Calico dresses, and were rarely seen without a *tiputa* or upper garment of some kind. (207-208)

5. For a sense of Colvin's objections to Stevenson's preoccupation with South Sea cultures, see Fanny's letter to Colvin in *Letters* 7: 79-80.
6. See the 1872 diaries of the Reverend James Chalmers (LMS Archives ms. 162) in which Chalmers talks about the practice of fines for putting a flower or a feather in the hat. It is probably important to mention that he thought the fines a bit ridiculous and encouraged the native preachers to stop enforcing them.
7. Claxton. 'Island Life at the Antipodes' 432.
8. An example of one of these passages can be found in Lamont:

   > They [the Penrhyn Islanders] endeavoured to push their legs through the sleeves of a black dress coat that had been mine, after the manner they observed I wore my trousers, till I showed one of them how to wear it properly. As an evidence that he thoroughly understood my lesson, the illustrious ambassador, seizing a pair of black trousers, stuck his arm through them, and ensconced his head in the body so that he could not find his way out till he roared for assistance .... trousers were evidently an incumbrance .... Coats (which they adopted on state occasions) were worn after their own fashion — that is, with the sleeves fastened round the loins in front .... Sometimes they were to be seen with one boot or shoe, and nothing else. Stockings were usually left to the women, by whom they were worn as a kind of cross-belt, secured, top and toe, on the shoulder, and occasionally even used as a dress turban on festive occasions. (127-28)

9. For Stevenson's references to the Half-Caste Club, see *Letters* 7: 247, 249.
10. Graham Balfour in his *Life of Robert Louis Stevenson* describes the public balls that were held in Apia and to which Samoans, half-castes, and whites were all invited and intermingled. See 2: 153. Isobel Strong's drawings of these dances illustrate this fact. Her watercolor sketches of these balls are at the Beinecke Rare Book and Manuscript Library, Yale University.
11. S. R. Lysaght of Samoa recalled that Stevenson's 'appearance on horseback was amusing — dressed in white, with riding boots and a French peaked cap, chivalrous in his bearing, but mounted on a horse which would not have been owned by any self-respecting English costermonger' (Masson 265).
12. The account of Reverend John Williams dressed in native costume appears in Prout 132.
13. On a recent visit to Edinburgh, I was delighted to see exactly the same headdress and the fighting club from the Marquesas at the Museum of Scotland (in the Polynesian Case on the fifth floor).
14. In the LMS Archives is a pamphlet by J. M. B. entitled *He and She from O'er the Sea: Missionary Recitations and Hymns for Twelve Boys and Girls*. London: London Missionary Society. n.d. On the title page the Society announces that 'the costumes and curios can be borrowed free, after due notice, from the Mission House for use at Meetings held on behalf of the L.M.S'.
15. In the nineteenth century there seems really to be no record of how the inhabitants felt about having their pictures taken while dressed in Western clothing. It is a relief to note, however, that the island inhabitants occasionally had their revenge and got to laugh at the Westerners and their costume. Churchward records a time a circus (Woodyear's Electric Circus) came to one of the islands of Samoa. As part of the performance a trick monkey appeared dressed 'for all the world, as similar as possible' to the British Consul. The response from the natives was immense roars of laughter (150).
16. Stevenson died from a blood clot on the brain. According to his stepson, Stevenson had been helping Fanny, his wife, to prepare the evening meal when 'suddenly he put both hands to his head and cried out "What's that?" Then he asked quickly. "Do I look strange?" Even as he did so he fell on his knees beside her' (Bell 263).

Chapter Three

Colonies of Memory

...so sadly, the changes come (*In the South Seas* 21)

Introduction

Nineteenth-century Western observers of the South Seas often worried that the islanders were losing touch with their past and were forgetting the traditions of their forefathers. In writing about their concerns these commentators frequently identified the missionaries as being responsible for this loss. To a certain degree, their perspective was correct, for one does not have to search far to find examples of the missionaries' culpability. However, if one looks more closely, one learns that the missionaries (especially those representing the London Missionary Society) also preserved part of what they had destroyed by studying and gathering artifacts from the island cultures they had invaded. As time passed these missionary collections became important to anthropologists, for they were visual reminders of an older, almost extinct Polynesian culture. They became a means through which to recall the past.

This circumstance is worth dwelling on, for the association of these artifacts with memory suggests ways of thinking about the psychology of memory. In particular, the parallels between what happens to these objects once they are removed from their indigenous surroundings and what befalls the contents of individual remembrances through time recall the alienation and the ultimate mutability of memory — two characteristics that undermine our hope that this faculty may hold the past in some kind of uncontaminated state. These characteristics also remind us that our personal memories (especially the memories of those who, like myself, are exiled from their own culture), like the Pacific islanders and their possessions, are all too readily held in the custody of others' desires and perceptions. With these reflections in mind, one turns naturally to the South Seas experiences of Robert Louis Stevenson. Just as the missionaries provide a context for thinking about the subject of clothing, so do they offer a framework for considering Stevenson's attitudes toward the nature of memory and recollection, concerns that often dominated his imagination.

A Crisis of Memory

When Stevenson sailed among the Pacific islands and atolls, he traveled in realms where, according to Western observers, a new order of things was believed to be subverting, if not replacing, older ways. These commentators feared that because of foreign pressures the indigenous peoples were relinquishing a devotion to primitive traditions and losing their cultural memories.[1] They worried that forgetfulness was slipping into the seat of memory. As early as 1829, William Ellis, a LMS missionary who had lived in Tahiti, was concerned that a new generation of Polynesians was 'growing up in total ignorance of all that distinguished their ancestors from themselves' (vi-vii). And later in the nineteenth century, one anxious friend of Stevenson's suggested that the minds of the inhabitants had already become a 'perfect blank'. ('Missionary Methods in the Pacific' 149). The threat of human as well as cultural extinction was a widespread preoccupation. Individuals with interests as disparate as those of John La Farge, the romantic painter (*Reminiscences of the South Seas*), the methodical collector J. Edge Partington (*Ethnographic Album of the Pacific*), and the naturalist/traveler Charles Hedley fretted over the 'slow extinction' of these islanders' past (46). They issued warnings about the growing scarcity of traditional objects, and their concern found a certain confirmation through a parallel preoccupation with a decrease in the population on a number of islands. An April, 1893 article in *The Chronicle of the London Missionary Society* addressing the 'sad' decline in Rarotonga from 7,000 inhabitants in John Williams's time (1820s) to 1,900 in 1892 is typical (88-90), and so, in fact, is Stevenson's chapter on depopulation in *In the South Seas*, where he talks of the Marquesans, the indigenous Hawaiians, and the Maoris as 'perishing like flies' (31).

The London Missionary Society (LMS) Missionaries

Among the people most frequently held accountable for this rubbing out of indigenous culture were, of course, the missionaries (a view that persists, perhaps even more strongly, today in popular thought).[2] In spite of the fact that there were discourses on the merits of these individuals (Darwin's approval of the LMS missionaries on the islands of Tahiti and New Zealand in the *Voyage of the Beagle* is one), a number of nineteenth-century texts on the South Seas did not hesitate to pose the scathingly critical and obvious question whether it would not have been better for the Fijians 'to be left alone in their old savagedom' and remain 'in their old heathen faith' (St. Johnston 326). Nor did they fail to rebuke the missionary 'who merely indulges in evangelical dreams and devotes himself only to the destruction of practices and beliefs which he classifies as "pagan"' (Hickson 178). Yet the fact is that a significant number of missionaries were keenly sensitive to the crisis of memory — to the disappearance of traditions — and eventually functioned not only as the destroyers but also as the preservers and protectors of a compromised culture.

Because of the missionaries' early history in the South Seas, this sensitivity seems paradoxical, for one cannot forget the dogged determination of the first London Missionary Society representatives, sent out in 1797 to Tahiti, to wipe out everything that did not conform to its doctrines and to eradicate the dark ages of paganism. One cannot ignore their official reports, as well as those written by a second generation of missionaries on other islands, applauding the destruction of idols and documenting their successes in creating a void which they then filled with their own structures and institutions — an activity that became literally true when the missionaries in Rurutu took away the inhabitants' ceremonial spears and converted them into staves to support the balustrades of a pulpit staircase or when the missionaries in Samoa confiscated the clubs and spears from the armory of the gods to build a railing for the courthouse.[3] The early missionary literature is replete with passages relishing the conflagration of *maraes* (idol temples), the driving of large herds of pigs into sacred enclosures, the hanging of gods disrobed of their apparel, the public burnings of idols, the drowning of ritual mats, the throwing of the gods made of coral into the sea, and the forced eating of food thought to contain the spirit of a god.

These acts and accounts have a horrifying resilience and reflect awful truths, but they do not represent the whole experience or impact of the missionary presence in the Pacific. If one reads more closely and widely in the missionaries' diaries, reports, letters, notes, and books, one discovers a more complex and provocative reality. In particular, one becomes aware of a contrary impulse on the part of these individuals to study and save what they and others were demolishing. Even in the beginning, when the LMS martyr John Williams was ostentatiously encouraging the breaking up of sacred objects in Tahiti, he was salvaging them for posterity. For instance, on the Vavau Islands, Williams saw five goddesses hanging by the neck (an 'execution' that was part of his campaign) and decided to ask the chief to give him one. Proudly Williams recorded: 'I have brought it to England, with the very string around its neck by which it was hung' (319-20). Later Williams placed this and other relics he obtained in collections back in London. Around the same time, Ellis, who motivated by his religious convictions could be heard speaking of 'malignant deities' and 'the deafening roar of idol worship' (1: viii, 62), was also methodically gathering traditional objects and noting, in detail, the ways and beliefs of the people he was converting. He was eager to leave an authentic record of the peoples' customs and rituals before they became 'obsolete' (vii).

As those familiar with it know, Ellis's subsequent study of the South Seas, *Polynesian Researches* (1829), served as a major reference text for ethnographers and, in addition, set a precedent for subsequent LMS missionaries in the nineteenth century who wished to 'preserve and elevate' Polynesian culture (Gill, *Life in the Southern Isles* vi). It motivated those like the Reverend

G. Pratt, who had been in Samoa since 1839 and had studied Old Samoan, to gather the results of his own researches. With the Reverend T. Powell, he salvaged and published vestiges of old Samoan traditions and songs. In their introduction to *Some Folk-Songs and Myths from Samoa*, they emphasized that their materials were collected many years before Europeans had become numerous on the islands and altered the way of life, and that they wanted to give readers a valuable insight into 'the manner of life of the Samoans long ago' (196). Ellis also influenced missionaries, like Stevenson's acquaintances Reverend Hiram Bingham and the Reverend S. J. Whitmee, who carefully studied the dying dialects of various Polynesian languages, and either created lists of words (after Bingham had collected two thousand words on his own, he paid a young convert a dollar for each additional one hundred words) or composed comparative grammars and dictionaries.[4]

Following Ellis's lead other missionaries took profuse notes and published books about the islands and their inhabitants. Among the papers of Reverend J. E. Newell (Newell officiated at Stevenson's funeral in Samoa) are numerous manuscript pages written in an earnest hand detailing the burial and marriage customs, the religious beliefs, the legends, and the dialects of the Samoans, the Gilbert Islanders, the Kingsmill and Ellice Islanders, and the people of Katadi, New Guinea. Knowing these would be 'of special value and interest to students of ethnology' (LMS Archives), Newell addressed his 'Notes: chiefly ethnological' to the Secretary of the Polynesian Society. Another of Stevenson's acquaintances, the Reverend William Wyatt Gill, wrote in *From Darkness to Light in Polynesia*, 'I have been the more anxious to put these things on permanent record, as the correct knowledge of the past is rapidly fading away, and will probably soon become extinct' (9). Stevenson's adventurous friend the Reverend J. Chalmers also spent considerable effort learning as much as he could about the Pacific cultures. In his books, he reveals an extraordinary eagerness and, occasionally, an uncontrollable curiosity. On one occasion he entered a darkened temple alone, and, after his eyes had grown accustomed to the lack of light, thrust his hand into the open frog-like mouth of a seven by nine foot wicker god to discover what was inside. He was 'somewhat startled when out flew dozens of small bats, which disturbed those in the other images and soon the whole place was full' (10). Collectively the frightened bats soon packed the interior. The next day Chalmers returned to take another look.

When the LMS missionaries were avidly collecting or purchasing pieces of the culture they were intruding upon, they did not necessarily confine themselves to salvaging objects related to traditional beliefs or to displaying the folly and sin of idolatry. They were also gathering items from a larger context: samples of hair (Reverend George Turner counted nearly seven hundred bunches of hair on the head of one young man and compared his appearance to that of an Assyrian sculpture), canoes, clubs, cooking utensils, baskets, and clothing — in a word, what is now called 'material culture'. Even Williams did not confine himself to relics of idolatry. Following the pattern of explorers and seamen he also collected natural history specimens. Williams once complained that because his ship had leaked, he had lost his snakes which he was conveying home. Some forty years later the tradition among missionaries of amassing curiosities continued, for the Reverend Gill secured a specimen, weighing sixty pounds, of the fruit from a gigantic palm tree; and the Reverend William Y. Turner with the Reverend Lawes collected lepidoptera and other insects. Just before leaving Port Moresby (New Guinea), someone brought them an animal of whose existence they were ignorant. Turner recalls: 'The specimen was a young one: the animal has a duckbill, small eyes, burrowing feet, and bristles over the body. Mr. Lawes preserved it in spirits and sent it to Professor Rolleston of Oxford' ('The Ethnology of the Motu' 27).

The shipping of this platypus was no exception; other LMS collections survived the long voyage home, not only to raise money through their sale, but also for experts to dissect, stuff, measure, assemble, and classify. Most of Turner's delicate butterflies arrived safely and added to the cluttered cases of the British Museum, and so did Chalmers' crates crammed with nose rings, girdles, tongs for turning wood in the fire, fibre belts, implements for opening coconuts, and a wooden step for the mast of a canoe. These joined the specimens of Samoan sea-worms that the Reverend John Stair had donated to the British Museum in 1847. All these curios sent to England were part of an active interchange these missionaries enjoyed with members of the scientific communities and learned societies. In the South Seas, for instance, they escorted British expeditions investigating the growth of coral formations — a subject that had earlier been of interest to Williams and Ellis and was currently fascinating Newell. And in England, on furloughs from their duties in the South Seas, the missionaries not only spoke about their adventures to the converted at missionary soirées or missionary conversazione held in chapel halls and Sunday school rooms, or displayed their exotic objects to Christian societies; they also served as respondents at scholarly functions and addressed members of the Zoological Society of London, the Royal Geographical Society, the Royal Anthropological Institute, the Philosophical Society, and the Philological Society of London.[5] Their papers, published later in these societies' proceedings and journals, resonate with their commitment to ethnographic and linguistic studies. Even in pieces about widow-strangling (a custom on some islands that the missionaries sensationalized), these missionaries silenced the clichés about the dark night of heathenism, muted alarming phrases deploring disgusting, barbaric, provocative practices and gestures, and refused to reassure the LMS officials that this research was not done at the expense of their duties as missionaries — a topos one often discovers in their books. Their sentences reveal a careful and measured hand that admits uncertainties and banishes the authoritative, judgmental tone of the LMS reports. Newell, for instance, frames his notes with apologies for their brevity, discursiveness, and partiality.[6]

Because of their long residences in the South Seas and widespread contacts with local populations, the LMS missionaries had extraordinary opportunities not readily available to the voyagers, naturalists, and tradesmen whose ships remained in port for relatively short periods. They were 'intelligent witnesses' (Buzacott and Sunderland, vii) who had an expertise upon which others depended. Nineteenth-century anthropologists and explorers, consequently, spoke of their indebtedness to Whitmee's linguistic and ethnological work and paid tribute to Reverend J. Atkin's 'most curious specimens of hair' (Davis 101) or spoke generally of the missionaries' contributions to 'the advancement of science' (Tylor 292-93). They praised the missionaries for their 'mass of facts' (Hickson 238) and their journeys into the unfamiliar recesses of an island's past unavailable to the outsider and almost lost to the indigenous peoples themselves, caught as they were in the changing circumstances of time and necessity. As Christopher Herbert points out, these missionaries essentially laid out 'the whole modern program of ethnographic research based on the unique efficacy of total cultural immersion, of verbatim quotation of informants, and on linguistic competence as the sine qua non of fieldwork' long before Boas or Malinowski codified these methods (164).

The London Missionary Society Museum

One missionary establishment that became important for preserving the cultural memories of the South Sea Islands and for the work of the scientific community was the London Missionary Society Museum in the Old Jewry, Austin Friars and then at 8 Bloomfield Street, Finsbury. The Museum was initially a repository for the trophies of Christianity. Even though 'benevolent' travelers contributed objects (1845 *Catalogue*), the primary donors were the missionaries (from China, India, Africa, and the Pacific) who for over a hundred years filled the rooms with the plunder of their conversions and the evidence and purchases of their researches. Glass-covered cases lined the walls and displayed the weird, the wonderful, the grotesque, and the commonplace.

Although there was nothing comparable to the inch-long flea chains of silver and gold with three hundred links, the mummified fingers, and the stuffed freaks to be seen in the *Kunstkammern* of private collectors, there were such curios as the club that struck the killing blow to the martyr Williams, a pair of shoes worn by Ellis in Hawaii, and a hat made by a sailor shipwrecked near the Marquesan Islands so that 'if any vessel passed in sight, he might be noted as a civilized person, and not a savage' (1826 *Catalogue*). There were also the spoils of curiosity collected by the South Seas missionaries: grass skirts, necklaces, a head-dress of feathers, bark cloth, breadfruit pounders, files made of shark skin, decoys for catching fish, warriors' belts, hair, ear-rings, combs, tattooing instruments, mosquito brushes, fishing nets, kava bowls, fish hooks, a red sash used at the inauguration of 'the greatest kings' (Williams 143), 'boisterous' and 'wild' drums (Ellis 1: 281), mats, wooden pillows, and instruments of war. There was also a case of insects (wild bees, black scorpions, and centipedes), corals, and sponges from the reefs in the South Seas. On top of the cases and cupboards with countless drawers perched model canoes, mounted mole rats, lions (of course, not from the South Seas), weasels, ant-eaters, and a dried snout of the Saw Fish; beneath the cabinets hid large baskets, some filled with stones collected by the indigenous people to indicate how many battles the Samoans had won, and on the walls spread fanned arrangements of spears barbed with sharks' teeth, paddles, and clubs.

3.1 'The Museum of the London Missionary Society'

In a museum initially devoted to displaying the spoils of conversion, there were, of course, a plethora of 'grim-looking gods', the '*horrible* IDOLS' calculated 'to excite in the pious mind, feelings of deep commiseration for the hundreds of millions of the human race, still the vassals of ignorance and superstition' (1826 *Catalogue*). On the floor under the north skylight rose a forbidding twelve-foot high idol, covered with bark cloth and ornamented 'with black zigzag lines', brought by Williams from Rarotonga. By 1845 these idols, torn from their surroundings, stood naked before guests from home and abroad who came to view these exotica three days a week (on Tuesdays, Thursdays, and Saturdays). They stared at these trapped objects and, from a safe distance, contemplated the plight and zeal of the missionaries in the face of such foreignness, ugliness, and superstition. It is as if by placing these savage pieces in the Museum, the missionaries had tamed them — even Reverend Gill could not resist the thought that the rival New Guinea gods Motore and Tan — now 'repose quietly' in the Museum (*Historical Sketches* 43).

This idiosyncratic jumble of specimens in the LMS Museum would seem to have had little use except for the Society's fund-raising efforts and to have been of negligible interest to those outside missionary circles who could view ethnographic exhibits elsewhere in Britain. But such a restricted picture of its appeal is not quite accurate, for in the second half of the century, the LMS Museum was in its own right attracting those wishing to study what was becoming unobtainable. Like the other collections, it too was catching the attention of those whose fascination with the South Seas was being encouraged by British economic and military interests. In a sense, the Museum was being transformed from a repository of Christian trophies to a collection of Polynesian memories. Anthropologists, especially, used its contents to reach into areas closed to them. They dipped into its cupboards to find examples of gods long gone, to illustrate and study details of a daily life long compromised, and to assemble ethnographic albums of the Pacific Islands (Partington's *Ethnographic Album of the Pacific Islands*, 1891). They were grateful to the missionaries for placing in their museum 'records of many tribes of which we have now only a traditional or written knowledge' (Altick 297), and paid tribute to 'the great historical importance of the London Missionary Society's Collection' (Read 139-40). Such was the significance of the collection to ethnographers that in 1890 concerned anthropologists suggested the Museum's contents be moved to the British Museum where the collection would receive better care. Apparently there was a fear that some of the objects were being neglected and were deteriorating. Charles H. Read in his article on the origin and sacred character of South Eastern Pacific ornaments (1891) discusses the decision:

> The Directors of the London Missionary Society, after due consideration, last year decided to accept the suggestion that had been made to them, to transfer to the custody of the Trustees of the British Museum the most important and valuable section of the interesting museum that they had gradually accumulated during the last hundred years at their well-known house in Bloomfield Street .... It is scarcely possible to exaggerate the ethnological importance of these specimens, an importance due in the first place to their intrinsic merits, and in the second to the fact that at the time they were obtained the religions and habits of the natives had been but little disturbed by European influence .... the museum was by no means unknown, and for its scientific value was frequently visited by foreigners. An ethnographical museum,

however, requires constant care for its proper preservation, and this it is
only likely to obtain where the custody of the specimens is a principal
object of the institution. (139-40)

In becoming the property of the scientific community and moving into the rooms of
the British Museum, these objects now more readily displayed the impulse of their
collectors to salvage and study the vestiges of the native cultures.

The Colony of Memory

When the missionary artifacts moved to the British Museum, they migrated as
inhabitants of a colony of memory. By this I mean they constituted a 'colony' in a
biological rather than in a political sense — not as a society that has been
established by the metropole and remains subject to it, but as a clump of cells or
spores that has detached itself from the parent organism and continues to exist in a
foreign environment. These objects represented what had been an integral part of
the traditional life. After nearly a century the weight of time had compressed and,
as it were, converted into fossils the multifarious layers of disparate objects that
had been lying on the LMS museum's shelves. As a substantial collection now
residing in the British Museum, they were resettled in corridors and rooms
exclusively dedicated to their study and preservation. In this museum, yet another
repository of memory, these artifacts served as visual reminders of an older,
partially extinct Polynesian culture.

This circumstance is compelling, for it takes the mind away for a while
from missionary history and leads one's thoughts to the psychology or experience
of recollection. As bearers and denizens of a social memory, the missionary
artifacts suggest ways of thinking about what happens, through time, to the
elements of an individual memory. The evolution of these artifacts has a striking
resemblance to what becomes of memories once they have left their original
experience far behind. My choice of the artifacts in the LMS Museum as a lens
through which to view certain aspects of memory may seem arbitrary, but the
analogy, although not always a perfect fit, is instructive. It elucidates the fate or
progress of those pieces of remembrance that are purposely recalled in order to
capture the past: the ones which, according to the Augustinian model, one
knowingly retrieves from the storehouse of memory.[7] The parallels between the two
illuminate the disturbing possibilities for alienation and the ultimate mutability of
conscious recollection. And, as we shall see in the last section of this chapter, what
happens to these artifacts also casts light upon Stevenson's experience of
recollection.

Alienation and Memory

As I have pointed out, when the missionaries first assembled artifacts of Polynesian culture, they destroyed as well as preserved artifacts representing the islanders' rites and customs. Their contradictory actions are poignant reminders that, like the objects collected by the missionaries, memory often originates in a landscape of destruction; that memory tends to keep company with and be dependent upon annihilation. Its images — its idols — are what remain after the breaking up, the tearing apart, and the selecting of pieces from a continuum of experience. Like the curios taken away by the missionaries, these remnants leave behind a ravaged and silenced context. It is not that memory is responsible for this damage to the past, but memory does make forays into the past in order to steal from it: its collections are the plunder to be sequestered and used elsewhere. In this role memory requires alienation. It needs to be as foreign as the missionaries were to the islanders. Without this sense of a certain alienation, it is impossible to impose 'schemata' (Bartlett 214), and thereby organize or exploit the past. The past really is another country; if it were not, it would be impossible to disentangle the objects that will inhabit memory from the intricately knotted clusters of the mind. Memory enters the culture of the present as a foreigner to it — as something that lives outside its time, its rites and customs — in order to support its reason for being. If the past were continuous and, therefore, not alien, memory would have no function. Although one cannot claim an actual parallel, it is helpful to be reminded that in a similar way the missionaries would not have felt it necessary to assemble what they did if they had not been acutely aware of their differences from the islands' inhabitants. It is significant that in their collections, the LMS missionaries rejected artifacts that showed signs of acculturation; they, like memory, were primarily interested in assembling objects that capture the otherness of experience. Although, for its short-term purposes, memory may hold on to anything and everything, one is reminded that recollection of what is long past rarely honors from a more distant time what merely blends into the present.

Once the pieces of memory are culled from the past, like the idols of Aitutaki that Williams attached to the yard-arms of his missionary ship to impress the inhabitants as he approached other islands, they come to shore to be displayed as trophies. Having left behind their vanquished companions, torn to pieces or drowned at sea, these gods will hang, illuminated by coconut lights, from the rafters of chapels. As trophies, they will later assemble to pose for photographs for others to see. And like Williams, carrying a spear and dressed in native costume, marching up and down his parlor before English friends, these spoils of the past will impose themselves upon the present. This sequence of acts launches these vestiges on their journey of alienation. Even when they attempt to hold on to the past and authenticate its experiences, these memories will lose touch with their original functional value and become, instead, curious pieces of exotic decoration, even to the one who has carried them back. In such a way, by capitulating to the demands of the present, recollection alienates the object from its indigenous identity and, in turn, the individual from the real experience of a former time.

3.2   Henry Anelay, 'The Reverend John Williams on Board Ship with Native Implements, in the South Sea Islands'

Memory and the Problem of Decontextualization

Anthropologists preoccupied with the concept of decontextualization also offer ways of thinking about memory's instability and the process of alienation. In her study of Reverend H. A. Robertson's late nineteenth-century missionary collection, Barbara Lawson points out that early critics of museum anthropology were attentive to the difficulties created by isolating objects from their specific context. For years critics have acknowledged that once the material culture is moved, a new order of meaning imposes itself on it through various systems of classification for storing and displaying. The gap between the new environment and the indigenous landscape is clearly visible in the LMS Museum during the early nineteenth century when specimens sent back by the South Seas missionaries sat on shelves between tusks of Indian elephants and stuffed African lions. The subsequent loss of those objects' specific locale and the ensuing geographic confusion foreground the exotic nature of the items by shifting them into the mode of some unfamiliar otherness that distorts any possible understanding of them. I cannot argue for an actual parallel, for I understand that in human personal memory there is one controlling intelligence that is not present in the case of artifacts:[8] still, one can see a similar trajectory when disengaged images from the past join others in memory to create a melange of pieces that obfuscates thoughts of their origins and obscures their indigenous relevance. An illustration showing Ferrante Imperato's cabinet of curiosities (Naples, 1599) vividly replicates this dilemma.

Specimens from various parts of the world fill the room: on the ceiling a grand, land-bound crocodile hangs upside down; surrounding it are arranged patterns of sea shells, lobsters, crabs, and starfish from a locale that has little to do with the crocodile. As in a universe that is reversed, these objects from the sea shine down like stars on the shelves below where there are small boxes containing minute artifacts from many other places. Through this strangely ordered chaos of specimens, this topsy-turvy, disparate world is homogenized into a dense space that overrides the history of the individual objects. Grouped among the remnants, the crocodile, now held in the custody of the awed viewers' curiosity, has lost all touch with its indigenous environment.

The anthropologist Nicholas Thomas is especially conscious of this problem of recontextualization in ethnology. His observations on the displacement and isolation of objects collected by the South Seas missionaries invite further thoughts about the instability and mutability of memory. In his study of 'entangled objects', Thomas remarks on the vacuity of meaning that surrounds a material culture once it becomes separated from its indigenous community. In his discussion he suggests that the vague labeling of specimens in missionary cabinets is one example of this emptiness that removes the specimens even further from their surroundings. To describe a Samoan spear as 'a curious spear, whereon a curious face was carved in the grotesque manner' (131) leaves room for almost infinite ambiguity and creates spaces into which crowd the cultural, emotional, and political interests of those who now look upon them and hold them in their power. The lack of specificity makes room for others to step in and appropriate the contents for their own ends. Within this context, it becomes even easier to understand how the missionaries looked at the idols. In their official publications they transformed and refigured these sacred items and implements into commodities (when they sold their spoils to raise money for their missionary work), into structural pieces (when they used the spears to construct balustrades for staircases), into terrifying images to demonstrate the ugliness of heathenism, into trophies to show off their successes, and by mid-century into legitimate anthropological pieces as well as into meaningless, silly objects to illustrate how frivolous the former traditional worship had been.

3.3   'Ferrante Imperato's Cabinet of Curiosities. Naples, 1599'

Bereft of their native surroundings, many such items in the museum fell prey to missionary propaganda and forfeited what was left of their ethnographic reality. For Stevenson's mother, Margaret Stevenson, who, as we have seen, was an avid supporter of the missionary cause, these curios seem to have existed primarily for the lessons they could teach about the valuable contributions of Christianity. In her 1890 diary, written upon her return to Edinburgh from Samoa, these artifacts have become nothing but 'things': On 29 January 1890, she records: 'St. Marks party. Etta & I showed some of the South Sea things' (Beinecke ms. 7304). In other cases, these 'things' were to become even more immersed in the missionary enterprise and its shifting requirements. Many years later, for instance, when some of the curios were exhibited at the 'Isles of the Sea' exhibitions and pageants (held at the Queen Street Congregational Church in Wolverhampton, 1921 and at the New Town Hall, Lewisham, 1933), they were shown for their 'glamour' (LMS Archives) and children in Sunday Schools were instructed on how to make plasticene models of the idols once thought to be untouchable. The earlier idea of horrid and disgusting idols has vanished under the protective clothing of a benign paternalism. In other people's hands, these idols went through more extreme metamorphoses. Stevenson's acquaintance Charles Warren Stoddard turned the idols into homo-erotic appendages for his 'baby cannibal' (his young male lover in his story 'My South-Sea Show'), and his friend H. J. Moors used them to decorate the South Seas exhibit (mainly a display of exotic dancing) at the 1893 Chicago World's Fair.

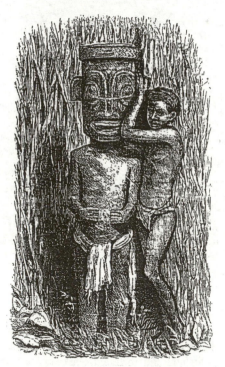

3.4   Wallis McKay, 'Niga and His Creed'

Through these examples one can readily understand why Thomas, thinking about this series of transformations, insists that objects are not solid entities, that objects change in defiance of their material stability. Although artifacts may remain the same in appearance, the shifting meanings attached to them continually alter their significance. Through this example, as I have said, one more fully appreciates the reality that conscious memory is not a stable entity either. It is, as Frederic C. Bartlett suggests, a living, developing, and 'complex expression of the life of the moment' (214). Like the artifacts, it gets caught by a current of mutability; it too gets swept away into the whirlpools created by its alienation, and, in turn, falls under the influence of the circulating present with its social and institutional needs that destroy or alter the structure of the original story. A recollection might superficially remain intact and give a false impression of longevity, but, as common sense instructs, it too is subject to retrospective constructions that deviate from the initial experience: Depending on the pressing demands of its new and various surroundings, what was marginal comes forward, what was singular converts to the plural, what was prominent seeks absence, what was elsewhere joins in, what was painful ripens into sweetness, what was facile grows still easier, what was simple turns more complex, and what was opaque becomes lucid. All depends upon who is subsidizing the recollection. In this sense, a conscious recollection is as much of a commodity as the curios collected by the missionaries; it is an item marketed by the circumstances of the present and the power of retrospect.

Memory and the Problem of Identity

The way curios and recollections are perceived influences how one discerns the identity or culture of a person. When the recollections mutate, so does an understanding of an individual's or a culture's nature. But no matter what the understanding, gatherings of recollections imperfectly define the individual or the society; selections of memories do not fully replicate a person's being. Just as the pilfered objects insufficiently represent South Seas societies, these transformed vestiges of the past will always be, in some way, inadequate and misleading.

Individuals conscious of the power of memory to create an identity are often aware of the way others, like the missionaries, plunder their culture — their past — and exploit it for their own purposes. As a result, in an effort to please or to win approval, individuals start manufacturing idols of memory for others to see or use. They fabricate, embellish, or restructure their recollections in order to pander to the pleasure, curiosity and predilections of others. Coming from England to the United States, as I did, at the age of 13, I found myself conforming (because I wanted acceptance) to what those in my new surroundings thought about my land. They believed, I thought, that people from my country are supposed to be polite, and reserved, so I found and still do find myself adopting that persona and recalling moments that subscribe to these prescribed qualities. Furthermore, I catch myself re-interpreting and transforming other memories so that they may display the features that others say they should. As a consequence, the actual photograph of myself as a seven-year-old child gripping the hand of a visiting refugee from

Czechoslovakia, becomes, in my own present recollection, nothing but a discreet, mannered handshake. I alter and compromise, even subjectively, what was originally there.

This kind of response brings to mind the inhabitants of New Guinea who, at the turn of this century, began making false shrunken heads for tourists and anthropologists intent on exhibiting them; the Samoans who started weaving mats and ornamenting clubs for the curious and acquisitive traveller to take home; and the residents of Fiji who produced 'cannibal forks' for nineteenth-century collectors. (Thomas reminds his readers that Partington in the late 1880s warned that 'special care' was needed to be exercised in buying these forks, for when he was in Fiji 'they were being made by white men for sale to travellers' [167].) These manufactured pieces of material culture take their cue from the expectations of the receiver. They portray a compromised history. In this way, the past finds itself trapped within an insidious cultural exchange and sacrificing what integrity it ever had.

The exchange is insidious because, once again, it compromises memory and, worse, because it causes memory to alienate the individual from him or herself (as I became separated from the boldness of my youth). One is left to cope with the disturbing probability that memory not only emerges from but also creates alienation. Those who might like to think that their memories are what designate the integrity of their being run the risk of being betrayed by the mutability of those recollections structuring their identity and by the fact that many of their remembrances are constructs determined by outsiders and conventions, rather than by themselves. This circumstance makes it difficult to entertain Hume's suggestion that identity of the self is a construct of one's own acts of retrospection that seem to show relations of cause and effect, and, in such a way, discover a unity, for, according to what has been suggested, identity does not belong to the individual; it is largely in the possession of others, or at best fashioned in an exchange.[9] Consequently, like the curios in the missionary collections, people, whether the South Sea islanders or ourselves, find themselves held in custody and placed in museums curated by others' desires and perceptions. In this sense, memory works against the ideal of itself, for it does not always do either what it promises or what one thinks it should. Instead of holding the past in some kind of uninterrupted, uncontaminated state, it undoes the ideal by faltering under the influence of the present. It also partakes in a strange paradox. In the manner recalling the procedures of the LMS missionaries in the Pacific, remembrance not only preserves elements from the past but also simultaneously annihilates, through forgetfulness and alteration, what surrounds those images. As the example of these missionaries' efforts and the history of their collections illustrate, conscious recollections in the colony of memory move from place to place, mutate, and betray their origins and the people whose continuity they were once supposed to guarantee. St. Augustine's metaphor of the vast cloister of memory with cells into which fit particular pristine pieces of the past waiting for the individual's summons is not always appropriate. Memory cannot always be a sanctuary, for others force their way in and plunder its images. They violate the images' shapes and distort their meanings for their own pleasures. We are not the only ones who control our remembrances.

Robert Louis Stevenson and the Colony of Memory

With these reflections in mind, it is interesting to turn one's attention to Stevenson's experience of memory. The context of his friendship with the LMS missionaries in Samoa offers an opportunity to consider how his thoughts about recollection conform to what I have suggested concerning the alienating character and mutability of remembrance.

Memory and Alienation

Obviously many of Stevenson's memories shared a berth with loss, for they depended upon his absence/his alienation from home and his sense of himself as an outsider among his new surroundings. Having first sailed away from Scotland in 1879, then again in the late 1880s, Stevenson, exiled in Samoa, found himself intermittently swamped by remembrances of his past. These poignant moments led him away from his barefooted life and out of the entangled tropical foliage approaching Vailima. They transported him back to the Highlands, to the sounds of old acquaintances' voices, to the familiar rooms of his childhood, and to the maze of intersecting streets in Edinburgh. In the South Seas, especially when writing about the history and the landscape of home, he consciously sought to resurrect their details by writing to Charles Baxter to request books, maps, or pictures that would prompt his memory. And sometimes, sitting at his desk in Samoa, he re-entered a dialogue with his friend and editor Sidney Colvin by looking up at Colvin's portrait hanging on the wall and letting the image's frown reproach him and his work. But these consecrated memories of people and places belonging to his past also stood before him without any prompting. Recollections flashed spontaneously into his mind and for that moment overwhelmed him so that he was no longer in the South Seas but suddenly, without warning, standing on Princes Street in Edinburgh or once more listening to a brook winding its way and tumbling over stones.

These recollections, however, whether conscious or spontaneous, did not dictate the nature of all his work, for during his six years on the islands, in addition to finishing up *The Master of Ballantrae*, starting *Weir of Hermiston* and *St. Ives*, and writing a history of both Scotland and his family, he was also actively thinking and writing about the culture, history, and traditions of the people he now lived and traveled among. As I have pointed out, when he was writing about his new surroundings, Stevenson, like the anthropologists, frequently sought support from the LMS missionaries, who having lived longer than he in these surroundings, possessed an invaluable expertise. They gave him information, assisted him with various Polynesian languages, introduced him to people, and, as friends, offered him their perspective on his subject.

In the South Seas is one project that benefited from the missionaries' help. As those familiar with this book know, for many years Stevenson struggled trying to compose what began as a serious, semi-anthropological study of the region. He worked and re-worked its chapters, agonized over its structure, and dealt with (and seems finally to have given in to) the displeasure of his wife and his editor who were afraid that the book was not entertaining enough — not anecdotal enough, 'a sort of scientific and historical impersonal thing' — and who thought it an inappropriate waste of his time (*Letters* 6: 303). Because Stevenson wanted the pages faithfully to represent the people he met, he feared propagating errors. Not wanting to be like the voyager who during the first week in a new place amasses falsehoods, and then leaves 'homeward bound and vomiting in a stateroom', Stevenson fretted that he had not enough time to study these islands properly and thought it 'pitiful, to come here an ignorant elderly ass and glance at them for [a] quarter of an hour out of a ship' (6: 213). He longed to address the very ethnographic and historical questions that preoccupied Whitmee, Gill, Chalmers, Newell, and Tylor about the origins of Polynesian peoples; like these missionaries he wished to learn the languages and dialects, understand the meanings of burial customs, and consider the pressing 'questions of race and civilisation' (6: 213). As if working in parallel with them, Stevenson spent hours, days, and months gathering legends, ballads, and traditional songs, many of which he attempted to translate. He also read scientific pamphlets, natural histories, and studies on the depopulation of the Marquesans. In the end, with the help of not only the missionaries but also native informants, the occasional colonial official, and white traders, he accumulated what he referred to as 'a mass of stuff' and found himself, as a consequence, 'staggering' under the weight of his research (*Letters* 8: 29).

Stevenson and Material Culture

Allowing for obvious discrepancies, Stevenson's massive assembling of information takes one back to these missionaries' enthusiastic, if not zealous, amassing of ethnographic data. There is, however, one significant distinction that reveals a difference in the composition of his and the missionaries' stocks of memory. In Stevenson's ethnologic materials there were no objects, no specimens from the islands' material culture. Unlike the missionaries who had and were still gathering a plethora of implements, clothing, hair, and models of canoes to send home, Stevenson was not interested in collecting such artifacts. Indeed he seems to have been annoyed with those who did. He especially disliked the missionary's habit of accumulating bits of the material culture, so much so that in one of his South Sea fables ('Something in It'), he criticized a rather dull and insensitive missionary by referring to him as the 'one that loved curios' (Jolly 255). Although he sent a few artifacts home as gifts to relatives — two mother-of-pearl shells to his cousin, Lady Kyllacky and Samoan fish hooks to others — and somewhat reluctantly, yet persistently, bargained for a sorcerer's basket which he sent to an eager Andrew Lang, Stevenson rarely felt compelled to acquire a curio from the islands he visited. His impatience with and his sense of the irrelevance of these South Seas trophies are bitingly clear in a July 1890 letter he wrote at sea between Ellice Island and New Caledonia.

> The ship [*Janet Nicoll*] wallows deep with barbaric trumpery collected by Mrs Stevenson [Fanny], twopenny spears are triced up in the rigging; whenever the ship rolls, I look to have a shark's tooth scimitar discharged upon my dead head; and as I walk about the cabin dictating to Lloyd [his stepson], my path is impeded by a Manikiki drum, vainly sprinkled on the outside with buhac powder, but supposed internally to be one clotted bolus of cockroaches. (*Letters* 6: 396)

Stevenson was not to be a John Williams sailing triumphantly to shore in a boat that ostentatiously exhibited his spoils. This difference between the missionaries' impulse to collect the material culture and Stevenson's unwillingness to do so emerges in part from the placement of his memory. It reflects his own sense of the crisis of memory. Living thousands of miles away from home and residing where a letter took seven weeks to come from Edinburgh to Samoa via Sydney, Stevenson's colony of remembrances was, naturally, primarily inhabited with recollections of the people and places he had left behind and replete with images he would not have liked to see vanish from his internal sight. Keeping these vestiges alive was for him a more pressing need than assembling and preserving material artifacts representing the traditions of his current surroundings. The result is that rather than being interested in collecting curios from his travels in Polynesia, he went to extraordinary lengths to fill his house in Samoa with the material culture belonging to his life in Scotland and England. In 1891 he arranged for shipments of his massive library, his Piranesi etchings, his Hogarths (reputed), two or three of his cousin Robert's paintings, Sir George Reid's portrait of Thomas Stevenson, a plaster group by Rodin, and his pictures from Skerryvore (his house in England). With the aid of his stepson Lloyd, who was sent home to select items and find a shipping company, Stevenson also had the furniture, china, silver, cutlery, and glassware from Heriot Row (the family house in Edinburgh) and Skerryvore packed and sent to Samoa. He even went to the trouble of transporting the contents of the wine cellar at Heriot Row. A year later, still gathering these curios from his past, Stevenson wrote to his friend Adelaide Boodle to inquire if she knew the whereabouts of a lantern belonging to the lighthouse [evidently a miniature one] that had stood on the porch at Skerryvore. He complained, 'For some inscrutable reason, Lloyd chose to leave it behind and we have the bare tower which is far from ornamental and the reverse of useful. If by any accident you can lay hands on it, do please communicate with Baxter [Charles Baxter] who will see it sent to Samoa ...'. As if pleading, Stevenson concluded, 'even if incomplete let us have the remains' (*Letters* 7: 355).

Stevenson understood that 'the remains' are all memory requires, particularly in the context of another country. Like the curios sent to the LMS Museum and like recollections in a foreign land, these assembled vestiges bumped into the incongruities of an alien setting. Yet, there was a difference, for they were protected by those who had known and lived among them in the past.

The Mutability of Memory

Not all the items, however, arrived in one piece. The objects shipped to Samoa either suffered damage or were ripped apart and reassembled for other purposes. First, the china arrived, and 'though, alas! a good deal had been broken', it still cheered their 'hearts to see the "home-things"' about them once more (*Letters from Samoa* 64-65). Stevenson was distressed over the condition of his library, especially his collection of fifteenth-century French history from which sheets and boards had been torn, like waste paper, to use as packaging material. Other older books had been stuffed in corners to steady chest of drawers within a shipping crate. As Stevenson wryly remarked, 'My library is arriving piecemeal ...' (*Letters* 7: 121). Almost resembling the idols broken apart and sometimes reassembled by the missionaries, these damaged books had been appropriated by others and put to new uses. Even the volumes that had not been damaged during shipment were threatened, for they now faced the debilitating humidity of their new, tropical home. In an attempt to protect them — to prevent the memories embedded within them from being devoured by some alien presence — Stevenson's mother set about varnishing their covers. She hoped the coating would deter not only the damp but also the paper-eating, burrowing insects eager to consume these vestiges of the past and home. Their fate reminds one that like the Manikiki drum Fanny took on board the *Janet Nicoll*, any object from the past, no matter what the circumstances, once removed from its original context, carries within its core a mass of cockroaches — clots of deterioration — that endanger the permanence of the thing and, worse, threaten to destroy the center of its significance. The incongruous companions, destruction and preservation, cling to memory.

Stevenson's sense of the vulnerability of these remnants and his consciousness of the vagaries of remembrance do not surface, though, in his writing about Scotland, for those essays and novels, composed in the South Seas, emerge from a sanctified repository exempt from time and circumstance. Contrary to what I have suggested about the experience of recollection, Stevenson's memories of home are unusually stable: certainly more so than those of the rest of us. As a result, they transport him, as if on a magic carpet, back to the shores, streets, lowlands and highlands of home. They are the record of a retrospective eye that creates a present of the past by being blind to the spaces and alterations inherent in memory. These remembrances do seem to reside in St. Augustine's sanctuary, for Stevenson can reach in to gather what he needs and then put it back for another time. He might alter what he takes for his fiction, but all returns as it had been. The treasure house of his Scottish memories is a safe place; little vanishes because the pristine memories wait protected in their cells for Stevenson to beckon them. Of course, when his recollections appear in print, others might appropriate or adapt them. But none of that activity seems to intrude upon Stevenson's sense of his own past.

Paradoxically, the point at which one discovers Stevenson's appreciation of the mutability and vagaries of memory is when he sets aside his nostalgia and reflects on the present condition of life in the South Seas. In these moments his eager eye shoots forward, like a voyager's telescope, to catch a glimpse of what awaits him on the shores of the moment. There is no looking back; instead, there is an immersion in the infidelities and convulsions of the present that jumbles and confuses the past. As he had done in his youthful *An Inland Voyage* (1878), rather than looking at the door for the figure that is gone, Stevenson, enthralled by where he is, waits to see what will enter.

The present that fascinates Stevenson is an unstable one; therefore, in his fiction and prose about the South Seas, he concentrates on episodes of transition. As I have discussed in the first chapter, he dwells on those occasions where one culture or group intrudes upon or intersects with another and disrupts memories and the seeming continuity of the past. Novels like *The Ebb-Tide* and *The Wrecker* (both written with his stepson), stories and fables like *The Beach of Falesá* and 'Something in It', his *In the South Seas*, and his study of the colonial and civil wars in Samoa (*A Footnote to History*) explore the diverse forms of encounter among traders, sailors, missionaries, beachcombers, Chinese servants, 'black boys' (*In the South Seas* 5), German, British, and American officers, and the indigenous populations. From its very opening *The Ebb-Tide* immerses the reader in the midst of a group of dissolute Europeans living in Tahiti who manifest an awkward and clashing intertexture of cultures; they dress like natives, yet retain 'some foreign element of gait or attitude'; sprawled on palm-leaf verandahs, they 'entertain an island audience with memoirs of the music-hall' (Jolly 123). Jumbling bits and pieces of their present and past, these beachcombers present a confusing, jarring picture.

In a similar manner, the first chapter of *The Beach of Falesá* places the reader at the scene of Mr. Wiltshire's arrival on an island where this white trader will clash with and alter the lives of other European traders, the natives, and himself. Throughout *In the South Seas* Stevenson takes his reader with him as he attends to sounds and images that represent this intermingling and that vividly illustrate the transitory state of these archipelagos. He listens to the natives speaking the pidgin language 'Beach-la-Mar' and hears them communicating among themselves through a version of a French-English or a 'scraped up' English (10) — Stevenson's eye glances at palaces built of 'imported wood upon a European plan', a modern lamp and a sewing machine in a native dwelling in the Marquesas, a cricket game played on a Samoan beach, the confused dress of a converted high chief (he wears western women's garments, his own attire, and epaulets of a European officer), and, bemused, watches a native army suffering while parading in misfitting European shoes and carrying European arms. As part of his preoccupation with these confusing cultural exchanges, Stevenson was also drawn to the sight of King Tembinok's collections of foreign curiosities: 'clocks, musical boxes, blue spectacles, umbrellas, knitted waistcoats, bolts of stuff, tools, rifles, fowling-pieces, medicines, European foods, sewing-machines, and, what is more extraordinary, stoves ...' (213) — an exquisite version and reversal of the European cabinets of curiosities.

Within this shifting context of incongruity, Stevenson was as conscious of change and loss as were his European contemporaries. And, as a consequence, he was as aware as they of a crisis in memory. When visiting the Gilbert Islands, he commented on the particulars of this dilemma: 'In the last decade many changes have crept in; women no longer go unclothed till marriage; the widow no longer sleeps at night and goes abroad by day with the skull of her dead husband; and, fire-arms being introduced, the spear and the shark-tooth sword are sold for curiosities. Ten years ago all these things and practices were to be seen in use; yet ten years more, and the old society will have entirely vanished' (*In the South Seas* 156).

Details like these form the backdrop for his Pacific writing. His story *The Beach of Falesá* is an especially vivid example of his fiction devoted to these changes. Its episodes record how the present is peopled by those who appropriate, contaminate, and qualify the old order of things; the story's events capture the gestures and actions of vanishing memories. The false marriage of Mr. Wiltshire, a white trader, and the tabooed Uma is one such moment. Their union is blessed by a fabricated and perfidious contract that has nothing to do with indigenous practices and has everything to do with both the missionaries' insistence upon such ceremonies and the corruption of that requirement. The ceremony compromises the memory of both the indigenous and the Christian traditions. But far more provocative examples surface when Wiltshire's rival trader and nemesis, Case, appropriates what was traditional and part of the island's cultural heritage for his own advantage, and therefore misrepresents and compromises the integrity of the past. Case is a forger of memory. Caring only for what profits him, he cleverly manufactures island curios which he sells to those who pass by and leave. As fabricated remnants, these objects have nothing of what Malinowski calls an 'ethnological reality'; no part of them touches what they are imitating. When they sail away from the island to distant lands, they disperse misunderstanding and create fictions about the past. But worse is Case's purposeful distortion of the inhabitants' traditional beliefs. Deep in the forest, using magic tricks and supernatural devices like an aeolian harp (banjo strings stretched over a wooden box that sound when the wind blows), by suspending brightly clothed figures with carved and ugly faces that have teeth and eyes made of shells that could be tugged and made to move, and by placing in a dark corner a large shining and smoking face splashed with luminous paint, the corrupt Case institutes what Stevenson calls a 'museum' of curiosities (Jolly 54) to scare and intimidate the natives. His barbarous idols are horrific caricatures of the real thing. Mimicking devils and indigenous spirits of the dead, they clank, radiate, swing, and moan among the leaves and branches so that Case may rule and always have the advantage. In a sense, Case's awful gathering of puppets and tricks is a parody of the LMS Museum during its early years when its collection of South Seas artifacts, with its emphasis on the savage and hideous idols, manipulated alarmed viewers so they would share and promote the official missionary agenda to bring the light of Christianity to those who worshiped these barbaric beings.

Conclusion

Perhaps Stevenson's character Case represents more the rule than the exception regarding the operation of memory. Not everyone has the alternative of Stevenson's sanctuary of memory — not all of us can dip in and out of memories that remain, untouched, within our minds. We do not have the recourse he enjoyed when thinking about home. Most of us find ourselves tripped up by the compromises and appropriations of the present, and we are left with recollections that are not as true as they once were; we live with memories that have become the fiction of others and that remove us from the very past we wish remembrance would bring us closer to. Therefore, if we cannot find sanctuary in our memory, perhaps we must fabricate it by playing tricks and manufacturing idols and curios to create an illusion of a past and an illusion of an identity and a sense of origin. We have to invent tradition by freely ornamenting our recollections to gain not only some sense of self but also the acceptance of others. Like the individual who recollects episodes to suit the demands of her audience, we embellish and distort what was natural and paint in what was not there. We must hang out those parodies of another time for others to see, or we must walk into the rooms of these collections in an attempt to experience something that resembles what once was. From time to time we find ourselves trapped in our own false colony of memory. The fate of the South Seas curios can be ours.

Notes

1. Depending on their ideological or economic orientation, nineteenth-century Western commentators blamed this crisis of culture on the intrusive behavior and policies of Europeans traveling in the Pacific regions: whalers, white traders, beachcombers, colonial officials, British, German, and American sailors from the ships-of-war, slave traders, and missionaries, all of whom introduced diseases and many of whom encouraged corruption and intemperance (early on even the missionaries were accused of driving the natives to drink). In one form or another the increasingly sustained contact with Europeans and the subsequent cultural exchange were culpable.

2. In *Culture and Anomie: Ethnographic Imagination in the Nineteenth Century,* Christopher Herbert remarks on the fact that often twentieth-century anthropologists have too easily condemned the missionaries, as well as the colonial administrators, for destroying native cultures. He suggests that these anthropologists are oblivious to the pioneering scientific contributions the missionaries made. Their efforts to spread the gospel as well as collect anthropological data in part preserved, while also destroying, native culture. Their work could even be self-contradictory: rather than converting the native, the missionary, as a result of immersing himself in Polynesian customs and beliefs, often found himself undergoing a 'transforming conversion' (173).

3. See John Williams, *A Narrative of Missionary Enterprises in the South Sea Islands; with Remarks upon the Natural History of the Islands, Origins, Languages, Traditions, and Usages of the Inhabitants*, 50. Also see George Turner's 1876 Diary about his visit to Tahiti, Ellice, and the Gilbert Islands. LMS Archives ms.168. SOAS, U of London.

4. Whitmee also collected ethnographic data and made ethnological maps of the Pacific islands. His map showing the ethnology of Polynesia can be seen in the map room of The Royal Geographical Society, London. The map was published in *The Journal of the Anthropological Institute*, 13 February 1879.

5. See, for instance: *Journal of the Anthropological Society*. Vols. 6, 7, 8, 10, and 18. 1877-1899. Also see *Proceedings of the Royal Geographical Society*. ns 1 (1879).

6. In the LMS Archives among Newell's personal papers (Box 9, Folder 2) are the following statements written by Newell concerning the inadequacy of his notes:

> The writer's Samoan experience, and his lack of personal knowledge of Western Polynesia cannot fail to have coloured his observation of the Kingsmill Islanders.
>
> The following notes are necessarily brief and discursive and partial. The time spent at each Island was largely occupied in Missionary work & would, apart from that fact have been much too brief for detailed enquiry into the origin and history of the peoples occupying this section of the great tropical belt that encircles the earth.

7. In Book X of his *Confessions*, St. Augustine speaks of memory as a storehouse, a treasure-house, of countless images of all kinds. One picks what one chooses and then returns the selected memory to its place in storage — to the cloister of memory. Memories can brought out and called back again. In this way memory is held in a vast sanctuary, protected until needed again.

8. I am indebted to Professor Regina Grol for pointing out this distinction.
9. See Section 6 ('Identity') of David Hume. *A Treatise on Human Nature*. Ed. L. A. Selby-Bigge. Oxford: Clarendon P, 1968: 251-63.

Chapter Four

Lighting Up the Darkness

Introduction

The missionary context of the South Seas also offers the opportunity to consider the role of darkness in the formation of Stevenson's imagination. As if taking his cue from the missionary insistence on 'lighting up the darkness', Stevenson develops his images and his prose from a background of shade and shadows. Just as the photograph emerges from a negative, so do his words and images materialize in the dark. Like the missionaries who required the notion of 'darkness' to justify their enterprise, Stevenson, very much in his own way, depended upon the presence of darkness in order to define what was significant for him. On the islands, where oil lamps lit the paths and where the rays of the moon paved the dark seas, Stevenson entered an environment that intensified his sensitivity to the play of light, darkness, and shadow, and that encouraged him to record their patterns with his words and photographic images, few of which have been published. These images and Stevenson's scattered and generally overlooked commentary upon them not only complement his written descriptions of the South Seas but also help us realize that, from Stevenson's point of view, darkness is the foundation of seeing.

The Context: Missionaries, Magic Lanterns, and Searchlights

According to the accounts of Stevenson's missionary acquaintances, the Polynesians gave precedence to the moon over the sun and counted by nights, not by days. The fluctuating moon and its varying play of light and shadow against a background of darkness structured their understanding of the passing of time and of their surroundings.[1] As if sharing in this perspective, the South Sea missionaries, who slept with a lamp faithfully burning by their beds (*In the South Seas* 174), also oriented themselves spiritually in terms of the light that falls on a shadowy night. They built upon the pervasive Biblical metaphor of the 'true light' (John: 1.5) and promoted the image of the 'gleaming light' of Christianity that brings truth to the 'dark-minded savages' (Murray 119).[2] Even in their informal handwritten diaries the convention persisted and served as the basis of reports the London Missionary Society representatives sent back to the LMS foreign secretary. Rather than abandoning the topos, Stevenson's acquaintances, the Reverend S. H. Davies and the Reverend J. Marriott, remarked on the 'lonely islands ... far removed from lands of light' (LMS Archives ms. 180).[3]

These missionaries, though, were not content to let this universal metaphor remain an abstraction. Wanting to make their role as bearers of light more literal and tangible (and, perhaps, more convincing to themselves), earlier generations of missionaries had announced their arrival on the shores of an island by firing rockets and burning blue lights (LMS Archives ms. 183) and by illuminating, at night, their roughly built chapels with candles and hanging chandeliers made from coconut shells filled with oil, or by placing in their sanctuaries large kerosene lamps that resembled globes in the midnight sky (LMS Archives ms. 160). The indigenous people were appropriately impressed, or at least the missionaries report it so. The Reverend John Williams was among many LMS missionaries to record the natives' astonishment at the ensuing spectacle. He recalled one witness who exclaimed, 'Look at the chandeliers! Oro [a Polynesian god] never taught us any thing like this!' (Williams 45). Some years later, motivated by a conscious impulse to make the notion of lighting up the darkness even more explicit, an American missionary in the South Seas, arranged for a long nocturnal procession of flaming torches that was to be 'a sort of celebration of the arrival of light and the deliverance from idols' (Bingham 401).

But no matter how impressive or intimidating were the fireworks and no matter how splendid the chandeliers or how wondrous the displays of flaming torches, nothing quite equaled the power of the missionaries' magic lantern to beam images of Christianity and Western civilization upon the blackness of the night. These entertainments lit up their agenda and increased interest in the religious services.

The Reverend Williams first introduced the magic lantern to the South Seas. Early in the nineteenth century, he was upset that 'Romish priests' were on their way to the islands with 'electrifying machines and other philosophical apparatus' (Smith 59). (One of these was possibly a model of the Virgin Mary which, when pulled by hidden strings, bowed down in acknowledgment every time the congregation uttered an *Ave Maria*.) Not to be outdone in impressing his potential converts, Williams ignored the LMS's disapproval of such magical gimmicks and thought it time to compete by exhibiting lantern slides. After procuring a machine and slides on Scriptures, English and natural history as well as a series of slides 'representing the tortures and deaths of the faithful confessors of Protestant Christianity' (Smith 59), he set off to convert the inhabitants of the Western Pacific islands. His subsequent memo to the home office reporting on the success of the magic lantern was to become one of many, composed by him and other South Seas missionaries, emphasizing the audience's extraordinary interest in the exhibition:

> At the natural history slides they are delighted; the kings of England
> afforded them still great pleasure; but the Scripture pieces are those
> which excite the deepest interest .... The birth of Christ, Simeon taking

the Saviour in his arms, and the flight into Egypt, indeed all that had a reference to the Saviour, excited prodigious interest, but when the plate of the crucifixion was exhibited, there was a general sobbing, their feelings were overcome, and they gave vent to them in tears. (Smith 59-60)

Nearly half a century later, following not only Williams's precedent and the example of other missionaries in China and India but also David Livingstone's practice of making his way across the African Continent armed with a magic lantern — the 'oxyhydrogen light of civilization' (Ryan 30) — , the South Seas missionaries continued to project light upon the darkness in the form of these exhibitions. In the 1870s, when the Reverend G. A. Harris and the Reverend James Chalmers, the missionary, whom Stevenson admired, paid their annual visit to the out-stations on the Hervey Islands, they came equipped with a 'very good and powerful' machine and 'nearly every description of slides' — not always an easy task in choppy seas and through coral reefs.[4] In his report to the LMS Foreign Secretary, Harris reiterated Williams's earlier enthusiasm for the lantern:

The whole village [Mangaia] was present on the occasion. The humorous & comic pictures were given first, but they evidently were not appreciated by the majority as the questions showed they did not understand them. It was far from so however with the scripture scenes & characters. Their interest manifested in these was most wonderful, in fact their absorbed attention quite affected me. They gazed in amazement upon Adam & Eve, upon the Ark of Noah and family, and so desirous were they of being impressed with the likeness of the Patriarchs & Prophets that they often asked Mr Chalmers to re-exhibit them. But the zenith of their excitement & interest was reached when they beheld the scene of the crucifixion. The whole meeting was here subdued to great feeling and solemnity. (LMS Archives ms. 169)

There tended to be a standard missionary order to these magic lantern shows. Often they opened with a series of slides depicting wild animals and displaying various other natural history specimens; then came the mandatory group of comic pictures, followed by slides of foreign kings, queens, princes, and dukes; then pictures of Western cities, and, finally, true to missionary fashion, a substantial group of Scripture pictures that seemed, as we have seen in the quoted missionary reports, to excite the audience more than the other images. Toward the end of the nineteenth century, these magic lantern slides were composed of hand-painted and brilliantly colored pictures on glass as well as photographic prints transferred to glass plates. Some of these were static, but many were mounted on wooden frames with levers and slips that moved and created the illusion that one was watching a moving picture.[5] The so-called humor of the comic images often depended upon these devices. One of the most popular of these humorous slides was the 'Human Rat Trap' depicting a snoring man with rats that jump into his mouth every time it opens. The moral was 'Don't sleep with your mouth open.' Another was the racist

'Topsy and her moving eyes', a picture of a Mammie-like figure rolling her eyes back and forth. Listed among the other humorous slides for sale in the magic lantern catalogues are the ever-available 'Sambo lecturing', 'Dentist drawing teeth', 'Man with growing nose', 'Before and after marriage', 'Woman beating man', and 'Countryman and dog changing heads'. (Later when Stevenson borrowed magic lantern slides from one of the missionaries, he received many of these.) Obviously much of the humor depended upon certain racial, class, and sexual stereotypes.

Whenever possible all these slides were shown via sophisticated magic lanterns with multiple lenses that made it possible to dissolve one view into another so that one had the sensation of seeing a succession of images without any interruption. So skillfully done were some shows (often it took two people to work the more complicated lanterns) that these devices really were the precursors of the cinema. I believe it is a mistake to think of the missionary magic lantern presentations as being simply earlier and cruder versions of contemporary carousel slide projector pictures. Some, of course, were, but because the missionaries' intentions were to gather and indoctrinate large groups of people, more often the performances were exhibited to hundreds of people, and for that number the machines had to be able to project bright and clearly defined images on screens of considerable size (as large as fourteen feet per side). As a result, whenever traveling conditions and finances allowed, the missionaries preferred to have lanterns that could display gigantic pictures to an audience of between four and seven hundred. They wanted their images (as well as their beliefs) to dominate and overwhelm an assembled crowd. For that they needed the most up-to-date lenses and lanterns fitted not only with powerful oil lamps but, preferably, also with pieces of lime that were set ablaze by mixing gas with spirits or by blending oxygen with hydrogen, a dangerous task that could result in explosions, burns, and fatal accidents. The resulting limelight emitted a powerful light. The missionaries were less satisfied with devices that only used the small oil lamps or kerosene lights that smoked and emitted considerably weaker and more static images upon hung sheets.

The magic lantern became a standard appendage not only for visits to out-stations but also for the London Missionary Society's annual May meetings and at fund raising events held on the islands. (At one of these events in 1893 Stevenson's mother, Margaret Stevenson, donated money towards the purchase of a magic lantern for a boys' high school and the district in which it was situated.) Such was the machine's importance that the *Report of the London Missionary Society* from 1892 and 1894 listed in its expenses the cost for traveling and lantern lectures (£1,058/16/2 for 1892 and £1,482/6/9 for 1894), and the Society's *Chronicle* carried requests for donations of projectors and slides. In May, 1892, for instance, the magazine pleaded for contributions so that the natives of Mangaia (a town in one of the Hervey Islands) could be kept free of liquor. The thought was that by amusing the inhabitants with magic lantern exhibitions, they would be kept out of trouble and away from temptation. One year earlier, with a similar hope in mind, Stevenson's close acquaintance, the Reverend W. E. Clarke of Samoa, had sent many letters begging Mr. Spicer, the treasurer of the LMS, and 'his wealthy friends' for £25 with which to purchase 'a really good oxy hydrogen lantern' and slides so he could hold nightly entertainments that would be more suitable than what was currently provided by the various 'European amusements'. Significantly Clarke recognized that the question of amusement had become a problem in Apia (the town near where Stevenson lived in Samoa) because the missionaries had prohibited 'native pleasures', such as cricket, a game that had been introduced by the colonials and had been blended into Samoan cultural practices. Sometimes the matches lasted two weeks and involved over one hundred people on each side. They also sought to halt the infamous night dances that the missionaries thought to be obscene. He trusted that good lecture slides would 'provide a night's amusement for natives in the town on the evenings of Race Days, & such times as the saloons are full & the street crowded with curious Samoans & dissipated Europeans.' He believed himself 'bound to try some counter attraction to the drunken pleasures of the night' (LMS Archives 23 June 1891).

Once permission had been granted and a dealer had offered a discount, Clarke sent a memo to Jas. Brown in Glasgow requesting a 'Metamorphoser' Lantern (a lantern fitted with excellent lenses and with the capability of showing framed slides one after the other without an interval).[6] The memo reveals just how informed Clarke was about the techniques of using the device, a disclosure that shows his interest was not just a passing fancy but rather one that frequent and sophisticated usage had produced. He wanted a lantern fitted with 'special quality (Dallmeyer) lenses & one that would give a fine clear picture well & sharply defined and illuminated for display to audiences of 400 to 600.' All these images were to be shown on a fourteen foot screen probably supported by bamboo poles to which the screen would have been laced. Willing to risk the sometimes deadly explosions that dogged the use of oxy-hydrogen lights at performances, he also requested extra apparatus 'for displaying by the oxy calcium spirit, light viz. — extra chimney, sliding tray [these would be for dissolving views], safety lamp, gasbag, retort, tubing, gas purifier, & best quality (3 dozen) cylinders in 3 tins hermetically sealed [the cylinders were small limelight cylinders — the size of bottle corks — on which the flame played. They had to be sealed or they crumbled]'. This additional equipment was a form of limelight burner in which the gas was mixed with spirit and went through a metal jet, which was lit. This burner, of course, gave the bright 'limelight' necessary for large-screen projection.

Clarke's appended list of supplies also indicates that he planned a varied night's entertainment featuring a wheel of life with six assorted subjects (a mechanical slide that had a sequence of silhouette images around a transparent disc, and a slotted disc over that. When the discs were turned, the projected figure appeared in animation on the screen), and chromatropes, another mechanical slide that had two glass discs, one on top of the other, each with spiral and other patterns in color. When the handle was turned, the discs revolved in opposite directions, giving a hypnotic swirling color pattern on the screen. He also requested a set of slides showing the 'Tabernacle in the Wilderness', and colored portraits of Queen Victoria in State dress, the Prince and Princess of Wales, the Duke of Edinburgh, 'Prince Bismarck', the President of the United States as well as 'two dozen assorted plain photographic views of London, & principal continental cities' (LMS Archives 23 June 1891).

Clarke's choice of slides with its emphasis upon imperial figures, such as Queen Victoria and the President of the United States, is a reminder that these missionary lantern shows were not only put on to entertain or to spread the light of the Scriptures and dissipate the darkness of sin but also to project an imperial world view. Even though there were many moments in missionary history when the missionaries found fault with Colonial practices, religion and empire also worked implicitly and generally in tandem. A grandiose, bright, and clear image of Queen Victoria in State dress superimposed upon a nocturnal Samoan landscape was a formidable prospect. Enormous portraits of the Queen, the princes, dukes, and presidents, all representing the various and often competing colonial powers resident in Samoa (Britain, Germany, and the United States), could not help but partially indoctrinate and intimidate the native viewer. These larger-than-life portraits coupled with the lantern itself, a machine demonstrating the so-called superiority of European technology, seemed calculated to keep the viewers in their place and to encourage them to be beholden to a colonial administration and rule. In this way the lantern, with its ability to display dissolving views that gave the illusion of motion, spread magical rays of 'civilization' across the darkness of these 'backward places' and helped keep an imperialistic order in the inevitable chaos accompanying a cultural invasion.

The powerful rays crackling, fizzing, and pouring out of the magic lanterns onto the pitch dark chapels, homes, halls, and grounds of the islanders were, perhaps, more benign and more modest variations of the penetrating and intrusive searchlights that the colonial ships beamed through the overvaulting darkness and onto the shores of the Pacific islands. During the 1890s the British, German, and American warships were prowling the coasts of the Samoan islands and, at night, demonstrating their force by directing a searchlight upon an unsuspecting village, town, or bay. For the naval officers, as well as for the missionaries, light could be used as a weapon that subjected a people through raking illumination and was an integral part of the process of conquest. As if purposefully breaking an Ellice Island taboo that prohibited the bringing of light into a dwelling place (Hedley 55) or refusing to acknowledge an Old Samoan ban that forbade the carrying of a lit torch past a King's dwelling (Stair 126), these vessels defied native traditions and penetrated the night to expose the landscape and potential enemies. Without regard for privacy or custom they imposed an imperialistic technology that during the 1890s was also being celebrated at the World's Columbian Exhibitions in Chicago and in Buffalo where the 'Great German' and the 'Great American' Search Lights surveyed the buildings and the midways (with their exotic South Seas Villages) lying in the path of their powerful rays.[7]

Electric search lights, powered by steam, belonging to the German warship and to the *H.M.S. Curaçao* [the spelling of the ship's name varies in Stevenson's papers] were especially in evidence in Samoa during the 1890s where there was a possibility of a bloody civil war and where there was competition among the various colonial powers for control of the Samoan islands. On several occasions Stevenson and his mother recorded seeing these piercing lights. Their reactions reveal their grasp of the threatening character of the practice, for they both emphasized the beams' harshness and compared the sight to violent phenomena. In her pocket diary (21 August 1892) Margaret Stevenson noted that she had spent the evening in Apia with Clarke and his family. When they had come out of church, they had seen 'something like a volcano rising out of the sea', a frightening spectacle that turned out to be the search light of the *Curaçao* outside the reef (Beinecke ms. 7304). Two years later during a crisis in the civil war (24 April 1894), Stevenson wrote to his mother and spoke of the bright searchlights that the German and armed British warships directed toward Apia Bay. He registered his sense of the alarming power emitted by these beams when he rather confusedly spoke of this being the 'most noisy' war 'that ever has been seen in these parts' (*Letters* 8: 278). Even when the circumstances were more benign and he was sailing as a guest on board the *Curaçao*, the searchlight was not an altogether welcome presence. Stevenson's words describing the occasion in a letter to Henry James (7 July 1892) betray his perception of its lurking threat:

> I had a cruise on board of her [*Curaçao*] not long ago in Manua [a small island of Samoa] .... Gradually the sunset faded out, the island disappeared from the eye, though it remained menacingly present to the ear with the voice of the surf; and then the Captain turned on the searchlight and gave us the coast, the beach, the trees, the native houses, and the cliffs by glimpses of daylight, a kind of deliberate lightning. (*Letters* 8: 313)

When daylight arrives, it is with relief that Stevenson disembarks on the island and minimizes the previous night's grand and imposing illumination by speaking of his subsequent two-day stay as an opportunity to catch a 'picturesque snap-shot' (a small, modest image compared to what he had witnessed the evening before) of 'the native life'. In a sense, by lighting up the unsuspecting shores of Manua, the British naval captain had given Stevenson his own imperialistic military version of a magic lantern exhibit. He had lit up the landscape and imprinted it upon the darkness and then, as in the exhibitions, let the image disappear into the void of night.

Electricity, whether in times of war or peace, had never been appealing to Stevenson, who, in an earlier essay, 'A Plea for Gas Lamps', had bemoaned the coming presence of the ugly, blinding, and permanent glare of electric lights that, like the searchlights, were forming a 'new sort of urban star ... obnoxious to the human eye; a lamp for a nightmare!' (192). Recalling the 'pale and wavering' lights of his youth that so easily allowed night to 're-establish her void empire' (189), he expressed his preference for the age of the gas lamps and celebrated the kindly, warm circles of light that spread along and mapped a city, creating 'biddable, domesticated stars' (190). In a sense his coming to the South Seas led him back to this landscape of his childhood where, in spite of the occasional searchlight, the stars, the oil and gas lamps still held dominion and where the 'old mild lustre' of the lantern illuminated the dark by degrees and not all at once (192). On the islands he was once more surrounded by moments of light that intermittently lit up a dense darkness without eradicating the mystery of the knowledge hidden within its shadows. It is interesting to note that in a letter to her sister, Jane Whyte Balfour, Margaret Stevenson remarked that one of the problems of returning from the remote islands and disembarking at Honolulu was re-entering the world of electric lights, a 'bewildering and unpleasant' experience (*From Saranac to the Marquesas and Beyond* 258).

Stevenson and the Landscape of Light and Darkness: Writing by Lamplight

Although Stevenson did not always fully agree with either the missionaries or the colonial officials and their policies, he seems not to have felt entirely alienated from their utilizing the image of light to situate themselves and to organize their surroundings. In his South Seas writing Stevenson positions both himself and his reader in a landscape oriented by lights shining in the darkness. As if he were still the child admiring the lamps that mapped the city of Edinburgh or the young boy carrying a bull's-eye lantern so he could illuminate the black night of a Scottish fishing village ('The Lantern Bearers'), Stevenson continues to follow the glow of lanterns or the sight of a young moon on his nocturnal journeys through the islands. As if using a draftsman's grid, he finds his way back from Apia to Vailima, his home in Samoa, by tracing the patterns of the phosphorescent dead wood strewn over the ground, 'like a grating over a pale hell' (*Letters* 7: 56).

These luminous points of reference shine not only upon the dense thickets and rough roads of the islands' interiors but also upon the 'wild, ill-charted and unlighted seas' that lie about their shores (*Letters* 7: 212). On board the schooner *Nakunono* Stevenson looks up at clouds, lit up 'from within like paper lanterns', that shed structural patterns, an image that suggests the idea of a map overhanging the caligenous, unfathomable darkness of the sea around Tutuila (HM 2413). Upon other occasions Stevenson and his family sail where torches mark the entrances through hazardous reefs, and where, at night, people signal each other from the wharf to the ship and the ship to the wharf by igniting German (lucifer) matches and creating hundreds of red, blue, and green lights (*Letters from Samoa* 50).

Light also alerts Stevenson to the presence of others: to the Vailima 'boys' whose lamps burn as late as eleven o'clock (*Letters from Samoa* 123), to his cook 'dabbling among pots' in the open kitchen (*In the South Seas* 221) and to the chief's wives counting sticks of tobacco late into the night. Only the sheen from the pipes smoked by the Paumotuans submerged beneath the sea reveals their presence. The glowing bowl of their pipes floating just above the surface of the water makes these aquatic smokers known to him as he passes by. Light in the darkness also marks events and arranges the surroundings. A hanging lamp serves as a focal point in a photograph of Stevenson and his family clustered around a table. This central light seems to dominate and bring all the rest of what is visible into its orbit.

In this context of a world oriented and dominated by lights shining in the darkness, Stevenson's daily habit of writing early and late by lamplight seems apt. He would arise as early as four and work until 'the lamp has once more to be lit' (*Letters* 7: 136) and would occasionally get up in the middle of the night to compose verses (*Our Samoan Adventure* 33). The lamp's rays overspread his manuscript pages, to reappear as scattered beams glowing in a green thicket (*The Wrecker*), as the street lamps' trembling reflections on the waters of the port (*The Ebb-Tide*), and as distant lights from fires and torches of many fishers moving on the reef (*The Beach of Falesá*).

In a sense Stevenson's continuing appreciation for the sight of a light penetrating the dark forms the very letters of his prose. In the opening passages of *In the South Seas*, when he describes his first sighting of the Marquesas, it is as if his words, like hieroglyphic silhouettes, emerge against the background of 'a radiating centre of brightness' at morning, within the disappearing gloom of night. The contrast between the light and dark brings into view the black lines of the horizon upon which stands a 'morning bank' as 'black as ink' (6) and reveals a prospect in which the dark peaks or needles of Va-pu show themselves in outline against the first rays of the sun. One of Stevenson's pencil drawings sketched on board the *Casco* shows the mountains appearing to write upon the sky, and illustrates how the contrast of strong, black lines upon a white sheet of paper creates a kind of vocabulary with which to delineate and realize what he sees.

These opening passages of *In the South Seas* give Stevenson the lines, the ink, and the letters with which to mark his arrival and to proceed. When he writes, his ideas and words emerge, bit by bit, as the dawn allows the landscape slowly to take shape 'in the attenuating darkness'. The prospect of light against darkness helps him describe what he has never seen before. They help him articulate what at that moment was 'a virginity of sense' (*In the South Seas* 6).

Ua-huna, piling up to a truncated summit, appeared the first upon the starboard bow; almost abeam arose our destination, Nuka-hiva, whelmed in cloud; and betwixt and to the southward, the first rays of the sun displayed the needles of Ua-pu. These pricked about the line of the horizon; like pinnacles of some ornate and monstrous church, they stood there, in the sparkling brightness of the morning, the fit sign-board of a world of wonders. (*In The South Seas* 6)

4.1   'Vaipuhiahi from the Harbour'

On his journey through the islands, he is never content to rest in the full white-washed blaze of day, but returns, as if to refurbish his vocabulary, into a landscape where he remarks on 'the hour of the dusk, when the fire blazes, and ... the lamp glints ... between the pillars of the house' (*In the South Seas* 15), and where the fronds of the palm trees 'stand out dark upon the distance, glisten against the sun, and flash like silver fountains in the assault of the wind' (78).

At sea off the coast of the Paumotus, he once more approaches and orients himself to a new island by concentrating on how the light punctuates and contrasts with the darkness. That evening on shore he looks up at 'clouds of inky blackness' (111) shattered at times by lightning. The style of his prose in this period has its genesis in these moments and in others when Stevenson, in the season of the full moon, walks 'perhaps till twelve or one in the morning' on 'the bright sand and in the tossing shadow' of the Gilbert Island palms (231). It is these episodes that Stevenson remembers when recalling the genesis and the growth of *The Wrecker* and *The Master of Ballantrae*. In his epilogue to *The Wrecker* he explains to W. H. Low that the idea for the book came to him on board the schooner *Equator* 'almost within sight of the Johnstone Islands ... and on a moonlit night when it is a joy to be alive ... ' (550). Later in an essay 'The Genesis of *The Master of Ballantrae*' Stevenson recalls that this novel began on a dark night: 'From a good way below, the river was to be heard contending with ice and boulders: a few lights appeared, scattered unevenly among the darkness .... For the making of a story here were fine conditions' (*The Master of Ballantrae* v-vi). It is significant that in 'My First Book', an essay about the composition of *Treasure Island*, Stevenson recognizes that knowledge of 'the place of the sun's rising, the behaviour of the moon' gave him his bearings in the landscape of his narration and helped lead him through his writing (*Treasure Island* xxx).

Intermittent Light and Shadows

Stevenson's fiction and imagination thrive upon the alternating, uneven dispersal of light and darkness. His characters seem to step out of the shadows onto the brightness of the page. Like the native women in *The Wrecker* who 'came by twos and threes out of the darkness' (15) and into the glow of the scattered lights, his characters emerge as if from oblivion onto the brilliant text.[8] Their succession of illuminated faces stirs his fancy and stimulates Stevenson to explore the mystery of what surrounds them. Stevenson continues what he had done before and transplants a style in which intermittent light is prominent. Just as when he had placed his characters in the half-lit streets and drawing rooms of London (*Dr. Jekyll and Mr. Hyde*) and had positioned Mr. Utterson, who waits for a sighting of Mr. Hyde, under the gas lamps that draw 'a regular pattern of light and shadow' (15), he must now enter areas where the hidden, the unseen, and the unarticulated press upon the edge of a sun's beam, or a moon's ray, or where a shining lamp punctures a dark place. As a result, his South Sea stories, like *The Beach of Falesá*, move from the full brightness of the morning (the opening of the story) to where the lantern, the candles, the torches, and matches punctuate the nocturnal landscape and reveal silhouettes of incomplete meaning. The story shifts from the sun-baked beach to the dark interior of the bush. The narrative's backdrop of contrasting light and darkness carries on what had been essential to his composing of *Dr. Jekyll and Mr. Hyde*, where most of the action plays on a shadowy set occasionally illuminated by a flame from a fire, the glimmer of a gas lamp, or the rays of the moon, and where Hyde prowls at night and Jekyll, when he is rid of Hyde, walks in the sunshine and works by day. Stevenson's style, especially in the first part when Mr. Utterson has the voice, represents this fragmented or partially lit perspective. Stevenson writes Mr. Utterson's narrative so that it progresses through fits and starts, and moves through disconnected details. What other evidence might be present to give Mr. Utterson a more complete view of what he is trying to understand is obscured by the night or the dark shadows of the action. When Stevenson describes what happens after Mr. Utterson, Poole, and the footman break down the door of the laboratory, he replicates this interrupted perspective by concentrating on detached phrases and illuminated objects to emphasize their incongruity against the backdrop of what we know about Hyde:

> The besiegers, appalled by their own riot and the stillness that had succeeded, stood back a little and peered in. There lay the cabinet before their eyes in the quiet lamplight, a good fire glowing and chattering on the hearth, the kettle singing its thin strain, a drawer or two open, papers neatly set forth on the business table, and nearer the fire, the things laid out for tea; the quietest room you would have said .... (61)

Stevenson's South-Sea letters and journals also portray episodes of interrupted darkness and discontinuous light in which metonymic figures and fragments replace the full, inclusive prospect. They describe the strange effects made by lanterns placed at intervals within the big shadowy halls at Vailima and the spectacle of natives dancing by the light of a dying fire that made it 'just possible' to see the nearest dancers and catch a glimpse of their shoulders 'polished in the glow' (Ms. Copy of Journal in Tutuila).[9]

Within Stevenson's metonymic field of vision, these partial images often seem to succeed one another like slides in a magic lantern show. Like the scrolls of lighted pictures that run through Mr. Utterson's mind when he recalls, at night in bed, what Mr. Enfield has told him about a Mr. Hyde, and like the pictures projected on a blackened sky by the missionaries, they come, one by one, between intervals of darkness, until night or sleep overtakes all. On the Gilbert Islands he follows the progress of a sunset when the shadows thicken to create a succession of luminous images, each splintered by darkness until the day is gone:

> It was then that we would see our Chinaman [the Stevensons' cook] draw near across the compound in a lurching sphere of light, divided by his shadows; and with the coming of the lamp the night closed about the table. The face of the company, the spars of the trellis, stood out suddenly bright on a ground of blue and silver, faintly designed with palm-tops and the peaked roofs of houses. Here and there the gloss upon a leaf, or the fracture of a stone, returned an isolated sparkle. All else had vanished. (*In the South Seas* 182)

At evening, outside King Tembinoka's dwelling, Stevenson watches as the Palace lanterns are 'fared off into all corners of the precinct, lighting the last labours of the day'. They illuminate, one after another, the departing 'prodigious company of women' and the scattered remains of extinguished lanterns (227-28). The contrast of light and darkness also outlines and isolates even sunlit images so that on the Gilbert Islands, from within a church (the 'great hall of shadows'), Stevenson, through the frame of an open door, sees in the 'intolerable sunshine' an 'ugly picture' of two women fighting (179). That night, as he lies outdoors in his hammock, the image of their hostile embrace, like a slide projected on the sky, haunts and disturbs his internal field of vision.

Because Stevenson had an enduring infatuation with patterns of light and darkness, he was naturally drawn toward light's protean attendant, the shadow. As in *A Child's Garden of Verses*, where the child watches his shadow go 'in and out' ('My Shadow') and waits boldly for its crooked presence to crawl in corners and march 'along up the stair' ('Shadow March'), Stevenson watches 'huge gorges sinking into shadow', and, during the day, traces the 'crude shadows in the sand' (*In the South Seas* 77, 135). When night comes (evening is 'that hour before the shadows' [174]), he stalks these shadows, though they lurk and terrify the Marquesan who believes in ghosts and alarm the Paumotuans who fear the dead might come to eat the living. He rides through treacherous and disquieting nocturnal landscapes where the moving light of a lantern tosses about a 'curious whirl of shadows' (*Letters* 8: 373) or where the dense shade of the trees makes the way confusing and populated with supernatural beings. A scene from *The Beach of Falesá* captures one such moment and revives Stevenson's sense of the shadow's menacing and animated autonomy:

> The light of the lantern, striking among all these trunks, and forked branches, and twisted rope's-ends of lianas, made the whole place, or all that you could see of it, a kind of puzzle of turning shadows. They came to meet you, solid and quick like giants, and then span off and vanished; they hove up over your head like clubs, and flew away into the night like birds. (Menikoff 89)

In Stevenson's imagination shadows are what animate their source. They extend, minimize, enlarge, and give movement to the object itself as well as to its surroundings. They infuse what they represent with life, dimension, and possibility. In so doing, they confirm the myth of the woman without a shadow who remains no more than a sterile body.[10] Furthermore they confirm the truism that an 1888 commentator uttered before the Anthropological Society in London when giving instructions on ethnographic photography: that the lighting of a picture needs the most attention, for every image is defined by the shading (Edwards 103).

In a sense shadows are the primary images, for they narrate the spirit of their origin and the shape they represent. And, like Fanny's shadow portraits of Ori a Ori (otherwise known as Teriitera), they are what gives substance to a person and character. In 1888, when the Stevensons were more than two months the guests of Ori a Ori in Tautira, Fanny (Stevenson's wife), whom the chief called *Jaffini Tuta* (the maker of shadows), made silhouettes of him by 'taking the shadow of his head on the wall, with the help of a lamp, drawing the outline and then filling it in with Indian ink' (*From Saranac to the Marquesas and Beyond* 242). These were the images that the Stevensons were to take away with them as a memento of their journey; and the silhouettes that Fanny made of themselves were also what they left behind, an impulse that suggests that shadows when captured like that permit one to remember, not the actual thing itself. In her pocket diaries, Margaret Stevenson noted that they 'bequeathed their shadows in memoriam' (Beinecke ms. 7304). Paradoxically, for something strangely insubstantial and elusive, shadows are what the mind retains. It should also be noted that shadows can be so solid and sharply defined that when Fanny was in Tahiti she found herself involuntarily stepping over them (*In the South Seas* xi).

Lighting up the Darkness: Photography

One of Stevenson's South Seas missionary acquaintances, the Reverend George Turner, recounts a Samoan myth about a lady who 'caught the shadows' and imprinted them on the water (Turner 101). This is an ancient legend that later informed the more general understanding in Samoa that to photograph is to 'shadow catch' (Claxton, 'A Samoan Boys' School'). In his own way Stevenson and his family took up photography to try and do just that. By exposing dark plates to the sun, the moon, and to the sudden glare of exploding flash powder, Stevenson not only continued to express his interest in the play of light on darkness but also caught images and shadows for others to see. These pictures, such as the photos of dancers in Apemama (cruise of *Equator*), capture their subjects and their shadows. Like the child's shadow in *A Child's Garden of Verses*, dark phantoms of the dancers' arms haunt the speak house walls. They loom larger than life to register the subjective experience of his subjects' movement and presence.

4.2   'Great Dance in Apemama Speak House'

Beginning with the first voyage on board the yacht *Casco* in 1888, photography was to be a significant accompaniment on Stevenson's various journeys around the islands, as it was for so many explorers and missionaries heading toward the lesser known regions of the globe (Ryan 29). Lists of 'photo things', and 'photographic goods' (Lloyd Osbourne's diary), and references to cameras and photographic expeditions regularly appear in Stevenson's letters, his mother's correspondence, and his wife's and his stepson's diaries. They tell of successes and disasters, as when Lloyd's photographic apparatus fell overboard from the *Casco* to the bottom of the sea, 'a terrible loss!' (20 July 1888 Beinecke ms. 7304). Divers came to retrieve the equipment but failed. Several months later (April, 1890) they speak of an explosion of fireworks on board the *Janet Nicoll* that destroyed 'a great part' of the photographs (*Letters* 7: 389). About ninety photographs were destroyed, but, fortunately neither of the two cameras was lost. According to Fanny, Jack Buckland had brought on board fireworks, including ten pounds of 'calcium fire' with fumes, for the entertainment of his native retainers in Auckland. The fireworks exploded on April 30 just as the ship was leaving Auckland harbor (*Letters* 7: 389).

Lloyd and Joe Strong (Stevenson's stepdaughter's husband) were the primary photographers, but, it should be emphasized, Stevenson did his share and often carried a camera. The Reverend Clarke's first view of Stevenson was of him with 'a cigarette in his mouth, and a photographic camera in his hand' ('Reminiscences of Robert Louis Stevenson'). This sighting was not to be the only time, for subsequently when Stevenson accompanied Clarke on a *malaga* (an outing) to more remote areas of Samoa, he took along his camera. In a typescript of his account of one such trip in 1889, Stevenson notes that 'after we had dined, we set out photographing' (Beinecke ms. 6556). It seems, though, that Stevenson was not confident about his technical skills and thought his negatives inferior. In his mind they resembled 'a province of chaos and old night in which you might dimly perceive fleecy spots of twilight, representing nothing' (*Letters* 8: 319). For this reason, he often took Lloyd along and placed the main photographic responsibility in his stepson's hands. In a December, 1889 letter to Charles Baxter, for instance, he informed his friend that 'Tomorrow I go up the coast with Mr. Clarke, one of the London Society Missionaries in a boat to examine schools .... Lloyd comes to photograph' (*Letters* 7: 346-47). Stevenson did, however, continue to show an interest in identifying subjects and composing the photographic shots. In her account of the voyage on the *Janet Nicoll*, Stevenson's wife not only records one such moment but also describes how the Penrhyn islanders mocked their photographic endeavors, a welcome subversion of the usual situation, in which the camera was used to exercise control over the people:

> Lloyd and Louis planted their camera stand in the centre of the village, and walked about to look for good points of view. While they were away a serious-looking man delivered a lecture upon the apparatus, to the evident edification and wonder of the crowd. During his explanation he mimicked both Louis's and Lloyd's walk, showing how Lloyd carried the camera, while Louis walked about looking round him. (*The Cruise of the 'Janet Nichol'* 57-58)

The photographs were to be used as illustrations for Stevenson's writing about the South Seas. On board the *Casco* (1888), they were equipped with at least one 'old broken' camera, developing equipment, and photographic plates Lloyd fitted 'as best he could' (Beinecke ms. 638). While in the Marquesas Lloyd had inadvertently dropped the camera into the sea, but thanks to a trader, Mr. Keane, an Englishman who had been a cavalry officer in India, a second-hand one was found. Because he had run out of photographic plates, Keane sold his camera to the Stevensons, but in order for the camera to function, Lloyd had to cut down his own plates so they could fit. In some of the photographs from this voyage, one can see dark lines and evidence of leakage of light around the borders of the developed pictures.

Whenever they disembarked, so did the 'precious camera' (*From Saranac to the Marquesas and Beyond* 134). They would set out early on photographing expeditions with the yacht's Captain Otis, especially Lloyd who, according to Margaret Stevenson, succeeded in taking a good many pictures: In Hiva-oa 'He did both the outside and the inside of the church, *Frère* Michel and *Père* Orenz, a large group of ourselves surrounded by natives, and a smaller one of ourselves with our new family' (*From Saranac to the Marquesas and Beyond* 135). Whenever circumstances made it possible, Lloyd developed his plates and printed some of his photos. In Hiva-oa, for instance, he got the use of a small dark room at the mission. Because they could rely on such available spaces, the Stevensons did not haul around the cumbersome black developing tents that many explorers took with them in other colonial areas. The resulting images, along with Stevenson's diaries, were deemed important enough to send home in case of accident. Certainly stories of ruin abounded, among them the fate of 'the Earl and the Doctor' [The Earl of Pembroke and George Henry Kingsley] who lost all their portable property collected on their three-year tour of the South Seas (Osbourne. Beinecke ms. 5267).

A few months later the Stevensons embarked on a second trip (June-December, 1889), on the schooner the *Equator*. This time their preparations for their photographic activity were more extensive, ambitious, and professional, for Stevenson had decided to include his son-in-law, Joe Strong (a professional painter and photographer), with whom there had been and were to be disputes and problems, but whom he considered a fine photographer. Stevenson's plan was that on this voyage Lloyd and Strong would take photographs. Many of these would be made into magic lantern slides. In addition, Strong would paint a series of watercolors depicting the people and the landscape. These paintings, based on his photographs, would form what Stevenson loosely referred to as either a diorama or a panorama, perhaps a mounted display representing places where they had traveled. (Often photographs served as models for the painter doing dioramas.) His idea was that the exhibition would be accompanied by an explanatory lecture given by Lloyd.

All the references to this short-lived scheme leave one with more questions than answers, for it is not certain exactly what Stevenson meant by the terms. Commentators tend to assume it was to be simply a magic lantern show, but I believe the diorama or panorama was conceived to be more than that. Stevenson's project was probably not meant to be what the nineteenth-century magic lantern catalogues call a 'photo-Diorama', long fourteen-inch slides projected on a screen, and certainly was not meant completely to duplicate the large panoramas and dioramas that were permanent features in major international cities (there were several mounted in Britain in the 1870s and 1880s). I suggest that Stevenson's idea was to construct a portable panorama (there were many in existence) that was closely linked to these popular (and money-making) nineteenth-century spectacles. It was to be a more modest version that would appeal to the public's ever-growing penchant for visual and exotic information. He hoped it would be easy to move around and, furthermore, be flexible enough so that he could add materials from his subsequent travels in the islands. All of his letters about the scheme reveal how concerned he was at this time about his finances and his need to find ways to raise money. In an April, 1889 letter to Baxter he explained: 'the idea is to get up a diorama and let Lloyd lecture, and try to start a little money, honestly got' (*Letters* 7: 285-56). Two months later Stevenson again wrote to Baxter: 'the idea is to begin the panorama there [Sydney], and when it is ready, carry it to some islands in style, and get more stuff for it; thus making it feed itself' (*Letters* 7: 315). This was the plan that Lloyd, in his June, 1889 letter to Baxter, said 'smelt of dollars' (Beinecke ms. 5267).

While the scheme lasted, the work was intense. The Stevensons must have started working on the photographic images in Honolulu where in a group of buildings was a room filled with 'tubs of water, negatives steeping, a tap, and a chair' and in another 'a picture of Joe Strong's upon the easel and a table sticky with paint' (*Letters* 7: 280). Supply lists at the back of Lloyd's diary reveal the seriousness with which they considered the project, for the photographic equipment appeared second after 'Mackintosh' and stood significantly ahead of such items as '6 bottles of brandy, laudanum, plaid, presents, tobacco, money, and clothes' (Lloyd's diary). Their earnestness and commitment to the project also surface when on 16 June 1889 Lloyd told Baxter how they were 'well-prepared for the panorama business' by 'taking a couple of cameras ... and one hundred dozen plates' (Beinecke ms. 5267), an obviously enormous number that suggests these were not plates that could be recycled and used again. All these 'photographic goods' as well as Strong's drawings, paper, oil and water colors took up considerable room in the Seamen's Chests. Unfortunately for us the panorama scheme eventually came to an end over a series of incidents concerning what Stevenson and Lloyd termed Strong's 'ugly', 'silly', and 'miserable misconduct' (*Letters* 7: 220n., 7: 346). In one letter to Baxter, written while in the Gilbert Islands, Stevenson indignantly and formally declared his dissatisfaction and frustration with Strong: 'I had to depose him from his office of photographer, which is now held in Commission by Lloyd and me: this incidentally blew up the panorama for I will never trust him in any business, if it was only to thread a needle' (*Letters* 7: 331). One of the later incidents was a quarrel over the use of a flash camera.

About four months later (April, 1890), now without Strong, Stevenson, Fanny, and Lloyd took their third Pacific voyage in the trading steamer the *Janet Nicoll*. This time Stevenson was hoping that by visiting more islands and returning to some, he could continue to collect more historical and scientific materials for his projected book on the South Seas. Once more the cameras came on board, and what few photographs survived the fireworks disaster returned with them. The enthusiasm for photography continued. Fanny remarks that even after taking pictures for a couple of hours, 'we ... reluctantly tore ourselves away' (*The Cruise of the 'Janet Nichol'* 30-31). At moments their fervor was tested by their subjects' fears at being photographed and standing before what Stevenson termed that 'one-eyed and unfamiliar spectator, the camera' ('A Samoan Scrapbook'). Fanny describes one of these episodes: 'Lloyd took the younger girl's photograph at the end of the bridge. I had to stand beside her with my arm round her for some time before she would keep in one spot long enough for the camera to be pointed at her.' Apparently oblivious of her insensitivity in forcing the girl to undergo this procedure, she observes casually, 'Though much less frightened, she was still suspicious' (*The Cruise of the 'Janet Nichol'* 101-102).

Photography and Writing

Ultimately the photographs taken on these voyages were important to Stevenson not because of their link to money-making schemes but because they were a necessary complement to his writing. They were, as I have indicated, a means of legitimizing or illuminating his words and of giving his readers a more particularized image to consider. He, like so many others, respected the authority of the camera. Stevenson wanted to correct the inaccurate, generic photographs frequently selected from banks of images that were generally available in books about the South Seas and often had little to do with the text.[11] He was displeased with the stereotypical images that more often than not came from what Nancy Armstrong refers to as a 'shadow archive' (30) that, in his mind, did not properly represent the reality he wanted to present. In this respect Stevenson was in the tradition of some missionaries and a number of anthropologists who went about with cameras collecting shots of 'new tribes and scenery' (Bevan 608), holding on to the belief that the camera was the most accurate means by which to portray a visible object.[12] Like them he considered that records made in writing were 'infinitely helped out by the camera' (Thurn 184) and that it was preferable 'not only to rely on written descriptions only, but to secure if possible photographs' (William Y.Turner 472); their importance was confirmed when Stevenson was able to send photos of gravestones to Andrew Lang so his acquaintance could confirm or contradict certain anthropological data. Fanny also expressed her belief in the authority of the camera. In a letter to Mrs. Virgil Stevenson Williams (November, 1888), she exclaimed 'all descriptions of Hivaoa, which is truly the fortunate Isle, I leave to Louis's book and Lloyd's photographs' (Beinecke ms. 638). And so did Belle Strong [Osbourne], her daughter, when she sent a photograph of a 'genuine Samoan beau' to Elizabeth Fairchild for fear that her correspondent was receiving a 'totally false idea' of Samoan people based upon her seeing the melange of South Sea islanders exhibited at the Chicago World's Fair (*Letters* 8: 130).

In a sense, for Stevenson these photographs bore a resemblance to the Samoan legend of the shadows. As if he were the lady in the ancient myth, he caught his images and imprinted them on the page to fill out or give meaning to his words and to confirm his observations. As a result, perhaps verifying Armstrong's sense of the 'mutually authorizing relationship between fiction and photography' (3), the pages of Stevenson's fiction often seem to develop from a photographic negative. One of the most vivid examples of this phenomenon occurs in the opening of *In the South Seas*. In these initial paragraphs he lets his readers follow his own eyes as he watches the landscape's particulars slowly come to light in the dissolving darkness. When he writes these opening passages, he is in the dark room of night and watching the shores gradually take their shape and become visible through the rising morning light. Once the fully developed image materializes Stevenson uses it to ground his observations so that the opening view of Nuka-hiva serves as a point of reference and a point of comparison for all that is 'so foreign' (*In the South Seas* 7) to the European eye.

Because the idea of the photograph plays an important role in Stevenson's orientation to the islands, it is not surprising that he turned to the camera so that he could not only situate himself in the center of his narration but also coordinate his thoughts with the photographic image. If one looks at the long list of pictures taken while on the *Equator*, a list meticulously recorded in Stevenson's hand, and then turns to look at a second column specifying their suggested use for his book on the South Seas — this time written in Fanny's hand (Beinecke ms. 6716) — , one easily recognizes both the intensity of Stevenson's commitment to the photographic image as a supplement to his text and the care with which he attempted to coordinate the words and the images. Still, there were moments when Stevenson felt the camera obtrusive and incongruous, especially in Apemama (the Gilberts) when, under a tree and surrounded by a magic circle, he submitted to the care of three native 'sorcerers' who tried to rid him of a threatening cold (*In the South Seas* 246-47). He thought the camera (the machine) and the cure (the magic) were not compatible.

Stevenson must have spent hours compiling and thinking through the hundreds of shots, a laborious task that unfortunately never reached fruition, for *In the South Seas* was eventually published without them. In the shorter pieces, though, Stevenson sometimes had the satisfaction of sending photographs and directing the use of them. His correspondence with Edward L. Burlingame is full of instructions about how to 'be very careful of the photographs' (*Letters* 7: 372) and of such pictures as a portrait of Tembinoka, a view of the King's palace, and the 'matted men' to be used as the bases of illustrations for an article in *Scribner's* (*Letters* 7: 366). Stevenson also sent Samoan photographs with the manuscript of *The Ebb-Tide* and strongly suggested that the engraver of the *Illustrated London News* refer to them. In addition, according to Clarke, he sent a snapshot of that missionary along with his manuscript of *The Beach of Falesá* so that the likeness between Tarleton (the missionary in the story) and Clarke 'might be correct'. Apparently Stevenson 'seemed quite hurt' that the missionary did not recognize himself ('Reminiscences of Robert Louis Stevenson').

Stolen Eyes

The photographs that resulted from the trips on the *Casco*, *Equator*, and the *Janet Nicoll* had little affinity with the popular commercial, almost pornographic, images featuring Samoan Belles lying invitingly bare breasted upon tropical foliage. Nor did they bear any resemblance to the anthropometric pictures in which travelers and ethnologists placed a naked native subject in front of a grid, against a screen, or next to a measuring rod so as to survey and classify the person's form.[13] Neither did his photographs approach Francis Galton's images of profiles that when layered, one on top of the other, produced a generic shape that supposedly revealed the features of a racial, criminal, or character type and, thereby, reinforced assumptions about ethnic categories and contributed to stereotypical notions about human behavior. Rather, Stevenson's images were snapshots of the instant. Most of them used 1/15 or 1/50 of a second exposures that illuminated episodes and caught fragments of light and experience when one focuses on a subject between intervals of inattention — when the mind wanders and does not see.[14] Some caught fleeting episodes like 'One detachment of the "talotasi" coming with songs and presents to meet us at Fagalo' and 'Mrs Stevenson being carried ashore' or 'Joe Strong taking out his false teeth before astonished natives.'[15]

4.3   'Mrs. Stevenson Being Carried Ashore — Apiang'

4.4   'Joe Strong Taking out his False Teeth'

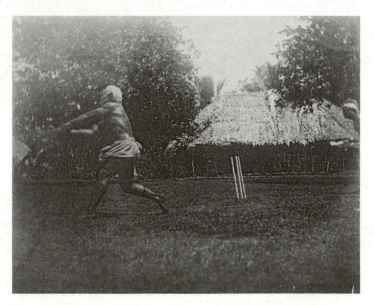

4.5   'Samoan Playing Cricket'

4.6   'Headquarters of Wightman Bros. — Butaritari'

Others featured the landscape and frequently registered the Stevensons'
presence in it as in 'Butaritari — RLS & Osbourne in interior of island' (the
photograph picks up the vigorous movement of the palm fronds); various
photographs, like 'Speak-House' catch the light that seeps through their openings.
Many attempted to represent the life of the natives like 'Samoan playing cricket' (the
exposure captures the light on the man's muscular body and ends when he finishes his
swing) or 'Headquarters of Wightman Bros.' showing natives carrying the bags of
copra from the wharf across the shallow water to the boats — the water splashes
during the exposure.

4.7   '"Equator Town" by Moonlight'

4.8   'Fanny, Stevenson, Nan Tok, and Nei Takauti. Butaritari, 1889'

As might be expected, given the class-consciousness of foreign travelers in the nineteenth century, a significant number of the surviving photographs also reflect Stevenson's consistent regard for the political hierarchy of each island he visited. These images were less spontaneous and reveal a more self-conscious, hierarchical eye. In these photographs Stevenson and Lloyd sought to picture those who had power and to place themselves in a position in which they were either seated with the chief (as in the photograph of Fanny, Stevenson, and Nei Takauti taken on Butaritari in 1889) or were, as Lloyd crudely put it, 'side by jowl with royalty' (Beinecke ms. 5267). They immersed themselves in the task of negotiating with the king or chief in an attempt to persuade him to pose, as when they were refused because it was a Sunday, and, according to missionary rule, no photographs were to be taken (*In the South Seas* 174). Once they received permission they exercised their so-called Western privilege and requested that their subjects dress up in native costume or, at other times, impatiently tolerated a king's desire to don elaborate and misfitting Western dress.[16] On one occasion, like minor colonial officials, Stevenson and Lloyd repeatedly marched, arranged and rearranged the troops of the sweltering and officially bedecked King of Butaritari and his wife, dressed in black silk, until all was well for the photograph. Similarly they asked people to come back and dance so that better photographs might be taken (HM 2412).

One of the early memorable photographic events was when Lloyd took a picture of Moipu, the former chief of Atuono. At first Moipu was reluctant, but after assistance from a missionary priest, he 'offered to go back to his house and change his clothes for his war dresses' on the condition the Stevensons send him a picture in exchange (Beinecke ms. 638). Later, seemingly pleased with the results, Moipu begged Lloyd to photograph his brother (*From Saranac to the Marquesas and Beyond* 139), swapped hats, and promised to 'make brother' with him (*In the South Seas* 102). What is significant about the episode is that Moipu's impulse to include Lloyd as a symbolic part of his family and, according to Fanny, declare 'thou art my name' (Beinecke ms. 638) was more fitting than initially seems plausible. It was not simply a gratuitous courtesy, but a metaphoric reality, for throughout the Marquesas, Lloyd, who had rarely been seen without a camera in hand, had come to be known as *Mata-Galahi* or Glass Eyes (*In the South Seas* 102), an appellation that acknowledges not only his wearing of glasses but also that a camera is a kind of eye. It suggests an oblique reference to an ancient belief that the photographic process includes the use of eyes stolen from children (Ryan 143). If one then recalls that Moipu was said to have been a notorious cannibal for whom a victim's eye was a dainty to be eaten or offered to the leading guest, then the taking of Moipu's name seems apt, for both Lloyd, as photographer, and the former chief consumed their victims by pilfering the eye. In a sense the Stevensons' photographic sessions were a kind of ritual (people assembled outside the church when they learned Lloyd was coming to photograph the former chief) in which their subjects were sacrificed to the photographer's and the viewers' taste and assumptions. The result is that Moipu, the so-called cannibal, was figuratively cannibalized by Lloyd's camera, which in the act of registering its picture stole its subject's eye and consumed Moipu's image. The camera plucked out his likeness, and with its prints offered them as delicacies for others, especially to Westerners who were curious to view and savor anything exotic. It is interesting to note that in the taking of a picture the camera often, particularly for longer exposures, literally consumed the pupil of the eye — eradicated it by blurring it; consequently, during the developing process, the photographer often had to scratch in that detail.

Within this context the taking of a picture can even be thought of as an act of revenge — an eye for an eye, so to speak. Stevenson suffered from what many travelers experience in distant places: he felt threatened and excruciatingly uncomfortable being watched by inquisitive islanders. His discomfort resembles that experienced by Mrs. Annie E. Breach, a missionary in Samoa (1899), who, after a *malaga* to an outstation, complained to the London Missionary Society Foreign Secretary that her every movement was watched by hundreds of eyes, and that she had had 'to exercise some ingenuity to make blinds of the girls' lavalavas, for one window ... was warped and perforated affording excellent peep holes for curious' and 'devouring eyes'. She added, 'one eats and lives in painful publicity' (LMS Archives ms.193). Her distress was also Mrs. Buzacott's, the wife of a missionary to Rarotonga who, by the way, had built a *camera obscura* so the

Reverend Williams could better see and make accurate portraits of the natives. Mrs. Buzacott saw eyes 'from every quarter fixed upon her', from every window 'eyes nothing but eyes' (Buzacott 28-29).

Stevenson especially felt uncomfortable when he could sense, but not see, the curious eyes upon him. One particularly disturbing episode was in the Marquesas when a gust of wind scattered the fans of the palms above his dwelling and revealed in two of the tops 'a native, motionless as an idol and watching us ... without a wink ... the thought that perhaps at all hours we were similarly supervised, struck us with a chill' (*In the South Seas* 19). The hidden observer, like the photographer bent beneath a black cloth, spied and stole their images with the wide-open lenses of his eyes that clicked shut when the palm branches closed again. Stevenson also expressed his aversion for the secretly vigilant policemen in Butaritari (181) who lurked, like seeing shadows, in the night. In addition, he disliked the dark promontory around which he sailed 'under the fire of unsuspected eyes' where 'an army might be hid and no passing mariner divine the presence' (113). He also had uncomfortable memories of the night on the Gilbert Islands when his was the only light remaining. As a consequence, his image hung in full view, as if suspended *in vacuo*, to be witnessed by invisible onlookers who passed by and lingered to observe him (182). Given this discomfort and anxiety, it is little wonder that Stevenson never forgot that island spirits sometimes tore out the eyes of travelers (144). Moreover it is understandable that, while visiting the Gilbert Islands, Stevenson eagerly fled the 'neighborhood of the red *conjunctiva*, the suppurating eyeball, and dreaded the beggar who pursues and beseeches the passing foreigner for eyewash' (219). The eye could also be a contaminating presence.

Taking pictures was a way of staring back and of reclaiming one's stolen eye. It was a way of not being infected by an alien presence, of sanitizing the other and keeping free of disease, and, especially, of retrieving the domination of the one who exposes the other. Photographs like 'Tamesae surrounded by war-chiefs', 'King Tembinoka with adopted son, standing in front of wives', and 'Two dancing girls from Little Makin' show native figures arranged very much under the authority of the camera's eye. They are clearly its subjects and vassals to its lens, a condition that becomes visually explicit in a photograph of some servants, entitled 'Three slave girls watching Mr. Strong painting'.

One of the two cameras belonging to the Stevensons that seems to have accompanied them on all three of their voyages added to this prerogative, for its possibilities gave them a feeling of even greater power. The apparatus allowed them to scrutinize without being observed and, therefore, to reverse what had been Stevenson's experience the night on the Gilbert Islands when his image hung displayed for all to see. This camera was a 'detective camera'. Lloyd describes the apparatus in a letter to Charles Baxter (1 June 1888): 'I have a detective camera — an affair you wear over the region of your heart' that allows one to take people 'without [their] knowledge'. If one looks at a picture of this kind of camera, one notices that it was worn underneath the shirt, that the lens peered through a stud hole

4.9 'Two Dancing Girls from Little Makin — Gilbert Islands'

in the front of the garment, and that the shutter was operated by means of pressing a button attached to a hose hidden in the photographer's hand. With this clandestine apparatus Lloyd hoped he 'should be able to get some very good results — beautiful young women surf bathing etc, and views' as well as 'illustrations of the customs and manners of the country' (Beinecke ms. 5267). In a later letter he gives the camera's dimensions as five by four inches (16 June 1889 Beinecke ms. 5267).[17]

But the device that dispensed just as much authority and control was the flash-powder apparatus that literally gave them the means to light up the darkness. For a fraction of a second, the flash revealed what was concealed and brought the subject into the photographer's territory. In a sense, on a smaller scale, it had the capability to mimic the search lights from the colonial gunships which would suddenly illuminate an unsuspecting Pacific village or bay as a display of force (*Letters* 8:313). The flash-powder, placed in a v-shaped metal container, usually held to the side of the subject, made it possible to photograph events normally inaccessible to the camera's eye. Strong's series of evening pictures displaying the 'Great dance' in the Speak House, Apemama illuminates a line of dancers and reveals details of their facial expressions. The initial shots register the dancers' unrehearsed surprise, even alarm, at the sudden popping and burst of light, and, eventually, seeming boredom with the photographic session.

Lighting up the Darkness: The Magic Lantern

During the cruise of the *Equator*, Stevenson also arranged for his own magic lantern shows in which he could project 'that great bright eye of light' (*Letters* 7: 372) upon a darkened room. Imitating what had become a well-established practice of travelers, explorers, itinerant showmen, and, as I have indicated, especially his missionary acquaintances, Stevenson took along a magic lantern and slides to entertain the natives he would be meeting on the cruise. His elaborate preparations for this activity bear out his stepdaughter's observation that he 'intensely' enjoyed both the lantern and the idea of amusing the inhabitants of the islands (HM 37985, 20 April 1889). Before they departed he requested and studied T. C. Hepworth's *The Book of the lantern: Being a Practical Guide to the Working of the Optical (or Magical) Lantern. With full and precise directions for making and coloring Lantern Pictures with Seventy-five illustrations.* He borrowed a 'fine magic lantern', a selection of comic slides, and a set of the life of Christ from the Reverend Francis Damien (in Honolulu) (*Letters* 7: 315). He also gave considerable thought to how the entertainment might proceed. His plan was that while the others worked the lantern and the slides gleamed and faded, Fanny was to play a hand-organ 'with what feeling and expression is possible' (Beinecke ms. 638); at intermission, Lloyd was to sing accompanied by his own taropatch,[18] Strong's guitar, and Stevenson's flageolet. The three formed a group Stevenson jauntily referred to as the *Island Nights Entertainment Troup* (*Letters* 7:315). Up to the final moments, even after the barrels of sauerkraut and salt onions, a bag of coconuts, as well as their 'native garments, tobacco, fish hooks, red combs, and Turkey red calicoes [all of the latter for trading purposes]' had been prepared to go on board the *Equator*, Strong was still finishing a last transparency for the magic lantern (*Letters* 7: 320). From the 1850s on slides made from photographs became increasingly prevalent.[19]

On the voyage of the *Equator* there seem to be only three recorded magic lantern exhibitions, two in a Butaritari church and one in Apemama where among other views Stevenson showed one of Windsor Castle. None of the performances completely followed Stevenson's initial plan. In Butaritari, the first (27 July 1889) was before an audience of three hundred, and the second (28 July 1889), and 'positively last appearance of the phantoms', was in front of a densely packed crowd. With no more room in the building, 'all round the church, groups sat outside, in the night, where they could see nothing', but where they could receive 'some shadowy pleasure in the mere proximity' (*In the South Seas* 198). Stevenson's exhibition followed the rather standard missionary order I have already described: First there were slides of wild animals (including a tiger) and then a group of humorous images. One that Stevenson used was the 'Human Rat Trap'.[20] Finally, true to missionary fashion, he ended with a group of gospel pictures that, according to Stevenson's remarks, seem to have moved the audience more than anything else. Upon seeing the images members of the audience exclaimed, 'Why then the Bible is true!' and later confided to others, 'these things all happened, we have seen the pictures' (194), obviously an instance of the easy authority of the image.

But what is most significant about these magic lantern exhibitions are what Vanessa Smith refers to as Stevenson's own ironic and somewhat aloof reactions to seeing the 'phantoms' (Smith 129). Maybe Stevenson's attention wandered because the slides were mediated by a rather incompetent native missionary (Maka) 'excitedly explaining the Scripture slides' (and not Lloyd). Maybe he lost interest because the images were not his, that is, not the ones based upon his, Lloyd's, or Strong's photographs. Perhaps Stevenson thought the gospel slides 'ludicrously silly', (*In the South Seas* 193-94), especially one depicting Christ before Pilate, 'the latter hovering on the screen like a many-coloured squall' (HM 2412). And maybe he found the slides to be less genuine than the music of a passing troupe of native singers (Smith 129). Consequently, instead of focusing upon the lantern slides, Stevenson engaged the peripheral play of light, darkness, and shadow that repeatedly took hold of his imagination. He turned his eyes from the screen and focused upon the passing singers emerging from the night. He was fascinated by the ways in which the lightening and darkening of the church arrested their movements, and how one by one they broke away to watch the images and then regrouped to disappear down a dark road. In a sense, the troupe's defection from their performance was also Stevenson's, for he too abandoned his show. While 'the lantern luminously smoked', rather than looking at the pictures, he watched as 'chance rays of light struck out the earnest countenance' of his cook grinding the hand-organ (*In the South Seas* 198), revealed a ghostlike vision of Strong (HM 2412), and created shadows in the hollow of the roof and the rafters. Enjoying the luxury of being for once unobserved, he stood in the rear of the spectators and spied upon the audience.

Photography at Vailima

When the Stevensons settled in Samoa, the photography continued. They took and had pictures taken of themselves, their native friends, and their staff for their acquaintances and family back in England and Scotland. In her pocket diaries of November, 1891, Stevenson's mother records one such occasion when 'Joe and Lloyd take photos of the house boys' (Beinecke ms. 7304), and a few days later in a letter to her sister remarked: 'We have been taking some photos lately; one large one of the whole party was done in the lawn, ourselves with our friends the G ___ s [Gurrs] sitting in front, the house-servants behind us, and the outdoor boys on the steps of the verandah still further back' (*Letters from Samoa* 106). These pictures mailed home became part of a more general transmission of Samoan images during the 1880s and 1890s, some of which reinforced racial stereotypes or, like 'Naughty Polly Samoan' played up to the idea of the compliant Samoan belle. Alison Devine

Norström points out that it was not just the Western military officers, the tourists, and the missionaries who were distributing photographs for publication and sale in the West but also commercial photographers. While the Stevensons lived at Vailima, for instance, the nearby town (Apia) had three: John Davis, Apia's first commercial photographer; Alfred John Tattersall, who had a large collection of postcards for sale, and Thomas Andrews.

It is perhaps fitting that two of these people, Davis and Andrews, were present in December, 1894 to photograph, for world-wide consumption, Stevenson lying in state and his grave surrounded by native mourners. Promising to send 'some of these views', Margaret Stevenson described to her sister the taking of one of these official pictures: 'When all was finished, Mr A _____ [Thomas Andrews] photographed the grave, first alone, and then with the Tongans … grouped on one side, and our Vailima and Tanugamonono friends on the other' (*Letters from Samoa* 323-24). In an earlier incident she had been fearful that a photo Davis had taken was ruined in a heavy shower (Beinecke ms. 7304). For her and for others the exposed dark plates were what helped to record Stevenson's death and impress its reality, like the shadows in the Samoan myth, on the minds of friends and admirers. These photographic images registered his passing. In an odd sort of way, one of their

4.10 Isobel Strong. 'Drawing of Margaret Stevenson's Room at Vailima [showing camera]'

Vailima staff, Lafaeli, had, some months before, anticipated this impulse to turn to photography, when, upon learning of his wife's death, he begged to have the black focusing cloth of the Stevensons' camera for a mourning garment (Neider 91).

Death and the Lighthouse Engineer

The day after her son died of a cerebral hemorrhage, Margaret Stevenson sadly noted 'but oh, we miss the light of our house!' (Beinecke ms. 7304). Although she was reverting to an overworked metaphor of the extinguished light, within the arena of Stevenson's sensibility her reaction shed the metaphor's hackneyed and prescriptive tenor; it drew closer to the truth. As a consequence, when Henry James wrote to Fanny, 'we have been sitting in darkness for nearly a fortnight, but what is our darkness to the extinction of your magnificent light?', his sentiment became both genuine and apt. Moreover when James added, 'He lighted up one whole side of the globe' (Neider 238), he was not merely subscribing to the rhetoric that death requires but expressing the fact that Stevenson's prose as well as his presence brought enormous foreign attention to the South Seas; so much so that in the late 1890s the explorer Mary H. Kingsley, while traveling in Lembarene (West Africa), referred to Stevenson's responsibility for the current fame of the Pacific islands (Kingsley 224).

Stevenson knew, though, that the attention he brought to the islands and the light he shed upon those he visited was imperfect and by no means complete. As much as he attempted to collect data, interview those who had been residing there longer than he, learn the various languages, and observe as best he could, he found it impossible to grasp the variety and the complexity of what was before him. Not wanting to be one of those travelers who dips into a place and then writes about it with pretended authority, he took extensive notes on such books as Dr. George Turner's account of his 1876 voyage in the Tokelau, Ellice, and Gilbert groups that included data on the population as well as on the practices of infanticide, cannibalism, adultery, and polygamy. As if anticipating Stevenson's penchant for violence and adventure, it also narrated tales of theft, kidnapping, and punishment by sending the accused out to sea (HM 2398). Stevenson also compiled lists of such medical details as the use of abortifacient herbs in the vagina, of piercing instruments to induce abortions, and of others with which to strangle infants. He noted that if the mother had a great affection for the condemned baby, it was, instead, buried alive (HM 20534). Moreover he jotted down significant key words and phrases such as *Re onohi o rapouoli* meaning 'the eyeball of the black night'; on board the *Janet Nicoll* he transcribed from memory anecdotes, legends, and practices missionaries, tradesmen, beachcombers, and natives had told him (HM 2398). These are a sampling of Stevenson's anthropological efforts of which the general reader is not always aware.

No matter, though, how diligently he read, listened, and watched, and no matter how persistently he resisted the critical, and sometimes hostile, remarks of his family and friends who grew impatient with his anthropological interests, Stevenson could eventually do little more than offer a partial, imperfect representation of his experiences. His *In the South Seas* is essentially a collage of illuminated spaces and images surrounded by areas of obscurity and dogged by shifting shadows of meaning and understanding. The resulting text honors the unknown, the unseen, and the unspoken as well as episodes of insight. The very chapter titles suggest the incompleteness and the discontinuity of knowledge and perception in these conditions, and at the same time the vague threat that haunts the little that can be known. For instance, the chapter titles from Part I: The Marquesas: 1. 'An Island Landfall', 2. 'Making Friends', 3. 'The Maroon', 4. 'Death', 5. 'Depopulation', 11. 'Long-Pig — A Cannibal High Place', 13. 'Characters', and 14. 'In a Cannibal Valley' give one a quick sense of the spottiness as well as the hovering menace.

In general, in Stevenson, as in the photographic negative, it is the dark, obscure moment that brings to view an event, a sighting, a consequence. It allows one to understand that darkness is the foundation of seeing and knowing. Without the dark, light is without significance. In Stevenson, light is really incidental to darkness. As in *Dr. Jekyll and Mr. Hyde* character, event, and revelation cannot exist without the background of night or shadow. Dr. Jekyll, and indeed also Mr. Utterson and Dr. Lanyon, must learn that the darkness that resides in Hyde is the foundation of our being. Significantly in *Dr. Jekyll and Mr. Hyde*, Stevenson also makes it clear that to have knowledge of something one can never rely exclusively on the fully-developed photograph. A photograph can never be sufficient. He is quick to point out that Mr. Hyde has never been photographed, and, as a result, intelligence of his appearance does not exist in the full light of stable particularity. There is only an indefinite sense that Mr. Hyde has some 'unexpressed deformity' (64). Although Dr. Jekyll's friends are curious to see Mr. Hyde's face, they never properly succeed, for they are constantly frustrated by its not being easy to describe and by its displaying an impression of malformation — his features are neither nameable nor fully illuminated. Obscurity must necessarily accompany revelation.

By illuminating segments of the Polynesian world for others to see, Stevenson not only completed and transformed his 'Creek Island, or Adventures in the South Seas', that he had begun at the age of twelve, into 'a Pacific reality' (*In the South Seas* ix) but also became the lamplighter of his *A Child's Garden of Verses*, fulfilling the desire of the child who had promised, 'But I, when I am stronger and can choose what I'm to do,/ O Leerie, I'll go round at night and light the lamps with you' ('The Lamplighter' ll. 7-8). With his observations and images Stevenson, like his forefathers, built his texts as if they were lighthouses whose intermittent beams shone upon uncharted isles and seas. His words guide his readers through the unknown. As the lenses of his understanding turn and the text proceeds, what was not visible emerges from 'the yawning blackness', and, as the hours 'keep running', the images disappear back into shadow and invisibility (HM 2394). These alternations convey Stevenson's sense that a full, resplendent, all-encompassing brilliance is not necessarily desirable; that the recording of experience, if it is to be close to subjective truth, must be full of interruption. It was, perhaps, his recognition of this truth that motivated Stevenson, as a young man still thinking of becoming a lighthouse engineer, to write his prize-winning essay, 'On a New Form of Intermittent Light for Lighthouses' (1871), and to describe how the intermittent beam illuminates for a moment what will soon become invisible and fall back into the darkness of the sea at night.

When in Samoa describing the toil of his Scottish great-grandfather, Thomas Smith, Stevenson drew close to the fantasy of his own life voyaging around the South Sea islands and attempting to find his way on horseback through the interior's rough, unmapped places. In his incomplete *Records of a Family of Engineers* Stevenson wrote: 'The seas into which his labors carried the new engineer were still scarce charted, the coasts still dark .... The isles in which he must sojourn were still partly savage. He must toss much in boats; he must often adventure on horseback by the dubious bridle-track through unfrequented wilderness; he must sometimes plant his lighthouse in the very camp of wreckers' (213). A century later, in the South Seas, Stevenson also rooted himself among wrecks and traveled among the 'partly savage'. Paradoxically, even though Stevenson was miles and years away from his past and from his predecessors' profession, in building lighthouses out of his prose he brought his life full circle, back to where his ancestors had been and back to where he, as a young boy, had accompanied his father on his tour of the lighthouses and the islands off the Scottish coast. His continuing awareness of the way light, darkness, and shadow alternate is testimony to that return. His orientation and sense of place was also theirs. His images of intermittent light, whether represented in words or on photographic plates, renewed and carried on what had been undertaken by earlier generations. In the end, the model of the missionaries' activities and the metaphors they employed recalled a precedent already entrenched in Stevenson's perception of his world.

Notes

1. Two London Missionary Society missionaries, the Reverend T. Powell and the Reverend G. Pratt, in a paper, *Some Folk-Songs and Myths from Samoa*, given before the Royal Society of New South Wales (5 November 1890) explained that the Polynesians, 'like the Gauls and other ancient nations, gave precedence to the moon, and counted by nights, not by days. The sun, they say, is "changeless", like a statue, and every day is very much like another, whereas the moon changes, and they can reckon by its phases' (213 n.7).

2. Following the example of missionaries in other lands, in the 1820s the Reverend William Ellis described his work in Tahiti in terms of a 'flood of light' that 'like rays in the morning' break 'in upon the intellectual and spiritual night' (Ellis 1: 260), and, towards the century's close, in 1894, the Reverend William Wyatt Gill paid homage to the convention's tenacity by entitling his account of his missionary life *From Darkness to Light in Polynesia*.

3. The Reverend Davies and the Reverend Marriott also spoke of converted natives who wanted 'to carry light back to [the] dark houses' of an island yet to be provided with a mission station (LMS Archives ms. 179).

4. This practice of showing magic lantern slide shows to converts continued into the 1890s and into the early decades of the twentieth century. For instance, on 2 February 1893 the Reverend William Ed Goward announced that at the end of March, 1893, the Reverend Whitmee of Samoa would be going through their district with a magic lantern and organ.

5. I am grateful to Jack Judson, of the Magic Lantern Castle Museum in San Antonio, Texas, who spent several days with me showing me these slides and giving me a sense of the range of images available to the public in the second half of the nineteenth century. He also allowed me better to understand how sophisticated the magic lanterns could be, especially those with more than one lens.

6. I am most grateful to Stephen Herbert of the British Magic Lantern Society who explained and helped me understand the technical terms in Rev. W. E. Clarke's letter.

7. For a description of the 'Great German Search Light' at the World's Columbian Exhibition see the 16 August 1893 issue of *Scientific American*.

8. One cannot help but be reminded here of Stevenson's account of his dreams in which he speaks of his characters in them as being independent of himself — as being the work of goblins. See 'A Chapter on Dreams'. *Across the Plains with Other Memories and Essays*. New York: Scribner's, 1896. 229-52.

9. This sight recalls that recorded by the Reverend Ellis half a century before, of 'a band of natives walking along the shallow parts of the rocky sides of a river, elevating a torch with one hand, and perhaps a spear in the other; while the glare of their torches was thrown upon the over-hanging boughs, and reflected from the agitated surfaces of the stream. Their own bronze-coloured and lightly clothed forms, partially illuminated, standing like figures in relief' (Ellis 2: 297-98).

10. For a reference to this myth, see Barthes 110.

11. For a fuller discussion about photography in Samoa see Blanton, Casey, ed. *Picturing Paradise: Colonial Photography of Samoa, 1875-1925*. Daytona Beach, Florida: Southeast Museum of Photography.

12. For an article claiming that the photograph is the most accurate means of understanding an object or a person, see John Thomson (instructor in photography at the Royal Geographical Society). 669-73.

13. John Thomson, the instructor of photography at the Royal Geographical Society, stated in 1891 that:

> In order to obtain a basis of measurement for any object to be photographed, a very simple device may be employed. If the object be ethnological, to wit, a racial type, where it is necessary to take a full face and profile view of the head, or a series of overlapping views of a number of types of the same family; a rod marked with one space of definite measurement will supply the required authority. This rod should be so placed in relation to the head, that it will fall into a plain bisecting the cranium about the ears for full face, and the nose for profile. The rod must then be photographed with the type, and the result will give a basis of measurement. This applies to full length figures as well. Its use may also be extended to any object where the value of the observation depends on proportioned measurement. (672)

14. I am indebted to Steve Mangione, Assistant Director for Production and Development at SUNY College at Buffalo, for spending several hours going through the Stevenson photographs with me and remarking on their technique. Steve Mangione is a specialist in nineteenth-century photography.

15. I wish to thank Elaine Greig of the Writers' Museum, Edinburgh for making these photographs and the scrapbooks of photographs available to me.

16. The reality was that by the time Stevenson was traveling among the islands, there was a confusion of Western and native dress. In the more populated islands, especially, many had abandoned their native garments.

17. If one looks at the photographic scrapbooks the Stevensons assembled, the one concerning the voyage of the *Casco* begins with photographs that are small and round, so are probably taken with the detective camera. These scrapbooks are housed at the Writers' Museum, Edinburgh. Many of the subjects in these early photographs are, however, posed.

18. There is some mystery as to exactly what a taropatch is. Some think it a stringed instrument, rather like a guitar.

19. According to *The Optical Magic Lantern Journal*, the popularity of these slides even reached royal circles. The journal reports that HRH Prince of Wales went 'kodaking' and had slides made of his negatives (1 August 1890).

20. In September, 1892 Stevenson took Arrick, one of his house staff, and Austin, his stepdaughter's son, to see a magic lantern show on an English ship-of-war that had come in to Apia. Among the slides was the unfortunate 'Topsy and her moving eyes'. According to Stevenson's perspective, this could have been Arrick's 'own mother or sister' (*Letters* 8: 372). Arrick reacted to the movement with both fear and excitement. It would be interesting to know if Stevenson were willing to exhibit moveable comic views of this type.

Chapter Five

Stevenson's Political Imagination

I like biography far better than fiction myself; fiction is too free. In biography you have your little handful of facts, little bits of a puzzle and you sit and think and fit 'em together this way and that, and get up and throw 'em down, and say damn, and go out for a walk. And it's real soothing; and when done, gives an idea of finish to the writer that is very peaceful. Of course, it's not really so finished as quite a rotten novel; it always has and always must have the incurable illogicalities of life about it .... Still, that's where the fun comes in. (Stevenson to Edmund Gosse: 18 June 1893. *Letters* 8: 104)

Introduction

When Stevenson reached Upolu on 15 September 1890 and began living at Vailima, he became a resident of the central and most important of the three principal islands comprising Samoa. He had chosen to live near Apia, the main harbor of the island, for several reasons: the climate was more suitable than Hawaii's (Stevenson invariably grew ill on his visits to Honolulu); Apia was a lively port with shops, offices, and support services (for instance, there was a regular and reliable mail service that brought monthly mailbags to the island), and there was a large white population. Moreover, H.J. Moors, a wealthy businessman and resident of Apia, persuaded Stevenson that this was the place for him. On the other hand, even before Stevenson reached the town, he was well aware that he was to become a part of a place that, in his words, was 'the seat of the political sickness of Samoa' (*A Footnote to History* 20).[1] He knew its history: its cumbersome and irregular forms of authority and leadership that created discord and that in 1888 had spilled out into civil conflict. He understood that he was entering a culture in which competing Samoan chiefs and clans periodically quarreled or coexisted in an uneasy truce and where foreign powers vied for control: because of Samoa's strategic position in the Pacific and because of its potential for economic development, the Americans had first shown an interest in the islands in 1839; the British and the Germans in the 1870s.

By the time Stevenson arrived, the pattern of outside interference was well established and frequently clashed with or, more often, overwhelmed the traditional Samoan practice of governance that was vested in a hodgepodge of communities and depended little on a central authority. Of the main Powers (the Americans, the British, and the Germans), the Germans were in the ascendancy, for they owned the largest plantations: they grew coffee, cacao, pineapples, and cocoanuts — they were the leaders in the Copra trade. The Germans were also the most aggressive of the three foreign presences. It was they who set up their own law enforcement agencies, occasionally fired upon uncooperative villages, and chose puppet kings who consequently, according to Stevenson, wielded about as much power as a president of a college debating society. The Germans, however, were not the only culpable intruders. The British were also guilty of firing upon Samoans and taking the law into their own hands. To make matters worse, all three consuls, representing Britain, Germany, and the United States, caused trouble and sowed discord by rarely being able either to agree on policies or to achieve an adequate understanding of Samoan culture and its language. Stevenson once observed that these officials added a fifth wheel to a place that was already 'all wheels and no horses' (*A Footnote to History* 6). From his perspective, Samoa was on a chaotic, destructive track that could do little but precipitate open hostilities among the various factions. Circumstances in Samoa cried out for some sort of stable, coordinated, and intelligent leadership. The country and its various parties struggled to find their way among clouds of ambiguity.

When Stevenson began his life in Samoa, there were two rival kings, neither of whom, as I have mentioned, had much to say about the running of his country: there was Laupepa, who enjoyed both the support of the Germans and the advantages of the terms of the 1889 Berlin Act (we shall talk about this later), and there was Mataafa, whom the Germans labeled a rebel (they confiscated his estates); yet, who was simultaneously Laupepa's friend and adversary. Stevenson far preferred Mataafa for being the more principled of the two. In Stevenson's mind, Laupepa was too easily 'the whip-top of competitive advisers' (*A Footnote to History* 291). Furthermore he was inconsistent, capable of being caring and judicious one moment and either treacherous or apathetic another. Mataafa, on the other hand, was trustworthy, and was, through most of Stevenson's life on the island, clearly committed to creating a more peaceful Samoa. Stevenson describes him as breathing 'a striking sense of order, tranquility, and native plenty' (312). Mataafa also seems to have displayed a certain dignity that appealed to Stevenson, as well as having an endearing touch of the pastoral about him: Stevenson recalled that when he stayed with Mataafa, he was awakened, at about four in the morning, by the sound of soothing notes being blown on a pipe. This, Stevenson explained, was Mataafa's way of attracting pleasant dreams, a practice he had probably learned from his father, who was described as a friend and protector of all living creatures. As we shall see, Stevenson devotes much of his political energy to championing Mataafa and working toward resolving the tensions among the warring factions.

It is not always easy to decide whether Stevenson's activities should fall under the heading of 'imperialist' or not: as my discussion in the introduction suggests, the question has no obvious answer. In fact, Stevenson reminds us that when one starts to look closely at the life of someone, not himself a colonizer, but living in a territory that is in the process of being colonized by his own country, one is bound to have complicated responses that disqualify the clichés of hindsight and that make the question seem irrelevant and naive. If an answer is required, though, one can respond by replying that in a certain, popular sense Stevenson did conform to what is thought of as imperialism. Particularly in his first years in Samoa, he did subscribe to the principle that if a non-western colony were to succeed, it required a strong and informed foreign leadership — otherwise the place would remain 'imperfectly civilised' (*A Footnote to History* 296). Yet, even such a generalization is misleading, for Stevenson also increasingly came to endorse Samoan rule, Samoan culture, and Samoan ownership of land. As a result, at the same time as he himself was hoping he might be given a position of political responsibility, he worked hard to deflate the corrupting power of the foreign presence (perhaps remembering England's rule over Scotland) and encouraged Samoans to take more responsibility for their future. Moreover, at times, rather than set himself up as a superior who looks down upon the natives as 'barbarous children' (*In the South Seas* 62), Stevenson was just as willing to accuse his fellow westerners of being childlike, naive, and uncivilized. In his story, 'The Isle of Voices', for instance, Stevenson observes that 'white men are like children and only believe their own stories' (*The Complete Shorter Fiction* 656).

Stevenson also consciously reversed the usual stereotype of the patriarchal foreigner who comes to exert his authority or his masculinity over the weaker, 'female' native culture, on one occasion actually presenting himself to Laupepa with a delegation of whites as the submissive wife of the benevolent husband, Samoa. Besides, he generally preferred to think of Samoa in terms of a country parallel to, and at times better than, his own, so that, for example, the clan system of Samoa and that of Scotland reflect upon each other, and the chiefs of each display similarities. In writing about the Marquesas, Stevenson observed that 'the grumbling, the secret ferment, the fears and resentments, the alarms and sudden councils of Marquesan chiefs, reminded me continually of the days of Lovat and Struan [Scottish Jacobite Chiefs]' (*In the South Seas* 12). For this reason, it is no accident that when Stevenson sets out to write about the South Seas, he goes back and forth between his Scottish and his Pacific subjects.

To follow Stevenson's political imagination is to trace the complicated course of a foreigner's trajectory abroad. The Stevenson who emerges is at once Scottish, British, English, and someone enamored of the various cultures of the Pacific. And, as we shall see in his campaign to oust certain white officials as well as one member of the London Missionary Society, the political Stevenson materializes, at times, as a tenacious, legalistic, and even vindictive figure. His political imagination was as complex as the situations it engaged.

The first part of this chapter, 'Stevenson and Samoan Politics', examines Stevenson's political role in Samoa; the second part, 'Libeling a Missionary', describes his campaign against the Reverend Arthur E. Claxton, one of the prominent London Missionary Society figures in Apia, who was also the fractious Natives' Advocate on the Samoan Land Commission. Stevenson's outrage at Claxton's behavior reminds one of the depth of Stevenson's involvement with the missionary society. And it recalls the extent to which the missionaries influenced the governing of the South Sea islands. Politics and missionary practice often worked in tandem. Much of the material concerning Stevenson's squabble with Claxton has never been published (it remains boxed in the London Missionary Society Archives). The story these papers tell serves as an example of the intricate and nitpicking quality of colonial politics that alternately attracted and repelled Stevenson.

Part 1: Stevenson and Samoan Politics

Shortly after the *Casco* reached Hawaii in 1889, Stevenson, although enjoying considerably better health than usual, lay briefly bedridden in Honolulu. When news reached him that a witness to the startling and surprising defeat of a German landing party in Samoa was staying at a nearby hotel, he immediately sent his stepson to fetch him. Even though he was ill, Stevenson wanted to hear a first-hand account of the bloodshed from John C. Klein, an American free-lance journalist, who had been in Fangalii on 18 December 1888 when the Germans had come ashore to protect their commercial interests and to disarm Mataafa's supporters.[2] What Stevenson learned from the journalist and what he was to glean from others in Hawaii, privy to Samoan affairs, — especially from David Kalakaua, the King of Hawaii — gave him the materials for what was to be the first of many hard-hitting letters concerning Samoan politics that Stevenson was to send to *The Times* and to governing officials throughout his remaining years. When 'Recent German Doings in Samoa' appeared in the 11 March 1889 issue of *The Times*, Stevenson had not yet decided to settle in Samoa. Yet he was well on his way to committing himself to its future and to engaging himself in a strenuous, time-consuming, and frequently frustrating campaign to rid Samoa of its irresponsible foreign officials and to try and reconcile the islands' warring factions.

People of Influence

That Stevenson should be so easily absorbed by the political life of Samoa is understandable if one realizes that being a white person of some standing as well as a landowner in the islands automatically placed one in a position to meet people of influence. Lloyd Osbourne once observed that the 'fun of this place' is that 'everybody you meet is so important' (*Letters* 7:99). From the moment the Stevensons disembarked on their various cruises around the islands, they were courted by and introduced to Queens, Kings, Chiefs, ship captains, naval officers, wealthy merchants, lawyers, commissioners, consuls, clergymen, and visiting dignitaries. When, for instance, they left the *Casco* in Hawaii, the Stevensons were at once embraced by the society surrounding King Kalakaua, 'the Royal set' already known to Belle and Joe Strong (his stepson-in-law), who was the official artist to the Hawaiian mission.

Once they began to establish themselves in Samoa, these connections proliferated and intensified. Before arriving in Samoa, Stevenson wrote to Edward Burlingame and playfully named his future companions: 'Three Consuls, all at loggerheads with one another … three different sects of missionaries, not upon the best of terms', and a variety of natives and whites (*Letters* 6:393). The list turned out not to be an exaggeration, for Stevenson in moving to a spot a few miles from Apia, a town largely occupied by white residents and administrators, was to encounter and do battle with more foreign government officials than he might have expected, and to immerse himself in a place ripe with not only local but also international intrigue and tension among the three consuls. When Graham Balfour, Stevenson's cousin, came to visit, he was quick to note how in Apia everyone knew everything as well as the chief persons involved, both white and Samoan, 'and knew all, and much more than all, that was passing between them' (Balfour 2: 161). A.H. Doudney, an acquaintance of Stevenson's who a few months later drowned at sea, declared with his customary bravado, 'You can be in a new conspiracy every day!' (Furnas 392). Such is the chaotic nature of an island culture, dominated by three competing powers (the Americans, the British, and the Germans) as well as the conflicting interests of the Samoan chiefs and Kings and a country not accustomed to a central government. It is, perhaps, not surprising that during the 1890s Stevenson would write a novel like *The Ebb-Tide* in which three disparate whites, acting as some unlikely, unwieldy triumvirate, are thrown together to command a vessel that has been plagued by disease and has a bogus cargo and which, because of the men's continuous machinations and weaknesses, sails a chaotic course.[3] Without wishing to overstate the comparison, one can see *The Ebb-Tide* as a sort of allegory of Samoa floundering and diseased at sea under the vulnerable leadership of the three consuls — at least, one can hear the cacophonous and contagious muddle of the social and political voices babble throughout the text.

Perhaps Stevenson best captures the compact clutter of Apia when in *A Footnote to History* he insists that his reader take a walk with him around its streets. Led by Stevenson, the reader passes by 'many varieties of whites, — sailors, merchants, clerks, priests, Protestant missionaries in their pith helmets, and the nondescript hangers-on of any island beach'. If the harbor is busy, he sees 'all manner of ships, from men-of-war and deep-sea packets to the labour-vessels of the German firm and the cockboat island schooner'. He also encounters 'all ranks of natives, chiefs and pastors in their scrupulous white clothes; perhaps the king himself, attended by guards in uniform', and, as he continues his stroll, the reader goes past the residence of the Samoan kings as well as by the stores, offices and barracks of the German firm. Then he comes to the German bars and stores and the German consulate. Farther on he reaches the Catholic mission and cathedral and eventually proceeds to the stores owned by H.J. Moors, the English mission, the office of the English newspaper, the English church, and the old American consulate. The walk ends when, 'on the line of the main coast of the island', the reader catches a glimpse of the British and the new American consulates (*A Footnote to History* 20-24).

In such a variegated and dense terrain, nobody could live a week without becoming entangled in local politics. A quick review of Stevenson's calendar when he was visiting Apia leaves one almost breathless and illustrates how someone in Stevenson's position was constantly in contact with and finding his way among the various factions. In November, 1890, Stevenson wrote to Sidney Colvin that he 'went down for the night to Apia; put in Sunday afternoon with our Consul [Thomas Berry Cusack-Smith] ... dined with my friend Moors, in the evening went to church ... back to Moors ... round to the Mission [The Missionary House of the London Missionary Society] to get Mr Clarke [the Reverend William Edward Clarke] to be my interpreter; over with him to the King's [Laupepa who, at the pleasure of the Germans, had replaced the ineffectual puppet Tamesese] ... back with Clarke to the Mission ... consulted over a queer point of missionary policy, just arisen, about our new Town Hall and the balls there [Stevenson was chairman of the Town Hall Committee] ...' (*Letters* 7: 20). Not only do the officials shift from hour to hour but so do the political issues. Later that month, on a Friday, Stevenson was 'all forenoon in the Mission House, lunched at the German Consulate, went on board the *Sperber* (German warship) in the afternoon, called on my lawyer [Richard Hetherington Carruthers] on my way out to American Consulate [Harold Marsh Sewall was the American Consul]' (*Letters* 7: 43). The cast of characters grows.

By 1892, the entries have a bit of more of an edge to them. In March, Stevenson writes to Colvin that he had ridden down to Apia on 'my endless business, took a cup of tea in the Mission like an ass, then took a cup of coffee like a fool at Haggard's [Bazett Michael Haggard, British representative on the Samoan Land Commission], then fell into a very painful scene with American Consul' [Stevenson actually shook him by the shoulders] (*Letters* 7: 249).[4] Later in September Stevenson recognizes the poignant, absurd humor that sometimes surfaced during these various encounters, especially those with the Chief Justice, Conrad Cedercrantz, another white official whom he despised, yet for whom he had a strong attraction. In a letter to Colvin, Stevenson remarks that it is 'Hard to imagine any position more ridiculous; a week before he [Cedercrantz] had been trying to rake up evidence against me by brow-beating and threatening a half-white interpreter [Charles Taylor]; that very morning, I had been writing most villainous attack upon him for *The Times*; and we meet and smile, and — damn it! like each other.' After the two had danced in a quadrille together, Stevenson commented that the Chief Justice 'has the charm of a funnily-pretty girl' (*Letters*

7:368). Among other functions, formal balls brought enemies and officials together. Stevenson's cousin Graham Balfour wryly remarked that at a fourth of July dance given by the American Vice-Consul, William Blacklock, 'all that gentleman's enemies might have been seen joining hands and dancing round him, while they sang, "For he's a jolly good fellow"' (Balfour 2: 154).

Stevenson did not have to go down to Apia to become enmeshed in its politics. At Vailima visitors with various concerns were always coming and going: white residents, officers and men from the German, British, and American warships, missionaries, captains from the merchant service, vice consuls, consuls, lawyers, land commissioners, plantation owners, and surveyors — all with their various partisan concerns. In August, 1891, for instance, Stevenson told Colvin that the Chief Justice [Cedercrantz], Henry Clay Ide [the American Land Commissioner], and Count Hans Wachtmeister, a Swedish travel writer, had come up for lunch, not an uncommon routine. White residents were, of course, not the only guests. In perhaps a rather romanticized account written for *Scribner's Magazine* (18 October 1895), Stevenson's cousin Balfour comments on the fact that Government chiefs, Kings, and rebels habitually found their way to Vailima to consult Stevenson with regard to policies of one kind or another:

> political letters were brought to him to read and criticise; his native following was so widely divided in party that he was often kept better informed on current events than any one person in the country. Old gentlemen would arrive in stately procession with squeaking pigs for the 'chief-house of wisdom', and would beg advice on the capitation tax or some such subject of the hour; an armed party would come from across the island with gifts, and a request that Tusitala [the Samoan name for Stevenson] would take charge of the funds of the village and buy the roof-iron for a proposed church. Parties would come to hear the latest news of the proposed disarming of the country, or to arrange a private audience with one of the officials; and poor war-worn chieftains, whose only anxiety was to join the winning side, and who wished to consult with Tusitala as to which that might be. (Balfour 2: 145)

Choice and Circumstance

The circumstance of living close to Apia, the center of the colonial political activity, as well as the proximity and accessibility to those white officials who were its central players, could perhaps have been sufficient reasons for Stevenson's engagement in the politics of the region. However, one must not forget that even before Stevenson arrived in Samoa he was primed for this commitment. It is worth being reminded of this fact, for generally, in the public's mind, the persona of the novelist all too readily tends to overshadow his political identity. Biographies devote few pages to his political preoccupations except when referring to Stevenson's support of Mataafa during his last years in Samoa. The consequence is that readers easily lose sight of Stevenson's love, as a student and a member of The Speculative Society of Edinburgh, for debates over such issues as free trade, the abolition of income taxes, capital punishment, and methods for solving international disputes. They run the risk of overlooking his legal training, a qualification that not only gets rehearsed in his final *Weir of Hermiston* and in details within novels like *The Wrecker* but also surfaces vividly in his formal responses to Samoan government officials and policy. Furthermore commentators usually pass over the letters to his parents about political matters (especially W. E. Gladstone's policies), written before he even thought about going to the South Seas and humorously signed, as he did in March, 1884: 'R. L. Stevenson, Politiker, His Sworn Opinion' (*Letters* 4: 249). It is interesting to note that in this particular letter, Stevenson expresses his fear that, in spite of his faults, if Gladstone, who was confined to his room because of a chill, dies, 'we may fall, like the French, into the impotence of four parties, any three of which can at a given moment, outvote the fourth. The result of this is impotence abroad and distraction at home' (*Letters* 4: 249). That anxiety foreshadows his later worry about the inadequacy and chaos accompanying the rule of the three inept Powers (the Americans, the British, and the Germans) in Samoa during the late 1880s and early 1890s.

About the time he was signing the 1884 letter to his parents, Stevenson was reading extensively on the subject of the Union between Scotland and England and the Irish Question. He composed the 'Confessions of a Unionist' for *Scribner's Magazine* but chose not to publish it. According to J.C. Furnas, Stevenson had wanted to prove to American readers that a 'well-meaning subject of Queen Victoria could think British rule in Ireland indecently stupid and yet oppose immediate Home Rule' (Furnas 240). He abhorred the tactics of the Irish Nationalists. In the spring of 1887 he also wrote a piece on socialism, 'The Day After Tomorrow', that appeared in *Contemporary Review*. But, more to the point, during this period Stevenson was in the midst of trying to sort out his reactions to the fate of British troops and the business of war and imperialism in South Africa and India. He even expressed an intention to write a history of the Indian Mutiny. Throughout he acknowledged how obnoxious the colonial power is to those it ruled, yet expressed an unease over the prospect of bloodshed and disorder in the absence of its authority. Both are concerns that were later to influence his reactions to the state of affairs in Samoa, where he longed for some intelligent authority or stability, eventually campaigned for Samoan independence, and tried hard to prevent civil war. In the Balfour Papers (Box 1, ms. 140) is an essay probably written in February, 1881 in which he reacts to the horrors of the Boer War, particularly to Sir George Colley's defeat and the thought that the General had been sacrificed in a dishonorable cause. Sir George with about 1,400 men had marched toward the Transvaal frontier where he was attacked by the Boers who had preceded him. Of the 554 men who constituted the British force, 92 were killed, including Sir George himself. The draft of what was probably to be a letter from

Stevenson to a newspaper begins to question the role of England in its imperialistic endeavors:

> I am beginning to be [*sic*] grow ashamed of being the kin of those who are now fighting — I should rather say, who are now sending brave men to fight — in this unmanly Transvaal war.... I am at the present hour — in company, I am sure, with all the most honourable and considerate of my countrymen — literally grilling in my own blood about the wicked business.

Stevenson continued, 'We are in the wrong, or all that we profess is false ... certainly the only chivalrous or honourable course, is for the strong to accept his buffet and do justice, already tardy, to the weak whom he [Gladstone] has misused' ('Protest on Behalf of Boer Independence' as quoted in McKenzie 19-20). During the same month Stevenson commented to his friend W. E. Henley that the war had been 'a damned, dirty, foul job ... God forbid this rotten old England' (*Letters* 3: 160).

Like many during 1884 and 1885 Stevenson had an intense interest in the British role in the Sudanese Campaign. Echoing his reaction to the defeat in Transvaal, he shared people's outrage that General Charles Gordon had received no support from the British troops and, consequently, had not only suffered defeat but had died. Stevenson reacted to the fall of Khartoum with bitter criticism of Gladstone and with a sense of public dishonor. He deplored the scene of political depredation and these 'dark days of public dishonour' (*Letters* 5: 80). His incensed letter of 30 February 1885 [?2 March] to John Addington Symonds exclaims:

> What a picture is this of a nation! No man that I can see, on any side or party, seems to have the least sense of our ineffable shame: the desertion of the garrisons .... Millais [John Everet Millais] was painting Gladstone when the news came of Gordon's death: Millais was much affected (this seems to throw a doubt on the truth of the anecdote); and Gladstone said: 'Why? *It is the man's own temerity!*' *Voilà le Bourgeois! le voilà nu!* But why should I blame Gladstone, when I too am a Bourgeois? when I have held my peace? Why did I hold my peace? Because I am a sceptic: i.e. a Bourgeois. We believe in nothing, Symonds: you don't, and I don't; and these are two reasons, out of a handful of millions, why England stands before the world dripping with blood and daubed with dishonour. I will first try to take the beam out of my own eye; trusting that even private effort somehow betters and braces the general atmosphere. (*Letters* 5: 80-81)

Stevenson was ashamed he had done nothing public to oppose the English policy that ignored Gordon's circumstances. Four years later memories of these events intensified his response to the plight of the Samoans, and Stevenson felt moved to write his first letter to *The Times* in an attempt to draw international attention to their troubles and correct his former silence. Later his cousin Balfour remembers talking with Stevenson at Vailima 'with great feeling about the death of Gordon' and noticing how he had 'never ceased to reproach himself that "I did not say then in the papers what I might have said before it was too late"' (*Letters* 6: n.250). Stevenson was tired of being a silent subject. He resolved to become as active as possible.

Now the martyrs of imperialism rather than the religious martyrs of his youth held his imagination. Moving from Britain to the South Seas seems to have released his political voice and given him the permission, the position, and the confidence to speak and write his mind to the public and to those in power. On the islands he was a more prominent presence. From Fanny's point of view, his life in Samoa allowed him to honor a yearning to be a politician. According to her, 'Louis became involved in political affairs because the profession of letters had been his second choice in life, forced on him by ill health' (Bell 255-56).

The Berlin Act

When Stevenson decided to buy land on Upolu in 1890, Samoan politics and economics (that is, those that impinged on European interests) were supposed to be managed under the provisions of the Berlin Act, signed 14 June 1889. The arrangement was to make the government less dependent on agreement among local representatives of the three foreign Powers by strengthening the judiciary, reorganizing public finances, re-establishing the municipality of Apia, ensuring the maintenance of peace among the Samoans, and offering the Samoan Government responsible and reliable European advisers.

The major innovation of the Berlin Act was the establishment of a Supreme Court with, however, only a single judge, the Chief Justice of Samoa, a foreigner to be appointed either by the three consuls, but in the case of disagreement, by the monarch of Sweden or Norway. The Chief Justice's decisions were to be final and binding, but the reality was that the Chief Justice's powers were both complex and limited. Even though he could take appeals administered by Samoan magistrates, he did not have jurisdiction over everything.[5] There were also municipal courts. And in many cases between or pertaining to Samoans, the issues were entirely outside the Chief Justice's domain, so, in effect, 'the Supreme Court as established by the Berlin Act was not at all supreme' (Gilson 399). Furthermore, in many instances concerning criminal acts of foreigners against Samoans, the foreigner often came under the jurisdiction of his consul: if, like Stevenson, the person were British, he was subject to the British Western Pacific High Commissioner; or, if he were an American who had committed an assault upon another foreigner, whether an American or not, the case would come before the United States Consular Court. Although the ensuing legal situation was intricate and full of residual loopholes, the Berlin Act, through the appointment of the Chief Justice, did attempt to set up a more stable means of settling civil disputes among foreigners that was not dependent upon the unlikely cooperation and reciprocity of the three Powers.

In addition to his appellate and civil legal duties, the Chief Justice was the official advisor to the King of Samoa, and, moreover, acted as arbiter and administrator in certain affairs of government and state. He was, consequently, the most important white official in Apia. In particular, he settled questions concerning the meaning and the application of the Berlin Act; he settled disputes between the Samoan Government and a treaty Power; he shared with the king the control over the leasing of Samoan land; he advised the Samoan Government regarding the passage of laws concerning the maintenance of law and order, the punishing of criminal acts, and the collecting of taxes. One can better understand why Stevenson, as we shall see later, was to feel so bitter toward the Chief Justice's failures and to be disappointed in his actions. The stability of Samoa seemed to depend upon him.

The Berlin Act also restored the municipal government of Apia that the Germans had earlier dissolved and with it a municipal council that appointed a magistrate and other local officials, that passed regulations concerning the sale and lease of land, supervised elections, and collected levies previously forbidden by foreign treaties. This municipal council was headed by a President (a voting chairman selected by the three Powers and, like the Chief Justice, a foreign official) who was also to serve as the chief executive of the municipality, the treasurer, and, at the King's pleasure, a general adviser to the Samoan Government. Unlike the Chief Justice, the President was permitted to receive instructions from the three Powers, but only if they were in agreement. Next to the Chief Justice then, the President/Chairman also wielded a lot of influence, and was supposed to bring stability to Samoa. For these reasons Stevenson was distraught when the President squandered the opportunity to effect some sort of working peace.

Stevenson's Political Activities

When Stevenson first moved to Upolu and built his home Vailima, he eagerly awaited the arrival from Sweden of Conrad Cedercrantz, the newly appointed Chief Justice, who, for various reasons, did not arrive in Apia until December, 1890 — many months after the signing of the Berlin Treaty. Similarly, he looked forward to the coming of the President, a Prussian named Baron Senfft von Pilsach who also did not appear until much later: April, 1891. The hope was, of course, that their appearance would somehow bring law and order to a place that was being pulled apart by competing foreign interests and was still suffering from its past civil strife, and, in Stevenson's mind, would allow for better treatment of Samoa's interests. Stevenson, though, was soon to learn that the presence of neither official was the answer. His frustration over the Chief Justice's and the President's ineffectualness, if not neglect, speaks loudly and clearly in a letter Stevenson wrote to Colvin in

September, 1891: 'Now for politics ... Cedercrantz, whom I specially like as a man, has done nearly nothing, and the Baron, who is a well-meaning ass, has done worse' (*Letters* 7: 247). Stevenson goes on to state his grievances about their exorbitant salaries, their squandering of the taxes, their not doing anything to help the Samoans: their refusal to fund such public works as building roads and to give a 'native' any position. Stevenson bitterly complained, 'They have forgot they were in Samoa'. He concluded: 'The sense of my helplessness here has been rather bitter; I feel it wretched to see the dance of folly and injustice and unconscious rapacity go forward from day to day, and to be impotent.' Feeling thwarted, Stevenson added that he 'was not consulted' by the Treaty Officials. Utterly discouraged that he is not a member of the 'blooming Municipality', Stevenson tells Colvin, 'the long and the short of it is, if the consulship could be got for me at the next vacancy, I would take it gladly, for I see now that (whether or not I have much common sense) I have it above the most of my contemporaries here; and I might possibly be useful' (*Letters* 7: 153-54).

Stevenson's disappointment in these officials came to a head on 5 September 1891 when Cedercrantz sailed to Fiji and left behind Senfft von Pilsach to settle the fates of five chiefs who, although they had declared themselves in support of Mataafa, the rebel King, had, in good faith, and at Mataafa's suggestion, surrendered to the authorities. They had been tried by a native magistrate and received a six-month jail sentence. When news reached the President that there was a plan to rescue these five men, he apparently arranged for dynamite to be brought from a wrecker ship and announced that if any rescue were to be attempted, the jail would be blown up, or, as Stevenson adds, 'such were the voices of rumour' (*Letters* 7: 169). Two days later the prisoners were deported and exiled in the Tokelaus. Stevenson was incensed with Cedercrantz for having deserted Apia when he should have been there to help out with the crisis, and was enraged with what he thought was Senfft von Pilsach's part in the conspiracy to blow up the jail and deport the chiefs who, after all, had surrendered in the cause of peace.

The dynamite plot resurrected Stevenson's resolve to do something about his feeling of impotence and to put an end to his silence. It occasioned his first political letter from Samoa to *The Times* (in May, 1891 he had written *The Times* about the fact that letters between England and Samoa were either delayed or lost). The letter about the dynamite scandal appeared in the 17 November 1891 issue and attacked the President not only for that fiasco but also for his intention to use native money to build himself a splendid house and for his sequestering the collected taxes beyond the reach of the municipality. Because of previously being accused of anti-German feelings and because of the tensions between him and the German community, Stevenson was careful in his missive to state that his quarrel was with Senfft von Pilsach, not the Germans. Furthermore, he hastened to add that the budget decisions were made by the President and the King without consulting the native Parliament — a pattern that eventually led to his increasing support for Samoan rule.

The assertiveness of the letter does not represent the ambiguities Stevenson could sometimes privately experience when dealing with those officials he criticized. As was often his practice, Stevenson stifled such thoughts in his official letters but readily revealed them in his correspondence with Colvin where he almost trips over his inevitable inclination to sympathize with or be attracted to those he was assailing. Just before composing his charge against Senfft von Pilsach, he confessed to Colvin:

> The next days were very largely passed trying to make up my mind how to write to *The Times*. It is now done, true enough, not false I mean — but quite un*true*; not telling for instance how this mild, wild little creature is as civil as a trick terrier, painfully eager to please — and came here (the poor soul) on his wedding jaunt with a pretty little wife no bigger than himself; and how there is no fault to find with him but sheer folly, and the dynamite was no doubt never intended to be used, and the man is too dull to see what harm his threat could do, but thought it bold and cunning, the poor soul! Such a difference between politics and history, between a letter to *The Times* and a chapter I shall write some day if I am spared, and make this little history-in-a-teapot living. (*Letters* 7: 164)

Some months later, in May, 1892 when Stevenson learned that the Chief Justice as well as the President were to leave in disgrace, he wrote to Colvin: 'Poor devils! I like the one [Cedercrantz], and the other has a little wife, now lying in! There was no man born with so little animosity as I. When I hear the C.J. [Chief Justice] was in low spirits and never left his house, I could scarce refrain from going to him. Yet the man is a rogue' (*Letters* 7: 282-83).

It was this ambivalent habit of mind that helped create characters like Loudon Dodd in *The Wrecker* (published 1892) who cannot help but be attracted to Bellairs, the shyster, even though he detests his principles: 'As I abominated the man's trade, so I had expected to detest the man himself; and behold I liked him. Poor devil!' (388). Just like Dodd, Stevenson in his dealings in Samoan politics periodically found himself falling 'into an ignominious intimacy with the man' he 'had gone out to thwart' (392). Similarly, the ambiguity recalls the dilemma facing Robert Herrick, who in *The Ebb-Tide* is simultaneously attracted to and repelled by the murderous Attwater.

The letter to *The Times* was not Stevenson's only political weapon. He also drafted a 'Petition of the White Residents to Baron Senfft von Pilsach concerning certain rumours current in Apia: presented 28 Sep. 1891' in which he attempted to elicit the true story about the dynamite plot. Addressing the municipal council, Stevenson declared that 'the rumours in their present form tend to damage the white races in the native mind, and to influence for the worse the manners of the Samoans' (*Letters* 7: 174). The response to this petition and to his letter was to be typical of many he received in subsequent months. His attempts were habitually met with arrogance from those whom he had named, and, even more frequently, readers, especially the foreign press, accused Stevenson of allowing his imagination as a novelist to interfere with or prejudice his understanding of events. In November, 1891 both the *St. James's Gazette* and *Punch* strongly suggested that Stevenson had 'thrown away ... a capital plot for a new story' and that he had wasted what could be good material for a novel on a newspaper article (McKenzie 102). These reactions persisted so that later, in July, 1892, when the British Consul, Cusack-Smith, wrote to the Foreign Office, he accused Stevenson of using his political campaign to promote or advertize his publications. Cusack-Smith's reaction was similar to the British High Commissioner's. On 16 August 1892 Sir John Thurston wrote to Cusack-Smith that Stevenson was basically intent on finding a 'Good subject for a new novel' (158). In 1893 such criticism of Stevenson's efforts continued so that *The New Zealand Herald* claimed that Stevenson had 'given the world no more proof of his fitness to fill the role of a statesman than he has of being able to win a wrestling match' (336), but at least *The Times* was beginning to admit that Stevenson's exposés of Samoan intrigues and problems were justified. On 18 May 1893, the newspaper was able to acknowledge that 'Mr. Stevenson has not written, it would seem, too strongly about the state of things in Samoa and the behavior of' Senfft von Pilsach and Cedercrantz. The editorial conceded, 'those who suspected that a master of historical romance and a humourist of rare ingenuity had, on a slender bases of fact, constructed a story of phantasy vying with' *Treasure Island* should read the Blue Book, the official record (338).

There were, however, at least two episodes in Stevenson's political career that might have encouraged the presumption that the novelist was in ascendancy, not the statesman. One of these was when Stevenson too hastily believed that Senfft von Pilsach had resigned. (The President had indeed sent in his resignation but the Foreign Office and the Embassies refused to honor it.) In October 1891, placing himself at the head of a delegation, Stevenson and a group of white residents (what Stevenson called his 'little band' [*Letters* 7: 180]) visited the German puppet King Laupepa to congratulate him on the supposed resignation of the Municipal President. (Recall that Senfft von Pilsach acted as official adviser to the King.) Stevenson had hoped that his exposé of Senfft von Pilsach's actions and policies had brought the President down, but he was incorrect. Aware of the support from the foreign powers, Senfft Von Pilsach had withdrawn his resignation. Innocent of this move, Stevenson presented the King with the following: (In his declaration, Stevenson chooses to describe his delegation by referring to them and himself as being the wife of the husband, Samoa — a gendered metaphor that is a welcome reversal of the usual stereotype of the 'masculine' colonizer who assigns his wife, the colonized country, a subordinate role. Here Stevenson depicts his white friends as humble and cooperative participants in a partnership with Samoa.)

> Your majesty — We are here certain white people who have taken up our residence, in Samoa. We have come to her as wives to a husband, and think her interest and peace our own. For some time we have been very much pained and distressed by advice, which has been given to your Majesty, which we think to be bad advice, and some of which we are ashamed should be given you by a white man of our race and of our civilisation. We have not intruded on your Majesty with advice; we do not require to tell your Majesty those things which your Majesty knows as well as we do. We have come instead to bring you our congratulations on a deliverance for your Majesty, ourselves, and for Samoa. Baron Senfft von Pilsach has given in his resignation; he is no longer your Majesty's adviser, that chapter is at an end, and if he should again attempt to advise your Majesty, it is as though a man should come up to you on the street and trouble you with counsels. (McKenzie 444)

Admittedly at the time Stevenson thought his action slightly foolish, if not a 'schoolboy step' (*Letters* 7: 180), and he might have still felt it imprudent even if the resignation had been honored. The episode does smack of the drama of historical romance, but it does reveal his deep concern for the responsibility of white rule and his continuing sense of shame when, as in the case of Gordon, the authorities let their side down.

Another episode, less excusable and better known to those familiar with Stevenson's biography where it often gets rehearsed, occurred in August, 1892 when Lady Jersey came to Apia at the invitation of Stevenson's friend Bazett Michael Haggard, the British representative to the Samoan Land Commission. This time, seemingly without as much self-consciousness or self-recrimination, Stevenson, at the insistence of Haggard and giving in to the strong desire of Lady Jersey (whom Stevenson seems not to have been able to resist), arranged for them all to visit the exiled King Mataafa — the ostracized chief whom Stevenson admired. The plan was obviously not smart, for news of the visit to Malie (the headquarters of Mataafa's supporters) of a member of the British landed gentry might disturb the tentative peace between the warring Samoan factions. However, Stevenson, if we are to believe his letters, seems to have been willing not to worry too much about this consequence and to have succumbed to the intrigues of the moment. He composed a letter (with a fictional date) to Lady Jersey in which he pretended she was his cousin (it was she who had proposed going disguised in the character of 'Miss Amelia Balfour'). The vocabulary of historical romance animates and punctuates his account of the charade. Stevenson speaks of the enterprise's peril, and suggests that to avoid detection, 'we should leave the town in the afternoon and by several detachments' (*Letters* 7: 358). In a letter to Colvin, he refers to 'the place of tryst' and to Haggard who, 'insane with secrecy and romance' shouted 'like a hero in the ballad' and took 'deliciously infinitesimal, precautions' (*Letters* 7: 360). Later Stevenson was to tell Lady Jersey that he had given her something better than a chapter from the Waverley novels. Moreover Belle, his stepdaughter, and he also made a scrapbook composed of caricatures and verses describing the adventure. The occasion was a huge lark, made even more ridiculous by the fact that everyone in the area was all too aware of Lady Jersey's disguise.

Although it is tempting to dwell upon these moments, one should not give them undue importance. For the most part Stevenson worked hard, tenaciously, and soberly to campaign against the indiscretions and irresponsibilities of the white leadership; and, of course, he was to crusade for peace and for his friend Mataafa. After his initial political letter to *The Times* Stevenson not only continued to write to that newspaper but also persisted in sending letters to consuls, the Chief Justice, the President, and other Treaty officials as well as to officials in the Foreign Office. He also corresponded with Laupepa about the problems of the Opium Trade and with editors of local newspapers concerning the misuse of Kanaka labor, an issue consequently referred to in the Houses of Parliament. Moreover he tried valiantly to prevent civil war by sketching plans to settle Samoa's problems (Beinecke Collection item #3121)[6], by arranging numerous clandestine meetings with both Laupepa and Mataafa, despite official displeasure; by offering his house as a safe place and himself as a suitable intermediary for re-opening discussions among the conflicting parties; and by helping others draft propositions and carry out exhaustive research so they could compose their lengthy revisions to the Berlin Treaty. Stevenson was a good mediator and, consequently, was occasionally asked to chair gatherings. One was a meeting of the municipality that took place on 1 March 1892, despite the fact that the German powers objected to the Chair being given to a frivolous novelist. Stevenson wrote the formal preface to the resulting report:

> Sir: At a public meeting held here last night, to the chair of which I was called, certain proposed alterations in the Berlin treaty were discussed, and I was instructed as chairman to forward, and have now the honour of enclosing to you, the text agreed upon. It was the request of the meeting that this should by you be transmitted to your Government, in the hope that your Government might be willing to consider the opinion of persons on the spot and immediately acquainted with the business and interests involved. (McKenzie 446)

The deteriorating state of affairs in Samoa compelled Stevenson to remain committed to his political activities, to attempt to take an influential role, and, of course, to begin work on his *A Footnote to History* that he completed in 1892 and that he hoped would better inform those abroad about the problems tormenting Samoa. He could not ignore the lack of cooperation among the parties of the Treaty Government in Samoa; Cedercrantz's refusal to oppose Senfft von Pilsach's buying, and therefore gagging, the island's only newspaper; the sequestering of the treasury, the swelling of factional struggles between Laupepa and Mataafa; Cedercrantz's preference for using arms rather than reconciliation; the misallocation of taxes; the high salaries of certain white civil servants; and the British Consul's enthusiasm for using force to settle Samoa's problems — a policy already shared and propagated by his American and German colleagues. Stevenson also fought back when he learned of the passing of the February, 1893 Sedition Regulation that threatened to fine or imprison any British subject 'who shall be guilty of sedition towards the Government of Samoa' and who shall 'embrace all practices, whether by word, deed, writing, having for their object to bring about in Samoa discontent or dissatisfaction, public disturbance, civil war, hatred or contempt towards the King or Government of Samoa or the laws or constitution of the country, and generally to promote public disorder in Samoa' (*Letters* 8: 25) — an act that seems partially to have been directed against Stevenson. Eventually, of course, the outbreak of violence in 1893 and 1894 intensified and confirmed his concerns.

Deportation or Consulship

Throughout his various political campaigns Stevenson was bold, even though the Treaty Officials intercepted letters between him and Mataafa, and occasionally appeared to threaten deportation. Their hostile presence shadowed him so that in June 1892, Stevenson wrote to Colvin saying 'there is great talk in town of my deportation, it is thought they have written home to Downing Street requesting my removal, which leaves me not much alarmed', and in December boasted to Henry James, 'On the hot water side, it may entertain you to know I have actually been sentenced to deportation by my friends at Mulinuu, C.J. Cedercrantz and Baron Senfft von Pilsach' (*Letters* 7: 305, 449). Stevenson also knew of the wrath of Cusack-Smith, the British Consul, whom he imagined jealous of his presence — and aware of Stevenson's threat not to pay his taxes. (There actually seems to have been nothing concrete about these fears concerning deportation. They were merely the offspring of rumor.)[7]

Strangely, at the same time, because of his persistent attention to the affairs of Samoa, Stevenson was subject to yet another kind of gossip: that he was to become the next British Consul. On 8 September 1892 the *Manchester Courier* reported that he was to be the next Consul and attributed the news to the publication of *A Footnote to History*. The false report seems to have been picked up by Pacific news agencies so that, for instance, the *New Zealand Herald, Sydney Morning Herald*, and the *Wellington Evening Post* ran the headline: 'Mr. Stevenson to be Appointed Consul at Samoa' (*Letters* 7: n. 387). Earlier in June, Stevenson had already heard talk of the possibility, for he wrote to Colvin that

> I should be quite prepared to accept the berth for £500 a year, might possibly go lower even, but I think it quite unnecessary that the point of view should be suggested to the authorities. The real reasons for the step are three: First, possibility of being able to do some good, or at least certainty of not being obliged to stand always looking on helplessly at what is bad. Second, Larks for the family who seem filled with childish avidity for the kudos. Third, and perhaps not altogether least, house in town and boat and boat's crew .... But I find I have left out another

reason: Fourth, growing desire on the part of the old man virulent for anything in the nature of a salary — years seem to invest the idea with a new beauty. (*Letters* 7: 311)

Although the words to Colvin are fraught with ambiguity, the truth is that Stevenson really did like the idea; in fact, so much so that when he heard about the rumor a few months later, he immediately asked Colvin to find out what he could about it. Stevenson was attracted to authority, and, undoubtedly he was ambitious. From the beginning of his residency in Apia he had expressed an interest in being assigned an official role. In September, 1891, frustrated by his helplessness, he had blustered to Colvin, 'if the Consulship could be got for me at the next vacancy, I would take it gladly ... I might possibly be useful, and I would always have a weight in my hand to throw into a trembling scale' (*Letters* 7: 153-54).

The rumor about the consulship was part of the culture of gossip that flourished copiously in his surroundings: from the moment he stepped on to the shores of Apia, Stevenson stumbled into a thicket of rumors — a fact he recognized in *A Footnote to History* when he suggested that 'should Apia ever choose a coat of arms, I have a motto ready: "Enter Rumour painted full of tongues"' (25). He was now dwelling in a situation in which people like Cusack-Smith or Thurston, the High Commissioner, might smile upon him in person but malign him behind his back. In a 16 August 1892 letter to Cusack-Smith, the High Commissioner suggested that the Consul 'leave him [Stevenson] (at least for the present) absolutely to himself. I incline to think that he is ill-advised and mischievous (these self-educated people always are) but he may want to be noticed as a terribly dangerous fellow' (McKenzie 158). It is not surprising that after the first few months of living in this political climate Stevenson wished he might have the liberty of returning to his private business (*The Times* 19 July 1892). No wonder that, at the end of 1892, he was complaining to Colvin: 'I am so weary of reports that are without foundation and threats that go without fulfillment, and so much occupied besides by the raging troubles of my own wame [home]' (*Letters* 7: 461). A month later in January, 1893, even though Cedercrantz and von Pilsach had been sacked and Stevenson had, therefore, realized a successful end to one of his campaigns, he commented, 'Politics leave me extraordinary cold .... Success in that field appears to be the organization of failure enlivened with defamation of character' (*Letters* 7: 463). When Stevenson wrote those words, he had just learned that Harold Marsh Sewall, the late United States Consul in Samoa, had written to the Foreign Secretary of the London Missionary Society to say that if there were civil war in Samoa, the blood would be on Stevenson's hands (*Letters* 7: n. 464).

Although subject to moments when he thought politics 'the dirtiest, the most foolish and the most random of human employments' (*Letters* 8: 106), Stevenson, as resilient as ever, continued with his efforts. Driven by his conviction that reconciliation between Laupepa and Mataafa was possible, and motivated by his conviction that Mataafa was a victim of injustice, stupidity, and thoughtless policy, Stevenson persisted in defending Mataafa and, through him, the Samoans' right to more independent rule. Toward the end of his life, Stevenson wanted the place rid of the irresponsible government of Consuls who disrupted any prospect of peace and who, on the contrary, through their policies and ineptness set the competing parties against each other. Later in April and May of 1894, he was to write to *The Times* and declare that three Consuls have 'no right under the Treaty to interfere with the Government of autonomous Samoa'. He insisted that these consuls 'cease from troubling, cease from raising war and making peace, from passing illegal regulations in the face of day, and from secretly blackmailing the Samoan Government into renunciation of its independence' (*Letters* 8: 229).[8] Finally, Colvin advised Stevenson to give up writing for *The Times*. In October, 1894 Stevenson replied, 'I know, my dear fellow, how remote all this sounds! .... I have my life to live here; these interests are for me immediate; and if I do not write them, I might as soon not write at all' (*Letters* 8: 373). Those last words say it all. Stevenson's political writing was absorbing him. In the last years he wrote *A Footnote to History* (completed August, 1892) and plunged into the depths of the islands' bureaucratic and governmental struggles through his lengthy, often vituperative, letters to the newspapers (he composed at least ten), articles, speeches, proposals, and proclamations. As if to keep his perspective and counteract the frustrations and disappointments connected with his political work, Stevenson also turned to his past and to Scotland, a place that, he was fond of pointing out, functioned as an antidote as well as an analog to Samoa. He found a refuge in the history of his family and focused upon their sturdiness, as lighthouse engineers, in the face of uncertainty, violent storms, and the tumbling chaos of the sea. The resulting *Records of A Family of Engineers* (published posthumously) elicits a center, whereas in Apia there was only an ever unraveling and confusing series of events and expectations; the family history invoked the memory of concrete results (the successfully built lighthouses that stand permanent and tall), an outcome more difficult to achieve in Samoa, where one faction seemed continually to dismantle the other and make the vision, let alone the possibility, of stability and permanence impossible. Things were just too easily wrecked.

Part 2: Libeling a Missionary

Introduction

Whenever Stevenson felt self-conscious about his immersion in Samoan affairs he referred to himself as a meddler. In May, 1892 he excitedly asked Colvin: 'I wonder if you can really conceive me as a politician in this extra-mundane sphere — presiding at public meetings, drafting proclamations, receiving mis-addressed letters that have been carried all night through tropical forests? It seems strange indeed, and to you who know me really, must seem stranger. I do not say I am free from the itch of meddling but God knows this is no tempting job to meddle in' (*Letters* 7: 277-78). From time to time, especially when he visited Mataafa in Malie, Stevenson did wonder whether his actions were appropriate, but, as he went on to explain to Colvin, 'You are to understand: if I take all this bother, it is not only from a sense of duty, or a love of meddling — damn the phrase, take your choice — but from a great affection for Mataafa' (*Letters* 7: 281). Much of what Stevenson did was obviously because of his deep attachment to and regard for Mataafa and the people of Samoa. One easily discerns his concern and respect in a letter to *The Times* in which he berates William Blacklock, the American Consul who replaced Sewall, for, among other things, disparaging the Samoans by calling their dwellings 'huts' rather than houses. The letter illustrates Stevenson's keen appreciation for the power of language to convey prejudices and reveal a speaker's assumptions.[9] And much of what he did was equally motivated by his sense of responsibility as a privileged white resident among a people caught in the snare of conflicting foreign interests that tended to discourage any form of independence or accountability. Stevenson was by no means just a meddler. I disagree with Graham Balfour's sense that his actions were merely, as Balfour says, 'interferences' (Balfour 2: 242).

　　　　Stevenson, however, was not always as much in control of his political demeanor as he or we might have wished. The ill-timed visit to Laupepa in late 1891 (when he prematurely congratulated the puppet King on the news of the false resignation of Senfft von Pilsach) and the August, 1892 excursion to Malie with Lady Jersey, as I have already mentioned, were presumptuous and foolish, but there is yet another episode that receives only passing attention and about which few know the full details: the libeling of the Reverend Alfred E. Claxton, a London Missionary Society missionary who had been, ordained in 1885 and had come to Apia in 1890, where initially he was in charge of English services in the church for white residents. The quarrel with Claxton reveals once more that Stevenson could fall prey to the rumors that circulated in the whirlwind of politics swirling through the streets of Apia, and, furthermore, that he could sometimes be high-handed and get trapped by his annoyance with the Treaty Officials. It also reminds one that just as the residents of Apia could not help but cross each other's paths, neither could the issues. The Claxton dispute is complicated by Stevenson's difficulties with the Chief Justice, the President, the Consuls, and the missionaries. These crossings sharpened a critical attitude in Stevenson that might, otherwise, have been more moderate. Even though the episode might seem to be nothing more than a passing embarrassment and too indebted to the trivia of detail, it throws a good deal of light on Stevenson's political identity as well as on the missionaries' role in administration.

Missionaries and Politics

That a missionary would become associated with political matters is not unusual. From the very beginning, missionaries in the South Seas found it necessary to establish themselves by courting the favor of the various chiefs on the islands. Then, in the name of religion, they attempted to Christianize the law of the land, especially those practices tainted with 'heathenism' by seeking such actions as the abolition of polygamy, the prohibition of certain marriage rites, the requirement of internal partitions within a home and the use of external blinds.[10] Politics and missionaries held hands from the start, and were still doing so in 1891, when some white residents in New Zealand started to campaign against church interference in political matters. These reformers especially campaigned against the rule that only church members could take office in relation to law and civil affairs.[11]

Obviously the partnership of church and state was not always comfortable, for the relations with Polynesian chiefs perpetuated controversy not only among residents but also among the missionaries as to what the correct association should be: should the missionary, for instance, be apolitical or should he quietly influence the governing of the community? The matter was complicated by the fact that on the one hand, the missionaries needed the protection of the chiefs and sought their patronage; yet, on the other, they did not want to be entirely beholden to these figures.[12] In turn, as R. P. Gilson points out, as the missionaries became more and more a part of the village culture, the chiefs, desiring the advantages, started to entrench themselves in church affairs (28).

When the mission stations became more permanent, the missionaries started to develop an attitude of political impartiality that, depending upon the context, seems to have been sporadically invoked. For instance, in the 1888 Samoan civil war when fighting broke out among rival native groups, Stevenson's friend the Reverend Clarke was adamant that the London Missionary Society House in Apia have what he called a 'non political ambulance' and that it receive an equal number of wounded from both sides (letters to Rev. R. Wardlaw Thompson: LMS Archives). There were, however, moments in the Pacific missionary history when such neutrality scarcely peeped out from behind the screen. The most infamous of these episodes featured Shirley Waldemar Baker, a Methodist missionary, who became the dictatorial adviser of King George Tupou I of Tonga and who, in 1880, became Prime Minister. Because of his increasingly overt political activities he resigned in disgrace from the missionary society and was deported in July, 1890 by Sir Thurston, the British High Commissioner (this too must have been in Stevenson's memory, especially when he felt himself similarly threatened by Thurston's displeasure).[13] Always attracted to strong characters[14] and also identifying with Baker's being the victim of rumor and accusation, Stevenson, in December, 1890, eagerly wrote to Henry James that Baker of Tonga had visited him: 'He is a great man here; he is accused of theft, rape, judicial murder, private poisoning, abortion, misappropriation of public moneys' (*Letters* 7: 65).

The above example is the extreme. More to the point is that because of the interlocking historical relations between missionaries and politics in the South Seas, the London Missionary Society (LMS) members in Samoa who were Stevenson's contemporaries could not completely detach themselves from political issues, nor did circumstances let them. Rather, most of them chose unobtrusively to influence and respond to their political surroundings. They still liked to maintain the official attitude of impartiality during hostilities, but they preferred to take a more covert role during periods of peace. Often the missionaries found themselves drawn into political matters because of their linguistic abilities. Stevenson was more than ready to call on Clarke to accompany him as both friend and interpreter so that he might talk with Laupepa (November, 1890), and when Stevenson resolved in May, 1892 to try and arrange some *rapprochement* between Mataafa and Laupepa, he did not hesitate to ask the S.J. Whitmee, yet another LMS member, to be his interpreter. Stevenson's decision was not simply based upon the convenient fact that Whitmee was an excellent linguist (Stevenson took language lessons with him) but because he thought Whitmee enjoyed the favor of the Chief Justice as well as that of the President. Such a circumstance would, of course, work in Stevenson's favor and make it easier to gain access to the puppet King, Laupepa, who was surrounded and advised by Government officials (*Letters* 7: 276).[15]

Like many others, Stevenson also consulted with the missionaries concerning political affairs. It is not unusual to find references in his letters to his stopping by the mission house to consult with Clarke about such matters as the dynamite plot (discussed in Part 1) and whether or not to send a letter to *The Times*. And it is not entirely unexpected to discover that in April, 1892 Stevenson and Whitmee seem to have exchanged position papers concerning the future of Samoa. They argued and eventually came to some agreement about many issues, except the notion of identifying a single foreign authority who should possess dictatorial powers and, thereby, put an end to the ineffectual triumvirate. Whitmee initially endorsed Cedercrantz, the Chief Justice, whose practices and policies, as we have seen, Stevenson despised. It is interesting to note that a few months after this exchange, the Reverend Ralph Wardlaw Thompson, the Foreign Secretary for the LMS, wrote to Whitmee apparently warning him about Stevenson and his politics: 'I should say, be sparing in expressing your view to Mr. R. L. Stevenson or others — I am not sure of that gentleman' (LMS Archives as quoted in McKenzie 152). The missionary wrote back on 11 July 1892 thanking him for his 'suggestion' regarding Stevenson. 'I know him well. He takes strong prejudices, is strongly opposed to the government officials & a great friend of Mataafa the opponent of the King' (LMS Archives: Box 42, folder D). As the letter reveals, the LMS also had its prejudices: Mataafa was a devout Catholic (the priest in Samoa was labelled the 'Keeper of the Conscience of Mataafa'); whereas, Laupepa was a follower of the London Missionary Society. Indeed in 1889 *The Times* had charged the mission with political alliances based upon these affiliations.

The Reverend Arthur E. Claxton

The reason the Foreign Secretary of the LMS was alarmed about Whitmee's relations with Stevenson was that during 1892 the Secretary had become increasingly aware of Stevenson's political interests through his letters to *The Times* and through a copy of *A Footnote to History* that Stevenson had sent to him. He was also not inclined to favor Stevenson, for Stevenson had been complaining about missionaries who overstep the missionary role rather than maintain their strict neutrality in politics. On 28 April 1892 the Reverend Thompson received a letter from Stevenson stating that 'It is my opinion, and my prayer, that the Mission should return to its old, traditional policy and maintain a strict neutrality in politics' (*Letters* 7: 255). The main reason, however, that the Foreign Secretary was on the alert whenever he heard from Stevenson or about his missionaries' dealings with him was that Stevenson had charged Claxton with a series of misdeeds and had set an awkward set of meetings in motion. Letters from Stevenson meant trouble.

Stevenson, Claxton, and Mataafa

From the beginning, Stevenson did not seem to be particularly attracted to Claxton, but he was careful not to offend him, since Claxton not only was part of the missionary community upon which Stevenson depended but also was interested in his story 'The Bottle Imp' that he later translated into Samoan ('*O Le Fagu Aitu*') and published in the missionary magazine (*O Le Sulu Samoa: The Samoan Torch*). Attempting to keep up a cordial relationship, Stevenson reluctantly and occasionally attended one of the missionary's services, but he was obviously not impressed. In November, 1890 he sent a chilly, grumbling note to Claxton griping that the church was too hot ('I went through more perspiration than I care for of an evening'), that Claxton's advice to the congregation '*sounded* dreadful', but conceding that the service was well designed (*Letters* 7: 30).[16] Their brittle relationship, however, was made even more fragile by the petty squabbles and rumors about the possibility of civil war that were swirling around them. At the end of May, 1891, Mataafa had settled seven miles down the coast in the village of Malie, arousing fears that he might defy the Samoan government; Stevenson and his family actually prepared themselves for a possible armed defence of Vailima.

In the midst of this uneasiness suddenly another set of rumors started to spread. In July, 1891, much to his horror, Stevenson heard a rumor that Claxton had proposed a scheme by which Sewall, the then American Consul, would trick the rebel Mataafa into coming to Apia from Malie where he was headquartered, arrest him, and blame the Germans for the deed — a plot that never materialized. In spite of this intelligence, though, Stevenson continued to see Claxton, corresponding with him about the translations of 'The Bottle Imp' and other matters concerning the missionary magazine. In late September Stevenson also sent Claxton a contribution to the mission, together with a polite note.

Claxton and the Land Commission

A month later, new causes of conflict between the two arose. Stevenson was already upset by what he considered to be the exorbitant salaries of the Chief Justice and the President; it now emerged that Claxton, who in March, 1891 had been released from most of his missionary duties so he might serve as the Natives' Advocate on the Samoan Land Commission, was to receive a salary of $300 a month in his new capacity as spokesperson for Samoans concerning ownership of land in Samoa.[17] Stevenson forwarded a letter written by his acquaintance A.H. Doudney protesting this extravagance, to the Foreign Secretary of the London Missionary Society, accompanied by a note of his own suggesting that the Society assume the costs of the Native Advocacy, instead of burdening the Samoan Government with that expense.[18] Stevenson had informed Claxton of his intended action before sending the letter, and, since Claxton was in agreement with Stevenson that the Society should undertake the expense of the Natives' Advocate, he raised no objection.[19] After the LMS notified Stevenson that his request had been approved, though, Stevenson still spoke of Claxton's 'original error' in his somewhat legalistic letter of acknowledgment to the Reverend Thompson.[20] Stevenson obviously did not trust Claxton, especially after being informed of his part in the plot to arrest Mataafa. Stevenson, however, did not actively pursue the charges. He either let them drop or tempered his responses, for he mistakenly thought Claxton was leaving for England in April, 1892 — apparently Stevenson thought he and Samoa were going to be rid of him for good.[21]

During the months of Claxton's absence, however, Stevenson never forgot the problematic missionary, for both Claxton's salary and his behavior on the Commission continued to be a topic of conversation. It was difficult for Stevenson to ignore the memory of Claxton who, while working in his official capacity, had undermined the effectiveness of the Land Commission to distribute land in more equitable ways. This was a body that, Stevenson hoped, would bring stability to Samoa as well as justice to the Samoans. Stevenson was already disturbed about the Chief Justice's various schemes to upset the Commission's authority and even more agitated by Claxton's willingness to be a spokesperson for Cedercrantz. Through this association, he believed, the missionary had betrayed and compromised the future of Samoa, particularly at a time when Stevenson sensed an increasing sense of crisis with regard to the state of Samoan affairs.[22]

Stevenson also despised Claxton for having pushed the Land Commission off track by accusing it of showing 'colour prejudice' when, indeed, from Stevenson's point of view, it did not — rather, the missionary was thinking more of his political advantage than that of the Samoans he was supposed to be representing. (Stevenson, of course, was increasingly invested in the principle that the Samoans be allowed to reclaim their land.) According to Stevenson's account in *A Footnote to History*, the missionary 'suffered himself besides (being a layman in law) to embrace the interest of his clients with something of the warmth of a partizan.' Stevenson explains: 'Disagreeable scenes occurred in court; the advocate was more than once reproved, he was warned that his consultations with the judge of appeal tended to damage his own character and to lower the credit of the appellate court. Having lost some cases on which he set importance, it should seem that he spoke unwisely among natives. A sudden cry of colour prejudice went up; and Samoans were heard to assure each other that it was useless to appear before the Land Commission, which was sworn to support the whites' (317-18).

According to the Missionary Committee's minutes, Claxton had sent a letter to Laupepa charging the Commissioners with 'studiously disregarding the interest of' the natives'. Laupepa had then forwarded the missionary's accusation to the Three Powers who, in turn, referred the matter back to the Land Commission for explanation. For Stevenson, who ever since his arrival in the South Seas had thought about the dangers arising from what he called the race barrier, Claxton had opportunistically nicked the culture's Achilles heel. He had been shortsighted and, because of his own political ambitions, had shut one eye to the realities, for he had defended some Samoans at the expense of other natives and, furthermore, had increased the feeling of instability by raising what Stevenson in this case deemed the unnecessary demon of color prejudice. With these circumstances at play, it is little wonder that Stevenson despaired when he later learned that the missionary had not permanently severed his ties with Samoa. He deplored the presence of someone he felt to be incompetent, divisive, and a spokesperson for the wrong interests.

Claxton and the Dynamite Plot

In the last months of 1891, when the issue of the missionary's behavior on the Land Commission was beginning to brew, yet another problem had developed that further discredited Claxton in Stevenson's eyes: this was the previously mentioned dynamite episode (October, 1891) that incensed Stevenson and set him at loggerheads with the Chief Justice and the President.

In the November following the exposé of the dynamite plot, Senfft von Pilsach, the Municipal President whom Stevenson held responsible, apparently attempted to make his peace with Stevenson. In a rather desperate and ineffectual move he sent an emissary to Vailima to confess that he, Senfft von Pilsach, had been 'a d___d idiot'. The emissary proposed that the President and Stevenson speak to one another, but Stevenson had replied that it was useless; he had nothing to say, for he had already tried to communicate with Senfft von Pilsach so the official might explain and apologize for his actions, but that offer had been 'very unpleasantly received'. The emissary piously replied, 'Well, but he really has had a severe lesson … I can assure you of that.' The conversation ended with what seems to have been the delivery of a threat: that Stevenson, by not accepting this offer, would be made 'a culprit against Germany' (*Letters* 7: 181). Unfortunately, Claxton was this very emissary. Claxton was now not only implicated in the scheme to kidnap Mataafa but also more openly associated with Senfft von Pilsach, Stevenson's adversary. By playing the subservient part of spokesperson for this Treaty Official, Claxton became, from Stevenson's perspective, increasingly untrustworthy.

It is amusing to note that when Claxton was at Vailima speaking to Stevenson on Senfft von Pilsach's behalf, Moors and Doudney arrived. The frightened and embarrassed missionary had to make a hasty and ludicrous retreat upstairs. Moors, who was to help incite Stevenson in accusing the missionary of the kidnapping plot, and Doudney, who had written the angry letter to the local newspaper concerning the impropriety of Claxton's generous salary as Natives' Advocate, did not depart until several hours later. Claxton was stuck upstairs until the two left the house. Such was the incestuous nature of the place.[23]

Claxton Returns

In September, 1892 Stevenson was upset when he learned that Claxton had not left the islands for good and that the troublesome missionary was returning to resume both his clerical and his Land Commission duties. Claxton had been in England merely on a five-month furlough. Stevenson, partially prompted by Moors, decided no longer to keep silent, especially about the missionary's supposed suggestion to the American Consul, Sewall, to lure Mataafa back to Apia and have him arrested and put out of the way. As a result, when Claxton returned to Samoa on 27 September, 1892, he was met with a thunderbolt, for he received the following high-handed and angry letter from Stevenson — a salutation I believe he did not expect. Recall that Stevenson, even though he had heard things that made him 'averse to shake his hand', had been cordial up to Claxton's April departure (*Letters*: 7: 276). The letter, as we shall later see, was to initiate an attempt to bring a libel suit against both Stevenson and Moors and to accuse them of slander.

> Revd Sir,
> I have to offer you my regret that I did not earlier what I find I must do now. When you left these islands, I trusted it was to be forever and held my peace. Since you have returned, it is my painful duty to advise you of the fact that there can be in the future no relations between you and me. Your interview with Mr Sewall (if there was nothing else) marks you as one of those men with whom I must either definitely break or cease to respect myself. (LMS Archives. Box 42, Folder 2)

The very next day the missionary replied with threatening words:

Sir,

Allow me to acknowledge your note of yesterday's date.

In reply I shall content myself, for the present, with doing these things. First, to assure you that when I left Samoa in April last I knew nothing of the slander which you have endorsed; and to remind you that you did not enlighten me when you said good bye. Secondly, let me remind you that you have gratuitously constituted yourself my judge, and have delivered sentence without allowing me the privilege of a hearing. (LMS Archives. Box 42, Folder 2D)

On 11 October Claxton also sent a defensive and vengeful letter to Thompson in which he informed the LMS Foreign Secretary that he had been 'cordially enough welcomed back here except by Robert Louis Stevenson and the Land Commissioners':

Mr Stevenson imputes to me a proposition for the entrapment of Mataafa, which, to use Mr Cusack-Smith's words to me the other day 'was heard on all sides at the time of Mataafa's secession to Malie, but which he never till now heard attributed to me.' I send a copy of a note received from Mr Stevenson the day after my landing, and a copy of my reply which will sufficiently describe what he has done. (LMS Archives. Box 42, Folder 2)

The stage for this abrasive exchange had been set at the moment of the accused's April departure from Samoa. At that time Moors, Stevenson's friend and wealthy businessman, had attempted to alert the London Missionary Society in England that Claxton had plotted to kidnap Mataafa. (Moors, like Stevenson, was a strong supporter of Mataafa.) On 15 April 1892 Moors wrote a letter, addressed both to Claxton and Thompson, that he planned to ship on the very same steamer on which the missionary was traveling, In the manner of a good novel, though, the scheme did not work, for Moors' letter did not get on board. In his hurry to prepare for a trip he was making to Nassau Island, Moors 'forgot to hand' the letter over to his secretary, Irving Hetherington (LMS Archives). Time lapsed before Hetherington handed the correspondence over to the first available steamer. Moors' letter and the copy destined for the missionary, therefore, did not reach either Claxton or the Society's Foreign Secretary until later. Moors had hoped that by informing the LMS and Claxton himself, the missionary might be prevented from returning to Samoa.[24]

Moors was not the only one to spread the story about Claxton. Even before the missionary left for England, Stevenson, perhaps encouraged by his rather cynical conviction that 'rumours have a knack of being right' (*Letters* 7: 252), went down to the Mission and informed Clarke about his colleague's misdoings. Father Didier, the Catholic priest, had also helped circulate the rumor and so had John La Farge, the American painter who had visited Samoa and taken the story with him as extra baggage to be deposited throughout his travels in the Pacific. His version betters Moors'. In his *Reminiscences of the South Seas* (1912), La Farge writes that in August, 1892, Sewall, the American Consul, had told him some 'charming details' concerning Claxton and a plot to murder the rebel King. The American Consul had supposedly asked La Farge, in the course of his travels, to alert Father Gavet, one of Mataafa's friends, to Claxton's proposal to assassinate Mataafa by encouraging him to walk on a road where it would be easy for the German sentinel to shoot him and legally so: 'consequently no one would be to blame, and Mataafa would be out of the way.' This scheme, La Farge asserted, 'the reverend clergyman thought could be managed' (La Farge 149).

Claxton and Libel

Upon Claxton's return, Stevenson's displeasure was soon to become more public and active. In his 11 October 1892 letter to Thompson, Claxton describes what he calls 'the strange steps' Stevenson and the Land Commissioners (most of whom were Stevenson's friends) 'in their frenzy of chagrin' took:

> The Land Commissioners on hearing that I had returned as Natives' Advocate hastened to petition King Malietua [Laupepa] to release them from my further presence in the Land Commission.
> The King introduced the Commissioner's petition to his parliament at once (and written without my knowledge), and by unanimous agreement of King and government in Mulinuu the petition of the Commissioners was negatived and a vote of confidence in myself carried. Had it been otherwise no change of Natives' Advocate would have been possible without the approval of the Chief Justice.
> On being confronted with Mr Stevenson's endorsement of Mr Moors' slander against me I laid the whole matter before Mr Cusack-Smith [the British Consul] and asked him as my Consul to inform me what steps I could take. He advised a demand to each of the above gentlemen Mr Stevenson and Mr Moors for an apology within 24 hours offering an alternative of a civil suit against both. Mr Clarke's disapproving of the advice I found on referring to the Society's Regulations that this is a matter cognisable by the District Ctte. S. 11. 86 and I have laid the matter in the hands of the Secretary of the Dist. Ctte. urging an immediate special meeting. A meeting has now been called for Friday next. (LMS Archives: Box 42)

It is obvious that the missionary fully enjoyed the favor of the Treaty Officials, especially that of Cedercrantz, the Chief Justice (Stevenson referred to him as 'Claxton's fast friend' [*Letters* 7: 386]) who made it clear to the Missionary Committee that Claxton 'would not be justified in giving up his duties' as Natives' Advocate and that Stevenson's friend, Edwin William Gurr, 'would not be justified' in replacing him (LMS Archives: Box 42). The missionary, therefore, stubbornly refused to give up his title until the middle of October when his fellow missionaries, after being pressured by the British Consul, asked their colleague to resign from the Land Commission. Because of the disagreements between the Three Powers and the Chief Justice concerning the missionary, the business of the Land Commission had come to a full stop. As a result, Cusack-Smith had earnestly urged the Missionary Committee to 'join with him in appealing to Mr Claxton to accede' and 'not attend the Commission for a time' (LMS Archives: Box 42).

The British Consul might have supported Stevenson's belief that Claxton should no longer serve on the Land Commission, but, as the above letter indicates, he did not appear to champion Stevenson's accusation that the missionary had advocated luring Mataafa to Apia so he could be arrested, for he suggested that the missionary either extract an apology from Stevenson or take him to court over the charge. The initial accusatory letters that both Stevenson and Moors had sent to Claxton were now subject to libel. When news of this possibility reached Stevenson and Moors, there was a commotion. The two scrambled to retain lawyers; they 'set a spy on Claxton's movements with a view to plead undue influence' (*Letters* 7: 386), and Stevenson fretted over the prospect of having to spend exorbitant amounts of money in his defense (seven or eight thousand pounds) and about the possibility of having to be dragged through a court system that was laborious and not necessarily sympathetic to him. Because Stevenson and the missionary were both British subjects, they would have had to appear first before the Deputy Commission Court in Samoa; then come before the High Commission Court in Fiji (Sir John Thurston who was hostile to Stevenson and had written letters against him to the Foreign Office was the High Commissioner), and finally, and this detail rather delighted Stevenson's sense of absurdity, and high drama, they would have to stand before the Privy Council in England. There was also the chance that the case would initially be heard by the Chief Justice. Given Cedercrantz's propensity to favor Claxton, this, in Stevenson's mind, was the worst scenario. Strange as it might seem, while these anxieties were grating in his consciousness and he was telling Charles Baxter that he was in for a libel action brought about by 'An accursed ruffian, a missionary by the vile name of Arthur Claxton', Stevenson's eyes were also glancing at the article in a New Zealand newspaper that declared he, Stevenson, was to be the next Consul in Samoa (*Letters* 7: 395). Such was the Jekyll and Hyde character of politics.

Stevenson did not just think of his own skin; an enduring loyalty to the missionary societies inevitably came to the fore, so that he also worried about the effect a libel suit might have on the Mission. He, therefore, at once determined to tell his friend Clarke that Claxton had no chance of proving his innocence concerning the kidnapping plot and would, therefore, lose the case. Stevenson wanted to spare the Mission 'the publication of its disgrace, and a considerable diffusion of dollars' (*Letters* 7: 386). He also sensed that the missionaries were not wholly on Claxton's side and that they might help him by bringing an end to the libel suit. Clarke evidently listened and persuaded Claxton to take less drastic steps and agree to let the Mission set up a special committee to deal with the matter. The Mission scheduled a series of meetings in which they would thoroughly investigate the charge. However, before Moors was willing to give evidence at these hearings, both he and Stevenson insisted that Claxton sign an agreement stating he would not press charges of libel. Through their lawyer, and using the intermediary of the Missionary Committee, Stevenson and Moors quickly set about drafting a document that would protect them from litigation. The result was that on 14 October 1892 they and the Mission proposed the following, which they hoped Claxton would sign. The Mission was just as eager as Stevenson to avoid the embarrassment and the cost of a law suit. One early draft of that document can be found in the Missionary Committee's minutes. It reads:

> Mr Claxton hereby pledges himself not to carry into a court of law the matter in dispute between himself and Messrs. Moors & Stevenson but to accept the decision of the Mission Committee and the Directors of the London Missionary Society. Messrs Moors & Stevenson also hereby pledge themselves that if in the opinion of the Society Mr Claxton succeeds in demonstrating his innocence they will publicly apologise and express their regret for having published Mr Sewall's charge and Mr Claxton will accept such apology. (LMS Archives: Box 42)

Already feeling prickly and irascible, Claxton could not accept the wording of the early drafts. He did not like the idea that the pressure was on him to demonstrate his innocence. He strongly believed that, rather than he, Stevenson and Moors should substantiate their charges. Hence, he requested that the Missionary Committee insert the words, 'if Messrs Moors & Stevenson fail to substantiate their charge' in place of 'providing Mr Claxton cleared himself of the charge'. The quibbling over the phrasing went back and forth between the missionary and Moors' legal advisors. Of course, Claxton objected to the alterations made by Moors' solicitors. The discussion continued. At a later meeting, Stevenson attempted to bring about a compromise by suggesting that 'the business in hand was to make his (Mr Claxton's) innocence apparent'. He argued that the alterations in the wording, therefore, were 'immaterial to Mr Claxton'. The missionary capitulated and accepted those changes; however, the sparring was not over. Claxton persisted in recommending 'one change after another, neither of which' according to the minutes, 'at all altered his own position', and continued to insist 'that as he gave up his right to bring an action for libel, it was necessary that the document should contain evidence of the existence of that right.' The exhausted note taker, the Reverend A. Hunt, concluded his minutes by admitting that the discussion lasted a long time and that 'Messrs Moors & Stevenson at length gave way and accepted' the inclusion of the word 'published' (LMS Archives: Box 42). Stevenson later admitted to Baxter that he was not so 'bitterly averse to apologizing' — he preferred apology to payment (*Letters* 7: 422).[25]

Of course, Stevenson was concerned about libel because he had also published his account of the kidnapping plot in *A Footnote to History*, a circumstance made worse by the incongruous fact that Stevenson was having trouble getting hold of the book. For some reason he owned no copy of *A Footnote to History* and, therefore, could not even check the wording of his charge against Claxton. In a wry, perhaps exaggerated, note to Edward L. Burlingame, Stevenson complained that there was one copy of *A Footnote to History* but 'that in the pocket of a missionary man who is at daggers drawn with me, who lends it to all my enemies, conceals it from all my friends, and is bringing a lawsuit against me on the strength of expressions in the same which I have forgotten and now cannot see' (*Letters* 7: 402).

The Missionary Committee Hearings

With matters, more or less, settled with regard to the agreement, the hearings before the Missionary Committee began in October, 1892. The Reverend J. Marriott, the Secretary of the Samoan District Committee, and Whitmee, who was to head up the investigation, came up to Vailima to ask if Stevenson would give evidence before the Mission Committee and, in addition, pledge himself to accept the final decision of the London Missionary Society Directors. Wanting to avoid a lawsuit and also desiring to save the mission from a public scandal, Stevenson readily agreed. The very same night, therefore, he, Moors, William Blacklock (then the American Vice-Consul), and I.P. Harper (the American Consulate's Clerk), appeared at the Mission House before the Mission Committee, composed of the Reverends Whitmee, Marriott, Clarke, Claxton, Hills, Goward, A. Hunt, and the Misses Wilhelmine Franzeska Louise Valesca Vanessa Schultze, Elizabeth Moore, and Agnes Eunice Large — teachers and missionaries representing the London Missionary Society. Between October 14 and 17, and from 8 p.m. until midnight, these four defendants delivered their testimony and were cross examined by the accused. Stevenson's account of the proceedings is lively. In a letter to Colvin, harsh insults, a biting tone, sexist phrases, and a sense of the absurd as well as a love of the dramatic mask the rather serious, yet simultaneously trivial, episode, or, as Stevenson called it, 'the Mission racket' (*Letters* 7: 407). Stevenson's description catches both sides of the situation. In addition, at times he seems to be distancing himself from the affair not only through his devastating, fictionalizing humor but also by referring to himself in the third person:

> In the library of the Mission a long table was laid with writing materials and lamps. On one side of it the Mission — eight persons, and three of them old maids; on the other we four, who were made to figure as the culprits. Claxton is a big, handsome, fair, blue-eyed fellow like the hero of a lady's novel; his head (the lady novelist would say) like a Greek god's — only it ain't; his legs (says Haggard) would be a disgrace to any livery. The cream of the affair was his cross-examination of R. L. S. which must have lasted at the very lowest estimate an hour and a half and was characterised by extreme bitterness on both sides. He is clever enough to have learned a lot of cross-examining tricks, and just not

clever enough to understand that they were worse than useless against
me. (*Letters* 7: 405)

Stevenson's portraits of the other participants are equally damning.
Claxton speaks in the style of 'a very bad Old Bailey counsel'; Clarke is referred to
as an 'extraordinary mixture of ass and angel'; Marriott is 'an amiable mutton', and
the three 'plain looking' women missionaries are characterized as having crushes
on 'the beau Claxton', and of looking at Stevenson with 'the most singular
expression of interest and horror' (*Letters* 7: 407). The bravado of these comments,
though, is not absolute; it is qualified, if not overborne, by Stevenson's sense of the
excruciating awkwardness of the hearings. In particular he is uncomfortable at
finding himself being manipulated by Claxton to betray a confidence with his friend
Clarke in whom Stevenson had confided after he had heard of the kidnapping plot.
Stevenson detests Claxton, 'the rascal', not only for spreading evil words about him
but also for manoeuvering him into 'an attitude of opposition towards Clarke'.
Stevenson adds that if 'Clarke had not been the gentleman that he is', the evening
would have been 'very painful' (*Letters* 7: 405).[26]
    Such was the uneasiness that Stevenson's mother, not wanting to grace the
presence of Claxton, declined to go to church. Stevenson also confessed that he felt
'a great delicacy about entering the Mission compound these days', and told Colvin
that during the period of the hearings he had been literally spooked when one hazy
moonlight evening, he had met a 'white man' who turned out to be Claxton:

> 'Good evening!' said I. The white man bowed with a great sweep of his
> white hat. 'Who is it?' said I. — 'Claxton!' said he. And we passed on
> severally, but I with a hateful sense of the enmities surrounding me, that
> I should ride on such an errand [an interview with Dr. Bernard Frunk, a
> medical officer with the German Firm] and make such an encounter by
> the way. (*Letters* 7: 408)

In the midst of the investigation, the members of the Mission House were
also feeling uncomfortable. The missionaries obviously liked Stevenson and
respected him, even though at times there were divergences of opinion, so even
during the period of the hearings Miss Schultze, (in Stevenson's words, 'the narrow
ugly upright romantic German woman') who had supposedly glared at Stevenson
during his testimony, came up to Vailima of her own accord, for a friendly, if not
righteous, visit; and Whitmee and his wife had sent up notes that Fanny responded
to by sending them gooseberry pies. The gooseberries' strange acrid sweetness is
somehow appropriate.
    The main source of discomfort for Stevenson, though, was, perhaps, not
with the missionaries, but with himself. As he listened to the evidence, he had a
growing sense that the case to convict Claxton was not as strong as he had initially
presumed. To make matters worse the key witness, Sewall the former American
Consul, was now residing in the United States and, obviously, could not be present.

At first Stevenson seemed certain that he was in the right, especially since he had thought there was a witness who would confirm his and Moors' accusation: Sewall's consular clerk had supposedly overheard the conversation between the American Consul and Claxton and could attest to the truth of the kidnapping plot. However, as the days went by, Stevenson's confidence seems to have been shaken. He became more sensitive to the likelihood that there was too much hearsay, even though he had originally gotten the account from Sewall himself. As Stevenson pointed out, 'the story was told so explicitly, that it was either absolutely true or a lie, there could not have been any mistake about it' (LMS Archives: Box 42).

When one reads through the minutes recording the witnesses' accounts, one easily understands Stevenson's increasing unease. Blacklock's statement is replete with negatives and the burden of forgetting: 'I do not remember the part referring to the Germans …. I cannot remember the exact date, nor can I recall now what part of the day it was. I cannot remember the exact words used, but only the substance of them. I do not think I heard the story again until about Oct. 3rd/92' (LMS Archives: Box 42). The American Consul's Clerk's testimony that was supposed to be so conclusive grows weaker and weaker as it progresses. Harper begins by resolutely announcing that 'I was present when this conversation between Mr Sewall & Mr Claxton took place', but as the seconds tick by, his certainty becomes less solid and finally melts into inconclusiveness. He admits that he was not in the same room, that he was sitting at his desk on the far side of the adjoining room, and that 'The door was closed between the two rooms.' Furthermore the clerk concedes that he mainly remembers Sewall's angry and indignant tones and that he could not 'swear to any particular words or statement'. All he has is an impression; he 'cannot recall exact words' (LMS Archives: Box 42). To complicate the proceedings, the Missionary Committee was waiting for a letter from Sewall, the former American Consul, that was not to arrive until several months later.

Stevenson delivered his statement on October 17. In it, he attempted, understandably, given the context of libel, to emphasize the care with which he tried to confirm the report of Claxton's suggestion that Mataafa be captured and that the blame be placed upon the Germans. Stevenson told the Committee that in April, 1891 he had waited for Sewall's return (the American Consul had been away) so that he might 'ascertain the truth or otherwise of the report':

> I saw him at the (Amer) Consulate within a day or two of his return. I asked him if the story reported in the beach was true. He denied having used the expression to this effect 'I am a gentleman & therefore cannot do it' but all the rest was quite true. He appeared to be very indignant at such a suggestion having been made to him [by Claxton]. I asked if I might be allowed to publish the story in my book (in Samoa) and he replied 'Certainly, you have my authority.' I was very much upset at Mr Sewalls [*sic*] confirmation of the report …. When a man like Mr Sewall makes a statement to me in the way he did, I cannot doubt his word.

Toward the end of his testimony, Stevenson, however, bends a bit by saying that if indeed Sewall now says that any part of the story is a calumny, a lie, then 'we are prepared to do full justice to Mr Claxton' (LMS Archives: Box 42).

In the midst of his statement to the Committee, Stevenson expressed his strong disapproval concerning Claxton's attitude toward the dynamite plot. Stevenson's testimony confirms what I have suggested: that Stevenson did not trust the missionary because of his alliance with the Chief Justice and the President, and especially since, in Stevenson's eyes, such an association was not only dangerous to the stability of Samoa but also immoral. The two issues, the kidnapping and the dynamite plots, contaminated each other. Using an imperious tone worthy of the best of the adventure novels, Stevenson continued:

> I must remind Mr Claxton of a certain painful interview I had with him and in which I had to speak very plainly to him. In that interview Mr Claxton declared the proposed dynamite affair a very harmless thing, but said it was not intended to carry it out. Yes, Mr Claxton said that the story was an unbelievable one, but that was not the point at issue, which was, whether such an action was not an immoral one; on that point the dispute arose. (LMS Archives: Box 42)

Stevenson closed his remarks by berating himself for not confronting Claxton when the missionary had left for England in April, 1891 and for waiting until his return in late September to write that he wanted nothing more to do with him. Stevenson was upset with his own lack of courage — a weakness, one recalls, he berated himself for when as a younger man he had failed to speak out against the policies of the British Government toward its soldiers: 'I did not report it [the Mataafa plot] while Mr Sewall was in Samoa because I hate a row and did not wish to make one. I think I was very much to blame in not making the matter known to Mr Claxton before he went away, and confess I was wrong in keeping up friendly relations with him. I sent the letter of Oct 1st to Mr Claxton because I had reproached myself for so doing and resolved to prevent any further falsity between us.' A day or so later and laboring under a fever, he went down to the Mission House to read over his evidence, make a few amendments, and to sign it: 'I accept the above with the addition specified as a fair digest of my evidence. Robert Louis Stevenson' (LMS Archives: Box 42).

When the former American Consul, Sewall, eventually did send his letter of witness to Thompson in London on 13 December 1892, the clarity everyone hoped for was crushingly unavailable.[27] By now there was such a confusion of voices, not unlike the plethora of disembodied voices that haunt the Beach in Stevenson's 'The Isle of Voices' and accompany the bloodshed in the forest [civil war]. Sewall's account waffles along with the others in and out of blame:

> Mr Claxton did not seek to have me entice Mataafa to Apia, for I had already written my letter, which was my last effort in that direction. I am

quite ready also to endorse Mr Claxton's statement that he had no thought in his mind of carrying to me any such proposition as he afterwards made …. The idea that Mataafa should be seized at Apia apparently only came to him incidentally during the conversation. And I can understand how in the case of one who could make such a suggestion, it might not have impressed itself on his mind as it did on mine. I would even be ready to say, therefore, that after so long a time he might honestly have forgotten it, had he not reported so accurately the other leading points in our interview, concerning which I did not speak with half the emphasis I did on this. (LMS Archives: Box 42)

No wonder that when Stevenson read the letter, he told Colvin, 'as much as I love pickles and hot water [politics] … I shall take my pickles in future from Crosse and Blackwell and my hot water with a dose of good Glenlivet' (*Letters* 7: 446).

Stevenson and others now had to deal with the deviations between their statements and Sewall's. On 20 April 1893 — two protracted years after the incident — the Reverend Marriott, representing the Missionary Committee, had sent a copy of Sewall's letter to Stevenson to ask him what explanation he could give for the 'remarkable divergences' (as quoted in *Letters* 8: n. 64). Stevenson acknowledged that there was a split between Sewall's statement that he had already invited Mataafa to return to Apia and Stevenson's understanding that it was the missionary who had suggested that Mataafa be tricked into coming back. But, for the most part, he still insisted on the culpability of Claxton for suggesting the removal of Mataafa. Obviously wanting to be rid of the whole mess and recognizing that he and his fellow accusers were the casualties of rumor as well as of overheard whispers and exclamations, Stevenson on 24 April, 1893, wrote a final, formal letter on the whole affair to the LMS Foreign Secretary. Significantly, in the letter Stevenson refuses to capitulate. He still tenaciously holds to his belief in Claxton's basic but not provable culpability:

Dear Sir, In reply to a communication from your committee here, I have to say that I can see no 'remarkable divergences' between Mr Sewall's letters and our reports. It was all hearsay on our side; and it has all the defects of hearsay evidence when it is examined; but the facts are there.

Two questions are handed on to me. They are easy to answer, and should be asked at Mr Sewall, not at us. In the first we have foreshortened the story both in hearing and telling; and said 'Mr Claxton has suggested to him that he should invite Mataafa to Apia under promise, etc.' where we should have said 'that he should profit by having invited.' For the second I must refer you directly to Mr Sewall repeating as I do so my original statement. I am, Yours truly. (*Letters* 8: 64)

The Verdict

A few months later, the case was over and the missionary cleared. On 28 July 1893, the Reverend Thompson wrote to the Reverend Marriott that the LMS Board of Directors had accepted Claxton's denials, that the missionary was 'entirely innocent' and was entitled to be fully acquitted of the charges made against him. Stevenson had lost, but he had succeeded in avoiding a libel suit and ridding Samoa of Claxton's presence (and he was also to succeed in the firing of the Chief Justice and the President).

In late October, 1892 following the investigation, the missionary had requested a leave of absence from his duties as Natives' Advocate, and then on 28 March 1893, he had resigned his position in Samoa and shortly afterwards left for England. Stevenson exclaimed to his mother, 'Do you know (I think not) Claxton has gone? … Not many tears were shed' (*Letters* 8: 81). In another letter he confided to his mother that Whitmee had told him that 'in giving the verdict of the Mission, as President of the Commission, he had to tell Claxton that his brethren had had so many instances of disingenuousness on his part that they felt that they could not accept his account of the affair' (*Letters* 8: 114).[28] Of all the people with whom Stevenson disagreed, Claxton, I believe, is the only one not to receive any word of sympathy or momentary forgiveness. In many ways, this was Stevenson's most contentious battle. Stevenson found it hard to forgive a missionary, for, as we have learned from the first chapter, he foresaw that the missionary would be instrumental in helping to create a more vibrant and healthier Samoa.

Although Claxton's colleagues might have not trusted him, they showed some compassion toward him. Shortly after the missionary had resigned his official duties as Natives' Advocate, he had written a letter pleading that he might be given something to do. As a result a circulating letter went round from missionary to missionary in order to get their advice as to whether Claxton should be allowed to help Marriott at his school in Malua. Their responses are interesting to read, for they reveal both a rigid strictness and a sympathetic interest in his well being. Furthermore they address the concern that since the case is *sub judice*, if they were to give him a position at the school, both 'natives and foreigners will consider that we have practically settled the case' (S. J. Whitmee). Others, like Clarke and Miss Schultze, tended to disagree and thought it might be 'a useful & unobjectionable manner of employing the time', and Clarke particularly did not think that Claxton's work at the school 'would be misunderstood by foreigners'. Indeed, he suggested that if the missionary were not active that might 'cause misunderstanding amongst the natives' (LMS Archives: Box 42). All of them recommended that Claxton should go to England and on his way pass through America where he could meet with Sewall to try to clear his name. (They all believed that because of the charge, he could not work effectively.) That proposal, though, was complicated by debates over who should pay the cost of the travel and by Claxton's objection that it was not his responsibility to search out the former American Consul.[29] The discussion over this matter is perhaps not relevant to Stevenson's part in the investigation, but it does give one a window into the culture with which he interacted and that helped define the political life on the islands.

Conclusion

Claxton's departure by no means brought an end to Stevenson's political activities. While he had been sporadically preoccupied with the missionary hearings, other issues that I outlined at the beginning of the chapter were raging about him. He was to continue, in his political writing, to be as committed, irascible, devastatingly officious, and, paradoxically, as impartial and generous as he sometimes could be. His was a strong will that finds its reflection in his last novel, *Weir of Hermiston* (published posthumously).

When he began working on that novel in 1892 (the very same year in which many of his political activities were most intense), he was, in a sense, turning his attention away from the Chief Justice in Samoa to the fictional Lord Justice-Clerk in Edinburgh — a welcome relief of sorts. Although there is a tendency to consider this novel as a recasting of his quarrels with his father, I suggest that, given the context of Stevenson's political activities, in many ways, *Weir of Hermiston* reveals his own identification with the protagonist's father as well as with the son 'Erchie'. One might say that Archie's father, otherwise known as the Hanging Judge, reflects to some extent his own political personality. Like the dreaded judge, Stevenson, throughout his political exertions, was also capable of experiencing the kind of 'savage pleasure' (210) in attacking and judging those he deemed in the wrong (recall the glee with which he exposed the Treaty Officials' misdeeds); he too could command those around him with a formidable brow and well-aimed, tenacious words (recall his imperious and officious letters); and he too worked from a sense of honor and respect for the law. In addition he recognized himself in Archie who inherited from his mother 'a shivering delicacy, unequally mated with potential violence' (206). Stevenson could never just be the dreadful judge. In his dealings with those whose policies and stupidities he detested (as in his responses to the Chief Justice and the President), the discreet, empathetic, and fragile side of him would also rise to clash or alternate with his temper.

The consequent fraternizing of these disparate qualities is what makes thinking about Stevenson both alarming and intriguing, for it reminds one of the 'incurable illogicalities of life' that Stevenson spoke of to Gosse when he was writing about his grandfather's life (see opening quotation). Putting together the pieces of Stevenson's biographical jigsaw puzzle not only brings one into more intimate contact with the intricacies of his political imagination and the instabilities threatening Samoa during the late 1880s and early 1890s: it also gives one a sense of a personality who can be described adequately only through a long list of often incompatible adjectives. By studying his life during his last years in Samoa, we get a fuller view of Stevenson's volatile, tenacious, generous, authoritarian, playful, imaginative, and legalistic mind. He might not have been the Weir of Hermiston of Vailima, but, at least as far as one part of his character was concerned, the kinship is there for all to see.

Notes

1. Apia was the capital of the white colonial officials; Leulumoega was the capital of native Samoa.
2. In *A Footnote to History*, Stevenson qualifies the reliability of Klein's account. He suggests that the war correspondent's 'wisdom was perhaps not equal to his energy' (206-18).
3. David Daiches in his introduction to his edition of *The Ebb-Tide* points out that the story is essentially Stevenson's and 'while he put Lloyd's name on the title-page as co-author, in his letters he nearly always refers to it as simply his' (*The Ebb-Tide* xxi).
4. In a March, 1892 letter to Colvin, Stevenson describes the visit to the American Consul:

> Poor fellow, I like him ... [words erased by Colvin]. I stumbled into a remark that native war was no very dreadful thing for the natives, which it isn't, and that it was useful to the race as the only thing that woke them up, which it is. He, of course — if you knew him you would understand the of course — supposed I was concocting a war with Mataafa, and public-spoke till I was sick. In vain I told him it was an academic opinion. 'You have no right to say academic opinions to me. I am a serious man', said he. In vain I told him it was not my opinion that war at present could do anything by harm! he would none of me. He public-spoke. At last I was at the gate leaving. I took him by the shoulders; he had just been saying he had 'heard the knell of Samoa', and a lot of other rot. 'Suaese', I said (his native name) 'try to hear for once what I am telling you. I disapprove of any war at the present time, it would lead to nothing but ruin, and what I said to you, I would say to no Samoan.' — 'I hope so', said he. 'Stop a bit', I said. 'That is not what you say, when I am telling you what I believe.' — 'You have no right to dictate to me what words I am to use', said he. 'I am an official here. You have been the first to use insolent expressions.' (*Letters* 7: 249-50)

5. In *Samoa 1830 to 1900: The Politics of a Multi-Cultural Community*, R. P. Gilson explains that the Chief Justice of Samoa 'was to be nominated by the three Powers or, failing agreement among them, by the monarch of Sweden and Norway. The appointment of the Chief Justice was to be made by the Samoan Government, which was allowed no option of rejecting a nominee, and his salary of $6,000, per annum was, after the first year of the court's existence, to be paid from local revenue. The Chief Justice's decisions were to be final and were to be binding on all the residents of Samoa, and all four governments party to the Berlin Act. Provision was made, however, for any of the four governments to complain of his "misconduct in office", and given "sufficient cause", he might be removed at the request of any two of the treaty Powers, which term by definition excluded Samoa' (397).
6. In an undated and unsigned plan in the Beinecke Rare Book and Manuscript Library (ms. 3121), Stevenson begins to sketch a letter in which he proposes a way to bring peace based upon his conversations with 'several different chiefs'. Only item number one is present:

1. A declaration by the King backed by the proper authorities.

a) His Majesty to make an excuse of the menacing famine, to declare a general amnesty and to propose fresh election of Faipule throughout the whole country, Atua to meet in Lufilufi, A'ana to meet in Leulomoega, Tuamasage to meet at Kulinu'u ....

b) *Proper Authorities*

No doubt the proper authorities in this case would be the three Consuls. Their authority to order the Samoans to lay their arms down has been proven before and though it has been undeniably weakened of late it would doubtless again prove sufficient. At the same time we have been assured by a very influential chief that in this matter the proclamation of the Chief Justice alone would be at once obeyed both by the rebels and the loyalists, so great is the present distaste for war. It may become a question of fine policy for the Treaty Officials to decide on their course of action in this matter on which we feel that we can offer a suggestion. The cooperation of the Consuls would doubtless be highly important. Above all it will be necessary or at least prudent to issue regulations for the new election of the Faipule.

c) Two ways are open: in the first place an election of fresh Faipule from the ancient districts: in the second place, which would promise to be both cheaper and simpler, an election of delegates to a constitutive conference to be held at Mulinu'u and where all complaints could be brought forward and all details of administration under the Berlin Treaty could be definitely arranged; these delegates to be elected by a majority of the natives of each province voting by ballot. (McKenzie 470)

7. Because of Stevenson's public criticisms and frequent verbal attacks against the two Treaty officials for their fiscal policies and their exacerbating the instabilities tormenting Samoa as well as his own persistent efforts to make peace between Mataafa and Laupepa, Stevenson half believed that there were plots on the part of the British Government (the Foreign Office) to have him deported.

There was later in September to be another set of false rumors when a Berlin newspaper suggested that Stevenson, as 'a white meddler', was to be arrested (*Letters* 7: n. 411). The rumors also persisted in December, when Stevenson told Colvin, 'The two gentlemen of Mulinuu (the Chief Justice and the President) had decreed my deportation: they came to the German firm to get a vessel in which I was to be removed — whither I know not .... But the vessel was actually ordered and actually refused' (*Letters* 7: 444-45).

8. On 18 July 1893, three warships (with the Consuls aboard) escorted Laupepa's forces to where Mataafa was based and forced Mataafa to surrender. (Mataafa had begun an armed rebellion). The rebel King surrendered and was taken on board a German warship, the *Katoomba*, that, before taking Mataafa and his chiefs into exile (first to Fakofu atoll and then in November to the Marshall Islands under German rule), stopped in Apia. Stevenson and Lloyd were the first aboard. Later when the lesser chiefs were imprisoned in Apia, a place, Stevenson thought, not suitable to their rank, he not only sent them baskets of food but also tobacco, kava, and cloth. He also arranged to pay $100 bail for one of the older men who was sick. Moreover after a short absence in Hawaii, Stevenson kept on writing letters and visiting the jail in an attempt to persuade Cusack-Smith to release the prisoners.

9. In reporting in his letter to *The Times* on the burning of the island of Manona, Stevenson wrote:

> The burning of the island proceeded, fruit-trees were cut down, women stripped naked; a scene of brutal disorder reigned all night, and left behind it, over a quarter of the island, ruin .... The next morning in Apia I asked the same Consul [William Blacklock] if there had not been some houses burned. He told me no. I repeated the question, alleging the evidence of officers on board the *Katoomba* who had seen the flames increase and multiply as they steamed away; whereupon he had this remarkable reply – 'O! huts, huts, huts! There isn't a house, a frame house, on the island.' The case to plain men stands thus: — The people of Manono were insulted, their foot-trees cut down, themselves left houseless; not more than ten houses — I beg the Consul's pardon, huts — escaped the rancour of their enemies .... (*Letters* 8: 269-70)

10. In *A Narrative of Missionary Enterprises in the South Sea Islands*, John Williams admitted that 'while we [the LMS missionaries] gave the chiefs clearly to understand that our objects were purely of a spiritual character, under existing circumstances it was as much a duty to direct them in the formation of a code of laws as it was to instruct them in the principles of Christianity...' (128).

11. On 12 August 1891, for instance, Frederick J. Moss, a member of the House of Representatives in New Zealand, wrote to the Foreign Secretary requesting that the native government affairs be quite free from church control. He strongly urged instituting a change 'which will allow men outside the pale of the church to take office' (LMS Archives: Box 40, Folder 6B).

12. For a full discussion of these matters, see Aarne A. Koskinen. *Missionary Influence as a Political Factor in the Pacific Islands*. Helsinki, 1953.

13. Stevenson had met Baker and, as was true with many other strong, authoritative, and daring characters he met, found him interesting and was sympathetic to him. In a December, 1890 letter to Colvin, Stevenson writes about a dinner party where Baker was one of the guests. He described him as 'the much accused Man of Tonga and his son, with the artificial joint to his arm — where the assassins shot him shooting at his father'. Stevenson noted that 'I found he and I had many common interests and were engaged in puzzling over many of the same difficulties' (*Letters* 7: 61). Baker, of course, was not the only instance of the missionary's mixing of the political and the spiritual. Another example is the figure of the Reverend George Pritchard who was the British Consul of Tahiti, the adviser of Queen Pomare, and a tradesman and preacher in Samoa. For an account of his character see William Shaw's *Golden Dreams and Walking Realities*. 1851.

14. Recall Stevenson's attraction to figures like the Reverend George Brown and the Reverend James Chalmers. See the section on heroes in Chapter 1.

15. Stevenson did not succeed in gaining access to Laupepa. Intimidated by the Treaty Officials who had learned of Stevenson's intentions, Laupepa failed to appear at the several meetings Stevenson attempted to arrange.

16. When Stevenson did offer Claxton an explanation for his negative reaction to the service, it was rather blunt, and one none of us would be pleased to receive:

I am sorry I wrote you so hurriedly the other day; I know after I had begun I should leave a false impression — that your sermon had really something to do with my heat; but I was too deeply engaged to begin again, and let it go. I do not know why you should care; but indeed I had fault to find. Only the strong statement — how shall I say — wearied me. (*Letters* 7: 31)

In 'Stevenson as I Knew Him', Claxton recalled meeting Stevenson the day after the service.

I remember meeting him one Monday afternoon in the town, when he broke out with these words: 'I say, Claxton, that's a hot shop of yours; you nearly boiled me last night.' I asked him if he alluded to the physical temperature, or was it the theology that made him so hot. He replied, 'No, I don't think it was the theology that made me say that; I really meant the physical heat' (we had an iron roof then to the building, which did not get properly cool till about midnight); 'but', he went on: 'I must say that you stirred me up when you said that a man should realise he is accountable to God all the time, even when he has put his slippers on at the end of his day's work.' (LMS Pamphlet, 1908)

17. This Land Commission was yet another consequence of the Berlin Treaty. The Commission, made up of one representative from each of the three Powers, assisted by a Natives' Advocate, was to investigate claims by foreigners to the ownership of land in Samoa and to register titles of claims. The position that Claxton held was significant because as Natives' Advocate, he was supposed to act as spokesperson for Samoans and their interests.

18. Stevenson's letter to the Reverend Thompson reads:

I inclose a letter which I understand, in a less mangled form, to be making the round of the white residents, and which I think the Society ought to see.
I fear I shall be thought to intrude, but I cannot refrain from adding how glad I was when the Society consented to accept this duty of the Natives Advocate, nor from expressing a hope that the Society may likewise see its way to bearing the expenses.
P.S. The marks in the inclosed are by its writer, a Mr Doudney. (*Letters* 7: 168)

19. At the same time, Claxton did object to Doudney's presumed misrepresentation of his own actions and motives and wrote to the Foreign Secretary complaining of Doudney's extravagance and impertinence. Claxton's January, 1892 letter to the Reverend Thompson reads:

I am glad you did not believe all that was in Mr Doudney's letter. It was so extravagant in statement that the local editor refused to insert it in his paper. It was then sent to several leading men in Ms. Mr. Stevenson told me he had received a copy and asked if I would mind his sending it to you to give force to his suggestion that the Society should 'undertake the expense' of the Native's [*sic*] Advocate. As this was what I wanted I offered no objection. Mr Stevenson characterised the letter as 'impertinent both as to time and matter'. That was the general opinion of the leading men who received copies and whom I consulted about it. Mr Doudney knew no more of my intentions than of what I had already done. (LMS Archives: Box 42, Folder C)

20. In his letter to the Reverend Thompson, Stevenson wrote:

> With regard to my former letter, I think it only just to Mr Claxton and myself that you should know it was written with that gentleman's knowledge and approval. I think we are both guilty of an error in judgement, and that (for both our sakes) this fact should have been mentioned at the time. It is not now too late to repair the omission. I believe that happy consequences have flowed from the change effected; and it is perhaps not too much to hope that Mr Claxton's original error may be forgotten. Certainly I have not heard the salary referred to by natives since it has ceased being drawn. (*Letters* 7: 255-56)

21. In a letter to Colvin, Stevenson wrote about the plot to arrest Mataafa in the most general of terms. Rather than naming Claxton, he used the pronoun 'They':

> There has been a lot of trouble, and there still is a lot of doubt as to the future; and those who sit in the chief seats, who are all excellent, pleasant creatures, are not, perhaps, the most wise of mankind. They actually proposed to kidnap and deport Mataafa; a scheme which would have loosed the avalanche at once. But some human being interfered and choked off this pleasing scheme (*Letters* 7: 142).

Stevenson also inserted the incident, without naming names, into his *A Footnote to History* that appeared in August, 1892.

22. In May, June, July, and August 1892, Stevenson's quarrels with the Chief Justice and the President had become more intense and so had his campaign to rid Samoa of them: 'Politics are on the full job again' (*Letters* 7: 252). He referred to himself as being at 'daggers drawn with the Government' (*Letters* 7:384).

23. In one of her letters, Fanny describes the awkwardness of that Sunday:

> Last Sunday Mr. Claxton came up plainly from the president, who has at last awakened to his danger. He tried every way to induce Louis to agree to meet the president and have an explanation; the offer came too late. we learned afterwards that at the same time Mr. Rose [the next five words are suppressed in the manuscript], a horribly low, vulgar fellow, the president's secretary, had spent the day with Mr. Gurr [Edwin William Gurr: friend of the Stevensons, lawyer, banker, and in 1892 the Natives' Advocate], intent on the same errand [to get the President to meet with Stevenson]. Neither was successful. The same ludicrous scene took place at both houses. Here, the American men-of-war officers dropped in, followed by Mr. Moors and Mr. Dowdney. The unfortunate missionary had to remain upstairs alone, in hiding for the better part of the afternoon, being at daggers drawn with Doudney. (Neider 109)

24. Moors' letter vividly reminds one not only of the strength of the heard or reported word but also of a fact I have already mentioned, namely that Stevenson and Moors never fully trusted Claxton because of his close affiliation with those powers, especially the Chief Justice and the President, who opposed Mataafa. Moors writes:

In July of last [1891] I returned from Sophia Island and soon after my arrival I saw Mataafa at Malie and advised him to try and comply with the request of the Consuls and disband the forces then assembled at that place. My suggestions were followed and the people who had assembled there in large numbers soon disappeared. Regarding his own personal movement he said, that he was afraid to enter the Municipality for fear of treachery for it was publicly reported that you [Claxton] had proposed that Mr. Sewall should entice him to Apia so that he might be seized, and summarily dealt with. Under these circumstances he was afraid to accept any assurances of safety. I had heard the same report and I therefor [*sic*] could give him no advice as to his personal movements.

This story to which I have referred has for many months been the common talk of Apia and it is said to have been a number of times confirmed by Mr. Sewall himself. It is to the effect that you suggested to Mr. Sewall that he should induce Mataafa to come to Apia under a promise of safety, and that while here he should be seized. Mr. Sewall is said to have replied that there was one great difficulty in the way and that was that he was a gentleman and could not engage in any such dishonorable transaction. In reply to this it is said that you remarked 'Oh do it in such a way that the Germans will be blamed for it.' Whether or not this is a correct report of your interview with Mr. Sewall I do not know, but it is the version that is continually told in Apia and which you should know of. Many people in Samoa look upon you as a very untrustworthy person, and they are glad to hear of your early departure for it is thought that your political interferences have alread[y] done much harm both to the Municipality and to the Government. (LMS Archives: Box 42)

25. It is appropriate to recall that Stevenson had previously, in February, 1890, sent an angry letter to the Reverend Charles M. Hyde who had publicly attacked Father Damien's character ('He is not a pure man in his relations with women, and the leprosy, of which he died should be attributed to his vices and carelessness' [*Letters* 6: 373-74]). Father Damien was the Catholic Priest who had devoted his life and brought order and hope to the lepers in the Leper Colony in Hawaii, on the island of Molokai. Stevenson visited him and the colony in 1889. Furious with its contents, Stevenson composed his famous 'Open Letter to Dr. Hyde' and published it. Stevenson, who had visited and observed Father Damien's running of the Leper Colony in Hawaii, knew that his blunt words and defense of the priest might be the cause of libel, but he did not really care, even though he worried about financial ruin.

26. In a letter to Colvin, Stevenson describes the moment when Claxton tries to embarrass his colleague:

Once he [Claxton] gravelled me entirely and the scene must have been really dramatic. He looked away, looked up at me quickly, and shot at me the question — 'Did you tell any of the Mission this story before my departure?' Now the trouble was that I *had* told it to Clarke, that I knew that Clarke had long kept it secret, and that I did not know whether he had even yet mentioned the circumstance. I sat a good while silent, then turned to the chairman [the Reverend Whitmee], said the question could have no effect on Mr Claxton's defence, and begged to be relieved from answering it. Claxton was not going to have interference, waived his question for the moment, turned to another subject, and sprang the thing upon me again with the same tricky suddenness.

Then up got Clarke. 'I think I should answer this question. Mr Stevenson did tell me of it the day before Mr Claxton's departure, as Mr Claxton very well knows since I have told him of it since his return.' (*Letters* 7: 405)

27. In December, 1892 Stevenson was writing to Lady Jersey that there was even a rumor that Sewall was dead. He added, however, that he had 'every reason to believe the rumour false', but that he was still waiting for Sewall's reply concerning the Reverend Claxton's behavior. Stevenson noted that the reply had probably not come because Sewall 'was up to the neck in the Presidential election [USA Presidential election] (*Letters* 7: 443).

28. Claxton never returned to Samoa. After he left Samoa he spent most of the rest of his life as a missionary in Chung King, West China. Ironically, later in life, when he returned to England, he became President of the Robert Louis Stevenson Society. It is interesting to note that his published memoir of Stevenson completely ignores the years of conflict between them. Instead, it focuses on their working relationship. If there is any bitterness, perhaps it shows up in Claxton's remarking that 'it had never entered into his [Stevenson's] imagination that among a people reputed to be half savage such a relation of trust and loyalty, not only between Mission and People, but also between hot combatants, could have been possible.' Some of his comments are incisive, especially those concerning Stevenson's choice of Samoa. Claxton quite rightly suggests that Stevenson was attracted to Samoa, for there was 'a race on the borderland between savagery and Western, and history in the crucible ready for the making ...' (Masson 248-52).

29. Claxton's response to the Missionary Committee on the matter of his being able to continue to work while the case is *sub judice* reveals how angry he was and how threatening he could be:

Acting on the advice of the majority I am helping Mr Marriott at Malua and shall await the decision of the Directors. The question of my continuance as Natives' Advocate is not one on which either Consuls or Land Commissioners have anything to say. And when Mr Clarke says he has no doubt that the Powers will uphold their Representatives (meaning the Land Commissioners) he forgets that the Chief Justice and the President are much more important representatives of the Three Treaty Powers. The question is precisely the same as when I wrote my circular last April viz; — whether the powers carry through the Treaty and support the Chief Justice in the position they have given him or whether they approve the intrigues of an opposition clique in which Consuls and Land Commissioners are involved.

If the Berlin Treaty of 1889 be a hoax as this clique asserts, then I beg to be taken out of the farce and to be allowed to spend my strength on something more useful, either by returning to England for furlough and deputation work or by joining Mr Chalmers in New Guinea till my furlough is due.

To subject myself to still further misrepresentation by any more interviews with Mr Sewall seems to me senseless as the view that the society's missionaries should travel about to refute slanders (not direct charges or accusations) instead of requiring that the slanderers substantiate their stories. Since Mr Whitmee has taken that view I regret that I did not insist on the words of my original draft of agreement with Messrs Moors & Stevenson.
Arthur E. Claxton
Nov. 8th 1892 (LMS Archives: Box 42)

Chapter Six

The Juvenile Missionary Magazines and
A Child's Garden of Verses

Introduction

One of the most poignant moments I have experienced while doing archival research occurred when I was turning a page in one of Stevenson's messy manuscript notebooks and found myself stumbling over early drafts of poems belonging to *A Child's Garden of Verses* (1885). My response was not just a consequence of seeing, in all their nakedness, the verses that had conversed with my childhood and that still spoke to me as an adult. It was what surrounded them. In the margins of Stevenson's draft and in between his scraggly, yet strangely neat, stanzas were notes, written to his doctors and family members, asking for a bit of pudding or wondering if the dosage of his medicine could be reduced.[1] These requests, jotted down when he was forbidden to speak for fear that the effort would cause severe bleeding, are an all too tangible reminder of the fevers and of the hemorrhaging that bloodied his sheets: of the persistent sickness that literally framed *A Child's Garden of Verses* and created the land of counterpane. They are also a reminder of the resilience with which Stevenson survived and transcended his circumstances — an enduring quality that helps one better understand the poems in the slender volume.

A careful reading of *A Child's Garden of Verses* not only reminds one of this elasticity but also offers one the opportunity to engage the fuller range of Stevenson's imagination. In particular, if one places his verses within the context of his argument with the missionary ethos voiced in the juvenile missionary magazines with which *A Child's Garden of Verses* often seems to be in dialogue, the flexibility, the modifications, and generosity of Stevenson's imagination become even more noticeable. Such a reading is a welcome antidote to the incongruously vindictive behavior that frequently characterized Stevenson's political activities examined in the previous chapter. It recalls a gentler, more forgiving heart.

As a kind of finale, this last chapter releases Stevenson from the complications of his colonial surroundings in the South Seas and places his imagination in a larger landscape less limited by boundaries and circumstances so that one may better observe the intricate and multiple movements of his mind at play. Still this chapter emphasizes once more Stevenson's understanding, characteristic of every stage of his life and work, that one is never complete unless one recognizes that what is beyond oneself — is alien to oneself — is part of and necessary to the community of self.

A Child's Garden of Verses

Stevenson began thinking about *A Child's Garden of Verses* in the early 1880s after his return from California, where he had married Fanny. This was a time when he and his parents were reunited — the breach that had widened when Stevenson left for America (without informing them) and had married an American divorcee was patched, if not healed; and this was also a period when Stevenson, with his new family, was back among his old haunts. Between 1882 and 1885 he wintered in Davos (he had already been there as a sick child with his mother), summered in Braemar (Scotland), lived in Marseilles and Hyères, and moved to Bournemouth where his father had bought a house for his new daughter-in-law. Bournemouth was chosen because the Stevensons thought that the South of England would offer a better climate than Scotland, and, therefore, would be better for their son's delicate health.

Although during this time there were moments of contentment and episodes in which Stevenson was prolific, there were also tenacious intervals of illness, relapses, consultations with various doctors (Stevenson dedicated *Underwood*, a collection of poems, to the several doctors who attended him), long weeks of tedious bed rest, and even thoughts that he might die. Writing from the Hôtel Chabassière in June, 1884 to W. E. Henley, Stevenson bluntly told his friend:

> I trust this finds you well; it leaves me so-so. The weather is so cold that I must stick to bed, which is rotten and tedious, but can't be helped.
> I find in the blotting book the enclosed, which I wrote to you the eve of my blood. That night, when I naturally thought I was coopered ....

Stevenson closed the paragraph with, 'I earnestly desire to live' (*Letters* 4: 307).

The combination of being closer to his parents, of treading familiar soil, of once more having a young person about him (Stevenson spent much time playing with his stepson, Lloyd), and of repeating the sick-bed scenes of his early years revived and made even more pressing his childhood memories — recollections that Stevenson never had to go far to find.[2] For someone frequently on the edge of life, these memories were, perhaps, more readily available to him than they are for many of the rest of us. It is not surprising that what he began in Braemar in 1882 and first called 'Nursery Verses', then 'Rimes of Innocence', then 'Penny Whistles', and eventually *A Child's Garden of Verses* emerges during this hiatus. I should add, as an acknowledgement of Stevenson's pragmatic side, he was also eager to write something that would win a popular market and allow him to be less financially dependent upon his father's generosity. Kate Greenaway's poems for children had, for instance, sold 150,000 copies in 1880.[3]

When commentators have thought about the verses, they have often remarked on their being autobiographical. Jenni Calder quite explicitly states that Colinton Manse, where Stevenson's maternal grandfather lived and where, as a young boy, Stevenson played with his cousins, 'is the child's garden'. She and others have, of course, also noted the poems' preoccupation with the child's loneliness and terror of sickness, with the 'half-real world' of his sick bed, and they have quite rightly mentioned the influence of the strict Calvinism of his father (Calder 30, 38).[4] They recognize how the stories told to him in childhood settle into the poems. All especially mention the power of his nurse's literary diet of vivid and bloody accounts of religious martyrs. In addition, they recall how his father's narratives of risk and peril as well as Stevenson's memories of publications like Captain Mayne Reid's *The Boy Hunters* (1852), *The Young Voyageurs* (1853), *The Bush-Boys* (1855), and Cassell's illustrated family papers contribute to the spirit of empire, pillage, and exploration that stalk many of the poems' lines.[5]

The Missionary Ethos and *A Child's Garden of Verses*

Certainly all these strands run through and tug at the very fibre of *A Child's Garden of Verses*. I believe, however, that one significant, and I might add, rather obvious yet overlooked, source for the verses remains unrecognized: the ethos that surrounded, informed, and found expression in the juvenile missionary magazines of the period. The culture of the missionary societies, familiar to Dickens's Mrs. Jellyby and her Borrioboola Gha settlement, was very much a part of Stevenson's upbringing and surroundings. It would be difficult to avoid its touch, its taint, and its metaphors. By tracing this presence in the verses, one can see how Stevenson negotiates, as an adult, the tenacity of this culture; one can also recognize not only his general indebtedness to the missionary imagination but also his own imaginative powers that superseded and gave direction to the missionary demeanor and demands. In the following discussion I am not suggesting that the contents of the juvenile missionary publications are directly employed in *A Child's Garden of Verses*, but that their preoccupations shadow the poems and offer a context for Stevenson's imaginative play. One might say that his verses exist in a continuous counterpoint with the fare provided for children in the missionary magazines.

The Young Stevenson and the Missionary Culture

As a young boy, Stevenson willingly participated in a pious household that not only took religion seriously but also respected the missionary cause.[6] As her donations to the city mission, her contributions to the teaching of girls in India, her activities in the Edinburgh Women's Association, and, as we have seen, her later devotion to the missionary stations in Samoa demonstrate, Stevenson's mother tirelessly supported the foreign and domestic missions of the Church of Scotland as well as the efforts of other denominations. Margaret Stevenson's pocket diaries documenting young Louis's (or 'Smout's' as his parents called him) prayers, his comments about God, Christ, and Biblical stories, and attendance at church capture her religious commitment. She proudly notes not only how 'Smout' built a tabernacle with his sticks (10 December 1853), talked about heaven and golden harps (26 June 1854), cried because he had forgotten to say his prayers (24 July 1854), but also registered shock that sheep and horses did not know about God and suggested that 'somebody should read the bible to them' (30 March 1854). She also records his anxiety about the state of the foreign missions and their influence over immoral practices. On 10 January 1858, she chronicles one such moment:

> Smout: 'The churches are very much to blame for not sending missionaries to convert the Arabs.'[7]
> Mama: 'But if people won't go what can the churches do [*sic*] will you go when you are big?'
> S: 'I think you've forgotten one word that was needful.'
> M: 'What is that'
> S: 'If I'm spared!' (Beinecke ms. 7304)

Obviously, at the age of eight, Stevenson had not yet qualified his youthful earnestness and fervor so that he might compose the opening lines of what was, perhaps, to have been a satirical poem: 'One man spends everything in Brothels, another in missionary societies, both live ...' and there, unfortunately, Stevenson's handwriting becomes indecipherable. Not even the manuscript librarian could untangle it.[8] These few remaining fragments stay knotted and unread.

Throughout Stevenson's youth the Church of Scotland and the Free Church of Scotland were constantly appealing to the wealthy members on behalf of such schemes as providing manses for their missionaries in India and South Africa (*The Missionary News* 1 October 1867), asking parishioners of all means to pray for the perishing souls of the heathen, and holding, as did a church in Edinburgh in 1844, 'great missionary' meetings in which three thousand children gathered in a hall decked with idols suspended from the roof. Weekly, monthly, quarterly magazines, and pages for youth rattled off the missionary presses to spread the word. With their lavish pictures and adventurous tales, these were the precursors of the popular, illustrated magazines for children that appeared mid-century. In Scotland the Presbyterians produced or contributed to the *Children's Missionary*

Record (Edinburgh 1839-48), *The Edinburgh Medical Missionary Society Quarterly Paper* (1872 —), *Free Church of Scotland Record* (1843 —), *Home and Foreign Missionary Record for the Church of Scotland* (1838 —), and *The Juvenile Missionary Record in Connection with the Church of Scotland* (1849-59). In England the Presbyterian and Congregationalist missionary magazines were just as abundant: *The Missionary Repository for Youth and Sunday Scholar's Book on Missions* (1839 —), *The Juvenile Missionary Magazine* (1844 —) [published by the London Missionary Society], *News from Afar: A Magazine for Young People*, the 'Young Folks' pages of the *Illustrated Missionary News* with its elaborate full-page etchings, and *The Juvenile Missionary Intelligencer* (1835 —).

If one reads enough of these periodicals, one soon realizes that no matter whether a particular issue originated in Scotland or England, its articles and features were interchangeable or indistinguishable. The magazines borrowed from each other, for the missionary culture knew few national boundaries. The culture determined its borders through its preoccupations and the set formulae of its perspective. The interdenominational magazines such as *Gleanings for the Young* (sponsored by the British and Foreign Bible Society) and the missionary recitations, hymns, and poems for children, like the *Children's Missionary Hymn-Book* (London: John Snow 1842) and the later *Hymns and Poems for Children* (Edinburgh: W. Oliphant & Sons) subscribed to the same prescriptions.

Whether, in addition to reading and memorizing Biblical parables, listening to his mother reading *Pilgrim's Progress*, or coloring the pictures in *The Child's Happy Sunday Book*, Stevenson actually laid eyes on any of the juvenile magazines listed above or learned by heart hymns from the *Children's Missionary Hymn-Book* cannot be determined from the record. What is essential is that he could not have escaped the influence of the ethos that informed these publications. Given the context of Stevenson's childhood it would have been difficult not to have absorbed the attitudes, perspectives, the concerns, and even the cadences of the missionary agenda. To grow up without swallowing the formulae and to remain deaf to the repeated choruses concerning heathen girls and boys would have been, I believe, impossible — especially given both the Church of Scotland's and his mother's commitment to the missionary effort. What is more, if one were at all aware of the phenomenon of empire and reading books like Peter Parley's *Tales About Empire: Asia, Africa, and America* (a missionary book given him by his aunt in 1856), one could scarcely ignore the missionaries' presence in foreign lands.[9] The missionaries were, of course, entangled in the building of Empire, and in their magazines featured full-page pictures of key locations such as the 'Harbour at Balaklava'. They set up out-stations that became the bases for the British to establish their place and eventually rule. We need only recall that later in the South Seas Stevenson's friend the Reverend James Chalmers explored the interior of New Guinea. Through his trips Chalmers learned the various languages, set up contacts, opened routes, and mapped uncharted places which eventually allowed the British to enter and establish their authority.

Missionaries caught people's attention by combining adventure and empire building, a union that would have engaged the youthful Stevenson. The Religious Tract Society capitalized on the alliance in such publications as *A Boy's Adventure in the South Seas or with Williams in Erromanga* by Frank Elias. A passage from that book is strangely evocative of Stevenson's own imagination; it would have stirred Stevenson's adventurous heart and appealed to his sensitivity to the way it describes light falling upon darkness. The passage describes the moment a young son of a missionary in the New Hebrides stares into the darkness that has set in at sea. He reports:

> But as we grounded I could feel the flash of a lamp near to my face, and could hear a call from the shore. Then the man in the stern stood up, and I had the horrible sensation of being approached from behind by one whose mind it might yet be to throttle, or otherwise murder me. I could feel him standing behind me and then was conscious of the full glare of a lamp turned upon my face. (165-66)

The missionary magazines also rarely missed the opportunity to seize a young reader's sympathy by emphasizing the perils of living in a distant land among cannibals, navigating past river pirates, sailing through violent gales and troublesome reefs, and surviving, with God's help, shipwrecks, the great danger of serpents, and savage beasts. It was not uncommon for issues to display pictures of man-devouring tigers and crocodiles (sometimes confused with alligators) pulling down a struggling victim. These images recall the details in 'Travel', one of the poems in *A Child's Garden of Verses*, details that were certainly not drawn from Stevenson's own experiences. In among the poem's lines, Stevenson's child dreams of a place

> Where the knotty crocodile
> Lies and blinks in the Nile,
> And the red flamingo flies
> Hunting fish before his eyes; —
> Where in jungles, near and far,
> Man-devouring tigers are,
> Lying close and giving ear
> Lest the hunt be drawing near .... ('Travel' ll. 21-28)

The Juvenile Missionary Magazines and *A Child's Garden of Verses*

With all these possibilities and conditions in mind, one cannot help but open *A Child's Garden of Verses* and pause when one comes to the verse, 'It is very nice to think/ The world is full of meat and drink, / With little children saying grace/ In every Christian kind of place' ('A Thought') and then turn to 'Foreign Children' and listen to the British child ask his brothers and sisters across the sea, 'Oh! don't you wish that you were me?' In these lines more is at work than the child's naively articulating an imperialistic egoism; the child is also obviously repeating the missionary formulae. Although one must not overstate the connection, similar preoccupations in many of the collection's poems erratically, yet forcibly, catch one's notice like a crack in a glass. In *A Child's Garden of Verses* the missionary material is visible and contributes to the whole, yet is distinct, of a different substance. This difference, as we shall discover, finally helps to illuminate the generous reach of Stevenson's imagination.

One component of the missionary consciousness that works its way into and through *A Child's Garden of Verses* is the persistent awareness of the presence of children in foreign lands, the sense of children being everywhere. Perhaps, more than anything else, this element distinguishes and defines the thrust of the nineteenth-century juvenile missionary agenda. A verse in a July, 1866 issue of the *Juvenile Missionary Magazine* catches this perspective.

> God bless the little children—
>   We meet them everywhere;
> We hear their voices round our hearth,
>   Their footsteps on the stair
> ....
>
> God bless the little children,
>   Wherever they may be! ('Hearty Wish' 8)

Such a view of the world populated, even dominated, by a community of children of all nationalities and races, in accordance with the precept, 'Suffer little children to come unto me', is the very image that introduces each issue of *The Missionary News* and *The Juvenile Missionary Magazine*. Sitting solidly above the bold letters of the journals' titles are the figures of children from many lands (American Indians, Eskimos, Turks, Africans, Chinese, and Arabs) surrounded by huts, wigwams, temples, mosques, minarets, and ships arranged on the arc of a globe — all, of course, illuminated by the word of God ('the light of the world'). In creating this world citizenry of little girls and boys, the magazine editors were fond of reproducing pictures of various children, like the drawings of the son of a Parsee fire worshipper and Chinese children, who look out of the page's frame, and with their inviting eyes, engage and bind to them their Western sisters and brothers. Full-page illustrations, such as 'Black and White', an etching showing a young African girl standing next to the white daughter of a missionary, also represent the dominant presence of children, each child in her distinctive clothing, but as 'loving as brothers'.[10]

The articles in these magazines extend and verbalize the various images' promise. Commentaries upon Afghanistan, Greenland, Persia, camel caravans and palanquins clutter the columns — details that find their way into Stevenson's poems. And letters from children in China, stories of young people in Siberia, accounts of orphans in India or Rarotonga, tales of Eskimo boys, of a little girl in Ceylon, 'poor black boys and girls', 'little Turks', Crow Indians, Abyssinian girls, Himalayan infants, and young Tartars fill the pages. In their magazines, the missionaries insist that their young readers transport themselves, through their imagination, to, say, a school in India, an interior of a home in Fiji, a harbour in Apia, or a classroom in the Sandwich Islands. As if taking their juvenile subscribers by the hand, the writers in these magazines lead British children into school houses to see what these foreign children are doing and point out that, for instance, on Thursday afternoon 'you may see groups of children coming to the school'; then they ask the children to imagine opening the little white gate and tripping along the path to the school-room door. Much like Stevenson in *A Child's Garden of Verses*, the writers constantly tug at the young persons' sleeves and ask, 'Should you like to go in with them, and see what they are going to do?' (*The Juvenile Missionary Magazine* 1844: 152). The missionaries' directive recalls the letters Stevenson wrote to Adelaide Boodle in which he invites her pupils to step into the life of children on the South Sea Islands.[11]

As I have said, the missionary impulse to create a community of children brings to mind *A Child's Garden of Verses* that often encourages its audience to imagine itself within a sphere inhabited by children from other lands, in poems such as 'Foreign Children' that speaks of 'Little Indian, Sioux, or Crow/ Little frosty Eskimo,/ Little Turk or Japanee'. Throughout the poems, the missionary agenda shadows Stevenson's own sense of a community of children. The young child thinks of the children saying grace 'In every Christian kind of place' ('A Thought'), contemplates 'Some deserted' foreign city which children had once inhabited ('Travel'), imagines boys and girls singing in Japan and Spain ('Singing'), envisages other little children 'a hundred miles or more away' bringing the speaker's boats ashore ('Where Go the Boats?'), and fantasizes about the toys of Egyptian boys ('Travel').

The missionary culture that asks the young folk to read articles about Hindoo, Palestinian, and Burmese children playing with their toys stalks the lines of Stevenson's verses. Its invitation to its 'Dear Children' (the juvenile magazine readers) to picture girls swinging in Tahiti, to identify with the young people singing on the banks of the Orinoco River, or to envision children playing on a Polynesian island are not far from view. It is not difficult to see that details in Stevenson's poems summon the missionary mandate that always required its young audience to consider the similarities between their lives and those of children abroad. For instance, at a general meeting of the London Missionary Society in 1842, the Reverend G. Pritchard reminded his youthful audience that the South Sea Islanders are on the other side of the globe, and, consequently, 'it is night with them when it is day with you. The Children in the South Seas are now asleep in their beds, and about the time you are retiring to rest they will be getting up' ('The Exeter Hall Meeting') — an observation that cannot help but remind one of

Stevenson's child who in 'The Sun Travels' says, 'While here at home, in shining day,/ We round the sunny garden play,/ Each little Indian sleepy-head/ Is being kissed and put to bed' (ll. 6-8).

One aspect of this gathering of children as depicted in the missionary literature that might have caught the chronically ailing Stevenson's consciousness was the practice of asking readers to pray for sick children and of dwelling upon their condition: on six-year olds who lie on their death beds in China and India, and on a little Tahitian boy 'taken ill by consumption' and not long for this world ('Tahitian Children'). They reflect upon a helpless South African three-year old seized with a 'severe illness' ('An Infant's Prayer in Africa'), a young Hottentot stricken with malignant small-pox ('For the Young'), an Eskimo child long ill with 'pulmonary consumption' ('For the Young'), and a sick nine-year old Armenian Turk ('Column for the Young'). These children pass peacefully away because, according to the missionary propaganda, they have been converted to Christianity. On the last night of their lives, they kneel down in the dark and speak of 'going home' ('An Indian Child Dying'). The emphasis on sickness (and especially on pulmonary diseases) as one means of creating a global community recalls the six-year old Stevenson who, according to his mother's pocket diaries, thought about a larger world of sickness and prayed 'that God would be near every person that was not very well' (5 February 1856).

The Missionary Culture and the Idea of Foreignness

As is not surprising, in spite of all the missionaries' efforts to persuade their juvenile readers to identify with foreign children and places — by even having them play the same games as their counterparts far away — they often seemed to contradict their message of brotherhood and sisterhood, if not turn it on its head, through qualifying remarks that reminded the British child not only of his superiority and good fortune but also of how alien children in other lands could be.[12] Stevenson's persona in *A Child's Garden of Verses* at times naively reflects this attitude, for instance when he remarks on foreign children who 'have curious things to eat' ('Foreign Children'). The child's comment distantly echoes the accounts of strange eating customs and food that one periodically runs into in the juvenile pages. In one magazine there is an article about a Persian garden party where the writer, armed with verbs calculated to disturb the palate, speaks of rhubarb 'cut in thin slices and eaten with salt quite raw' and describes guests who 'plunged their hands into rice' and 'tore off pieces of meat' while eating 'very much and very fast' ('Sketches for Girls'). In another there is the account of a Chinese dinner where one was offered dishes of 'cold, salted earth-worms', 'delicately-cooked "bow-bow"' and 'stewed rats' ('A Chinese Dinner'). More to the point, though, is that Stevenson's child persona also innocently acquiesces to the missionaries' rule that Christian children ought to be grateful that they are better provided for than children in heathen countries, that they ought to thank God they live in a 'happy Christian land — a favoured spot on earth' ('Do Not Forget the Heathen') and that they should sing the praises of being 'born on British ground' ('The Misery of the Heathen'). These are the sentiments that give birth to such exclamations in *A Child's Garden of Verses* as 'Oh, don't you wish that you were me?' ('Foreign Children').

Stevenson and the Missionary Imagination

It is important, of course, to remember that it is Stevenson's child persona, not Stevenson himself, who speaks the words of the verses and succumbs to and repeats the missionary clichés. These poems are not only autobiographical; they are about a child of Stevenson's imagination. With this in mind, it is interesting to note that in May, 1883 when Stevenson wrote to W. E. Henley concerning the possible illustrations for 'Foreign Children', he envisioned a child that was not completely himself. Rather, Stevenson pictured an aggressive English child 'pushing in the middle' while surrounded by

> foreign children looking at and showing each other marvels. The English child at the leeside of roast beef. The English child sitting thinking with his picture-books all round him, and the jing-a-ring of the foreign children, in miniature dancing over the picture-books. (*Letters* 4: 114-15)

The disparaging tone of Stevenson's instructions and, most particularly, the belligerent image of the English child 'pushing' in the center displays a critical distance from the naivete of the child persona. Obviously, in his thirties, Stevenson was better prepared to follow through on his observation as a six-year old that the second verse of a missionary hymn, 'I'm Not Too Young', was 'gross nonsense'. This incipient skepticism was reaffirmed when he added, 'it looks as if God only saw me when I sinned now I thought he saw me always' (Margaret Stevenson's Pocket Diaries, 24 February 1856: Beinecke ms. 7304).

By the time he was composing *A Child's Garden of Verses*, Stevenson had to negotiate the gaps between his early piety and his later skepticism if he was to write his verses. He had to create a kind of dialogue between the leaden tone of the missionary culture and the fierce, imaginative play of his childhood kingdom that fully enjoys the sight of a 'friendly cow' that defies the missionary agenda and like a satisfied cannibal eats the meadow flowers ('The Cow'). No longer is the field populated by cattle that Stevenson as a young child thought needed to be converted and have Bible stories read to them.

The Cow

The friendly cow all red and white,
        I love with all my heart:
She gives me cream with all her might,
        To eat with apple-tart.

She wanders lowing here and there,
        And yet she cannot stray,
All in the pleasant open air,
        The pleasant light of day;

And blown by all the winds that pass
        And wet with all the showers,
She walks among the meadow grass
        And eats the meadow flowers.

The poems of *A Child's Garden of Verses* bloom in the space of the meadow where the pastoral and the wilder elements of the landscape, the child, and the cow come together in verses that recognize not only the domesticity and sweetness of apple tarts but also the powerful impulsive wildness of a cow that gives with all her might, charges across the meadow, and is exposed to the winds blowing in the open air. The verses allow for the existence of the untamed child who intensely loves the cow and its freedom. Such layering defies the restrictions of the missionary imagination, breaks boundaries set up by the restraints of that monoculture, and allows Stevenson not only to soften the harshness of the missionary mandate but also to create a child persona that legitimizes the many intersecting conversations of childhood. Even though the missionary agenda prowls beneath the lines and occasionally speaks through the obedient child who behaves as the missionaries would have encouraged, and, in a mannerly way, refuses to speak an ugly word ('I never said an ugly word' from 'A Good Boy' l. 2), the dominant voice in the poems is a more complicated one.

Changing Perspectives

This configuration of the child in *A Child's Garden of Verses* reminds one of how important it was for Stevenson not to feel shut in by a system and confined by convention. His imagination yearned to travel beyond the suburban Edinburgh garden gate, and, as we have seen through his South Seas literature, enter territory that demands another way of understanding and perceiving one's surroundings. One of the pleasures of reading *A Child's Garden of Verses* is to come across poems that celebrate such a change in perspective. One I particularly enjoy is 'The

Little Land', in which the child, because he is a child, sees and hears what otherwise would escape his eye and ear:

> High bare walls, great bare floor;
> Great big knobs on drawer and door;
> Great big people perched on chairs.
> Stitching tucks and mending tears,
> Each a hill that I could climb,
> And talking nonsense all the time — (ll. 51-58)

The child's enjoyment in his different point of view anticipates Stevenson's own excitement when several years later he changed worlds by traveling to the South Seas. There, as I have pointed out in previous chapters, he realized he was stepping out of the familiar mythology and even spoke of himself as metaphorically putting on a diving suit and plunging into uncharted depths. (As if attempting to search for a new perspective, Stevenson actually did once don a diving suit.) Now a different paradigm takes him and the traveler outside the bounds of his own culture. No longer are the stereotypes, racial hierarchies, and European ways necessarily superior; neither the English child nor the Western perspective need be at the center. Even though he was not always able to do so, because of the prejudices of both his editors and his readership, Stevenson did seriously question whether the European is the more civilized. As we have seen, in texts like *A Footnote to History* he wanted to ask his readers to see life from the other side — as he had done when, as an amateur emigrant, he had left his own class and gone below deck into steerage.

As his directions for the illustration to 'Foreign Children' suggest, Stevenson had little time for a John Bull who, like the English child sitting to the leeward of a side of roast beef, insists on his beef and plum pudding, and imperiously dismisses those he dominates. In the essay 'The Foreigner at Home' Stevenson ridicules those who, stuck in their conceited ways, can admit nothing of value outside of themselves. Although he declares he loves her, he also takes a missionary named Miss Bird (one wonders if that is her actual name) for his target. He condemns her and her fellow missionaries 'who had come thousands of miles to change the faith of Japan and openly professed their ignorance of the religion they were trying to supplant', and damns her for her 'staggering pretension' when she declares 'the viands of Japan to be uneatable'. Miss Bird shares the Britannic folly that declares: 'We shall not eat the food of any foreigner; nor, when we have the chance, will we suffer him to eat of it himself' (6) — a sentiment that echoes the child's parroted disapproval of unfamiliar food in 'Foreign Children'.

This inclination to stretch and burst through the limits of one's surroundings urges its way past and across the clean, neat, and moralistic sentiments of 'Whole Duty of Children', 'A Good Boy', and 'Good and Bad Children' in *A Child's Garden of Verses*. The missionary imperative of identifying with children in foreign lands is transformed into a passion for the unfamiliar for its own sake. Throughout the other poems, Stevenson's child cranes his neck and climbs trees to peer farther and farther away. He crosses 'the dimpling river', sees where 'the grown-up river slips/ Into the sea among the ships' ('Foreign Lands'), steers a boat to Malabar ('Pirate Story'), travels to Eastern cities, to the Great Wall of China, and to the banks of the Nile ('Travel'), touches Ali Baba's rocks, and catches a glimpse of frozen Siberia ('Historical Associations'). Like the sun in 'The Sun Travels' that finds its way round the earth, and like the child and his friends in 'Keepsake Mill', he thinks of himself as breaking through the borders ('a sin without pardon') and crawling 'Out through the breach in the wall of the garden' to strange and enticing forbidden places.

Stevenson's Dialogical and Synthetic Imagination

Although Stevenson identified with the child who expands and alters his perspective and thinks it 'the pleasantest thing' to swing up in the air so he can see over the wall to where the 'Rivers and trees and cattle and all' spread over the countryside ('The Swing'), he also liked to go 'flying down again' and find his way back home. Many of the poems in *A Child's Garden of Verses* emphasize this wish to be home again ('Marching Song'), or celebrate the safe return to his room after steering in the dark ('My Bed is a Boat'), and relish the thought of returning 'out from the cold and gloom' into his 'warm and cheerful room' ('Northwest Passage').

As strong as was his longing to see beyond his immediate surroundings and attempt another point of view, just so powerful was his need for the familiar and the domestic. The movement of the child's swing in *A Child's Garden of Verses* follows the motion of Stevenson's imagination that endows his child persona with the ability to reconcile contradictory impulses and, in one graceful sweep, to yoke the domestic with the distant, the internal with the external.

    The Swing

    How do you like to go up in a swing,
        Up in the air so blue?
    Oh, I do think it the pleasantest thing
        Every a child can do!

    Up in the air and over the wall,
        Till I can see so wide,
    Rivers and trees and cattle and all
        Over the countryside—

    Till I look down on the garden green,
        Down on the roof so brown—
    Up in the air I go flying again,
        Up in the air and down!

In these verses, the child and his surroundings, like the cow, are both wild and familiar. Stevenson's instructions for the illustration of 'My Bed is a Boat' visualize this principle. In a letter to Henley, he proposes that the bed should sail, 'curtains and all' upon the sea, and that the child should awaken to find himself at home where the corner of the toilet is to be seen 'worked in to look like the pier' (*Letters* 4: 114). Throughout the poems, this blurring of boundaries and doubling continues so that a certain coziness or homeliness dwells among the pillaging and piracy: military banners ('Marching Song') are napkins, the fierce wind is a child ('The Wind'), his bed is a boat on which 'like a prudent sailor' he takes a 'slice of wedding-cake/ Perhaps a toy or two' ('My Bed is a Boat'), bats lie in bed at noon ('The Moon'), an icy hill and lake are 'frosted like a wedding cake' ('Winter-Time'), and the back of a sofa follows a forest track. In other verses, his storybook is the place where the 'roaring lions come to drink' ('The Land of Story-Books'), armies march in the embers of the domestic hearth ('Armies in the Fire'), and, of course, soldiers battle among the dips and folds of his counterpane ('The Land of Counterpane'). This imaginative binding later finds renewed expression in *The Beach of Falesá* in which, as Roslyn Jolly observes, a hybrid exists between the exotic, colonial and masculine spaces and 'the feminine realm of the domestic novel' ('Stevenson's "Sterling Domestic Fiction"' 463). Wiltshire, the protagonist, is as much committed to his marriage, family, and their ensuing domestic issues as he is preoccupied with the exoticism of his new situation.

Stevenson's dialogical imagination, that allows him to recognize the conjunction of the tame and the untamed, the familial and the undomesticated, the gentle and the boisterous, releases him from the strictures of the missionary context. As I have suggested, in spite of the missionaries' invitation to their followers to embrace a world outside of themselves, the missionaries' real tendency was to keep these brothers and sisters across the sea at bay and to shun their strange foods. In their scheme, children in foreign lands, even after being converted to Christianity, were inescapably alien. They were part of another landscape, of a society that was far away. And because of the distant land's associations with heathenism, cannibalism, infanticide, and other abhorrent practices, they remained irrevocably distinct.

Foreignness and Reciprocity

The missionaries' idea of foreignness helps one better appreciate Stevenson's contrary impulse to open up the imagination and to extend the familial self to internalize what is beyond it and bring it home. Even though Stevenson's child could be arrogant and participate in the imperialistic dream of wanting his own kingdom, as in 'Block City', where he will establish a city 'for me', in most of the verses there is little sense of his wanting to impose or export a way of life. Rather, there is a reciprocal dialogue, as in most of Stevenson's writing, an inclination to look beyond the self and, if not to import what he discovers there, to find parallels with his own experience and in that way to make a companion of it, not an alien. What lies outside of him he brings home by finding similarities between, say Scotland, its superstitions, its characters, and those of Polynesia. As I have mentioned in previous chapters, he finds parallels between Scotland's experience with the political power of England and Samoa where the colonial powers competed with and compromised its culture.

Stevenson clearly knows that what is supposed to be alien to him enriches and fulfills his being; it is really a part of him. Like the shadow in *A Child's Garden of Verses*, what seems to be outside of oneself is one's companion in one's own territory: it marches round the house and stares through one's own window-pane ('Shadow March' from 'Northwest Passage'). In the missionary literature, the gaze is not reciprocal. It is always the British Christian children who are given a 'peep' into the lives of foreign boys and girls, not the reverse. And, of course, like the shadow, foreignness intimately attaches itself to Stevenson's child; it 'goes in and out' with him and is 'very, very like' him 'from the heels up to the head' ('My Shadow'). What appears to be remote and alien is but an extension of himself, and is not something, as in the missionary and colonial agenda, that has to be made to resemble him.

The Idea of Duty

This reciprocity that is integral to Stevenson's imagination distinguishes his attitude from yet another aspect of the missionary sensibility. Echoing the nurse in Blake's *Songs of Experience* who demands that the children on the green come home, for their days are 'wasted in play', the missionary culture, when it addressed children, emphasized duty above all else and repudiated idleness and play as if they were the devil himself. Young people were instructed to sing hymns asking the Lord to give them grace 'that I may ever walk with Thee;/ And ever do Thy will;/ That in each duty, great or small, I may be faithful still'. ('A Child May Be Useful'). Children were commanded to 'Rise! for the day is passing', and required to read such poems as 'Play and Work' or Isaac Watt's well-known hymn 'How doth the little busy bee/ Improve each shining hour' (*Divine Songs for Children* 1715), later parodied by Lewis Carroll in 'How doth the little crocodile' (*Alice in Wonderland*).

> Who'll come and play with me under the tree?
> My sisters have left me alone;
> Oh, sweet little sparrow, come hither to me,
> And play with me while they are gone.
>
> Oh, no, little lady, I can't come indeed,
> I've no time to idle away;
> I've got all my dear little children to feed,
> And my nest to new cover with hay.

Pretty bee, do not buzz about over the flower,
But come and play with me, do;
The sparrow won't come and stay with me an hour,
But say, pretty bee, will not you?

Oh, no, little lady, for do you not see
Those must work who would prosper and thrive?
If I play, they would call me a sad idle bee,
And perhaps turn me out of the hive.

Stop, stop little ant, do not run off so fast,
Wait with me a little and play;
I hope I shall find a companion at last,
You are not so busy as they.

Oh, no, little lady, I can't stay with you,
We're not made to play but to labour;
I always have something or other to do,
If not for myself, for a neighbour.

What, then! Have they all some employment but me,
Who lie lounging here like a dunce?
Oh, then, like the ant and the sparrow and bee,
I'll go to my duties at once. ('Play and Work')

Obviously Stevenson's child does not conform to this standard. Although sensitive to the expectation that he should say what is true, when spoken to, and 'behave mannerly at table' — 'At least as far as he is able' — and, at times, attentive to a 'birdie' that cocks his head and says to the sleeping child, 'Ain't you 'shamed, you sleepy-head!' ('Time to Rise'), Stevenson's persona does not always heed the strident voice of duty. Rather, for this child and for Stevenson, it is play, and not play as conceived as the sin of idleness, that rules supreme. For them, play has no goal or purpose other than itself and is not entangled in the web of laziness and neglect of one's responsibilities. Throughout *A Child's Garden of Verses*, most of the poems, like 'My Kingdom', 'Block City', 'The Little Land', 'Pirate Story', 'At the Sea-Side', 'Bed in Summer', 'A Good Play', and 'The Hayloft', celebrate its passion and excitement. There is absolutely none of the guilt that comes with the missionary agenda. Obligations, productivity, and prostrating oneself to a higher authority are just not a part of his persona's consciousness. In the land of play, the only will is the child's, to seize the opportunities of the moment; adults are only on the periphery. They drift in and out or sweep through the door. For Stevenson's youngster, to buckle up in armor, to don a sword, and to march double-quick was not to be a Christian soldier or a member of a missionary band but to be immersed in the thrill of pretence that simply takes one round the village and home again ('The Marching Song'). The movement of the playmates is directed by the children and circles in its own pleasure. There is no point, no duty, mapping and superintending it. There is only the enviable state of being a child who, either alone or with allies, can take another's part and internalize his role.

Stevenson is nostalgic for the child because, unlike the adult, he is not haunted by a sense of duty[13] and can swallow 'the most staring incongruities' ('Child's Play' 157): a bed becomes a boat, a sofa a mountain, the stairs a ship, and a wicket a harbour. Adults cannot readily accept substitutes: they desire 'the thing itself' ('Child's Play' 160). One cannot help but contrast the child's ability and Stevenson's delight in it to the missionary literalness that could leave nothing to the imagination. When British Sunday Schools put on missionary exhibitions and pageants, children not only read scripted parts directed by adults but also wore imported attire, carried exotic curios, and acted on platforms burdened with confiscated idols, all sent back by foreign missionaries.[14]

The Movement of Children

The fluidity of Stevenson's and the child's imagination that dwells within a landscape where the land drifts into the sea and the night becomes day also finds expression in the movements of *A Child's Garden of Verses*. Rather than sticking to the formulaic sentiments and the horizontal march of the missionary line, Stevenson choreographs his verses and his thoughts so that they move like a child. They do not direct his motion or threaten to trip him with the weight of a sinful soul (as the missionaries had once censored the native dances in the South Seas). When Stevenson initially thought of *A Child's Garden of Verses*, he fancied a frontispiece of 'a little ring of children' dancing to the songs of the tin whistle (an instrument that Stevenson himself enjoyed playing). Throughout the poems young boys and girls whimsically bend their limbs in verses about delight, fear, loneliness, adventure, and wistful longing. The poems see-saw and swing high and back down again through the swaying of their metered feet and their alternating patterns of sun and dark, winter and summer, and rising and going to bed. The reader and child ride the lines, as if responding to the waves of the imaginary boat sailing on the meadow in 'Pirate Story', or, at times, like the three playmates, suddenly burst away to make a 'quick' escape from the charging and roaring cattle. Mimicking these irregular, sporadic motions, the child's shadow either jumps, shoots up, or stays behind. All these gestures spiral through *A Child's Garden of Verses* and counteract the deadly conventions and regularities of the Christianized pagan child who lies inert, cultivating the sanctity of his sickness, and comes, eventually, to a full stop.

The dance of Stevenson's children creates a circle of continuity and possibility so that the exciting wind gallops away and comes back again, the river flows forever, stars go round in the child's mind, and children join hands in dances that unite them. The movement of *A Child's Garden of Verses* recalls not only the essay 'Child's Play' but also the pleasure Stevenson had observing children dance in a French hotel and skipping rope in Hampstead. In 'Notes on the Movement of Young Children' he reminisces about watching little girls coming out into a cleared space on the ballroom floor and giving themselves over to a variety of moods and melodies with 'wonderful combinations and variations of movement'. Not one displays any 'be-end of orientation and conformity'. He delights in watching how suddenly 'an excess of energy' breaks the rhythm of the music as if 'their light bodies could endure no longer the restraint of regulated dance' (350, 352, 354). He is particularly drawn to the irregularity. He admits that when watching one child skipping rope, he could not help but be taken in by her imperfect motions and found himself moving his shoulders as if to imitate her — a reaction that seems to anticipate his writing of verses that imitate the child and attempt to get back into its body. The poems move sympathetically to the erratic motions of a child; their choreography gives voice to the rhythms of his young subjects. In a letter to Edmund Gosse, written in Bournemouth 12 March 1885, Stevenson notes how his verses form a regiment but hardly like the one in 'Onward Christian Soldiers':

> They [*A Child's Garden of Verses*] look ghastly in the cold light of print; but there is something nice in the little ragged regiment for all; the blackguards seem to me to smile, to have a kind of childish treble note that sounds in my ears freshly: not song, if you will, but a child's voice. (*Letters* 5: 85)

Stevenson choreographs these voices and rushes of energy so he may gather their melodies within the garden of his memory and let his persona romp on the lawn, haylofts, and meadows of Coniton Manse where Stevenson himself played with his cousins. This is the garden that assembles all that flourishes and grows within it, yet has walls to see over and breaches to peep through. It is an enchanted ground that in no way resembles the columned space of the missionary pages featuring 'The Children's Garden', where young folk, like Bertie or Alfred, plant potatoes and harvest a hundred cucumbers to raise money for missionary purposes ('Bertie and his Missionary Garden'). In the missionary garden, the purpose is to prevent idleness and to get young folk to spread the seed of Jesus's message. It is a place for cucumbers, not flowers.

A Multiplicity of Voices

When *A Child's Garden of Verses* assembles Stevenson's memories of his own boyhood, it reflects a self-awareness that further distinguishes Stevenson's point of view from the missionaries' perspective. For all the missionaries' talk of a guiding light that illuminates the way, their magazine articles display a terrible blindness that fails to recognize anything outside its own narrow purview. These publications represent an insult to many of the missionaries out in the field who, as we have seen in the first and third chapters, were fully prepared to deal with perspectives other than their own. *A Child's Garden of Verses* recognizes the critical presence of others: to begin with, the critical eye with which the child observes adults. In turn, as an adult, Stevenson will often look back from a distance and watch the movement of children, as he had done in a hotel in France. At other times, he must abandon the child entirely and become the experienced omniscient voice who, in 'Summer Sun', can speak generally about the sun as the gardener of the world, of good and bad children, and of unseen playmates. These various points of view criss-cross each other in the verses.

Sometimes these voices are tempered and shadowed by yet another group of perspectives: a set of observers from Stevenson's past who look over the shoulder of his verses, sit behind the lines, and potentially pass judgment on their accuracy. Stevenson names these figures in his dedicatory poem and the group of envoys at the end of the volume. In the prefatory poem to Alison Cunningham, 'From Her Boy', Stevenson addresses his childhood nurse and not only recalls his childhood sickness but also reaches out to young readers who might now be suffering as he had done: 'And grant it, Heaven, that all who read/ May find as dear a nurse at need,/ And every child who lists my rhyme,/ In the bright, fireside, nursery clime/ May hear it in as kind a voice/ As made my childish days rejoice.' At the end of *A Child's Garden of Verses* the multiplicity of voices increases with the set of 'Envoys' written to his cousins Willie and Henrietta, to his mother, to his Auntie, to another cousin Minnie, to his Name-Child, and, finally, 'To Any Reader'. These individuals comprise an audience of spectators who both see and speak to his past, present, and some unknown, distant time. Stevenson clearly senses that they will read his verses, recognize themselves, and either confirm the authenticity of his poems and his memories of a moment or think the same of 'another child, far far away' ('To Any Reader'). Their presence hovers about the verses — Minnie's especially, for Stevenson asks her to 'Reach down a hand, my dear, and take/ These rhymes for old acquaintance' sake!' ('To Minnie').

The Single Voice

A reader could potentially go astray among this plethora of prospects and utterances: those of the moral child; the spontaneous child; the authoritative child; the indifferent child; the adventurous child; the frightened child, and 'all the thousand things that children are' ('To Willie and Henrietta') as well as the cousins who are now grown up and are themselves parents; the mother; the memory of the Aunt; little Louis Sanchez (Fanny's sister's child); the distant, unknown reader; the occasional impersonal narrator who stands outside the child's room, and, of course, the adult Stevenson who acts as a surrogate for the child as well as for the memory of himself as a young boy. However, the charm of *A Child's Garden of Verses* is that the child persona manages to dominate all of these so that what prevails in the reader's consciousness is the impression of a single voice, and certainly not the specter of the various external presences that frame the poems.

What one really remembers is the solitary child who is pleased with his own life, who makes no excuses for himself, and who is thoroughly wrapped up in the moment or in the memory of it. The child's voice reverberates with the pleasures of enumerating his treasures (some nuts, a whistle, a stone, and chisel: 'My Treasures'), building a city out of blocks ('Rain may keep raining, and others go roam,/ But I can be happy and building at home': 'Block City'), wandering through an imaginary forest ('The Little Land'), creating a kingdom ('My Kingdom'), clambering in the haystack ('The Hayloft'), looking down on the garden green ('The Swing'), or steering through the dark ('My Bed is a Boat').

For all Stevenson's inclination to look beyond himself, the voice he gives his surrogate child is one that usually reflects a blissfully self-contained world where anything else is either irrelevant or a pleasant fantasy. In 'A Good Play', for instance, the child who builds a ship upon the stairs and who carries on sailing, even when 'Tom fell out and hurt his knee', is oblivious to a reader, to anything or anyone observing him. His enjoyment is engrossing and all-encompassing. And so are his fancies about looking forward to growing older so that he can tell other girls and boys 'Not to meddle' with his toys ('Looking Forward'). He speaks from within enclosures where confidence, comfort, and a harmless selfishness and a spontaneous generosity permeate the poems' lines. At the same time, as sanctuaries, the verses give the child the means and the freedom by which to venture beyond himself or his boundaries and to admit what otherwise might be excluded or regarded with suspicion. Moreover the child's voice tempers whatever aggression or condescension might be lurking within the territory of the verses, including echoes of the missionary directives. For instance, when he asks the foreign child, 'Oh! don't you wish that you were me' ('Foreign Children'), the tone is more generous and sympathetic than prescriptive. And when, in 'A Good Play', Tom falls, the accident is neither painful nor obtrusive; nor is it threatening in the playful and gentle milieu of this book. Stevenson lets his children be the true arbiters of an imagination in which the criterion of value is the fullness of the pleasure achieved. His children and his poems are a tonic that increases one's zest for life. For these young boys and girls that is the true morality.[15]

Throughout *A Child's Garden of Verses*, the regularity of the four-line stanzas and easy rhymes creates a simplicity that complements the primacy of the child's single voice. This uniformity rounds out each of the poems with a gentle closure, calms the lines' restlessness, and cancels or quiets the dialogue of voices. The concluding lines place the child's head on its pillow, take the child back home, reassure him that the spreading circles in the stream 'Will clear by-and-by' ('Looking-Glass River'), and let the reader share both the child's and the adult Stevenson's confidence that other little children will bring his boat ashore.

In this manner, the poems tender a safe harbor not only for the child but also for Stevenson so that he can preserve and stay in touch with the security and the landscape of his childhood. Protected by these poems, as an adult, he can now travel to foreign lands where he may, like the child, see 'apart and high', and, therefore, escape not only his sickbed but also, if need be, the blinding shadows of the colonial night. Like the conflicting highlander and lowlander who cease their quarrel when they meet abroad (in the essay 'The Foreigner at Home'), the various voices in these poems come to rest within the alien land of the verses and each embraces the other to form a closure and create a feeling of solidity.

Looking-Glass River

Smooth it glides upon its travel,
    Here a wimple, there a gleam—
      O the clean gravel!
      O the smooth stream!

Sailing blossoms, silver fishes,
    Paven pools as clear as air—
      How a child wishes
      To live down there!

We can see our coloured faces
    Floating on the shaken pool
      Down in cool places,
      Dim and very cool;

Till a wind or water wrinkle,
    Dipping marten, plumping trout,
      Spreads in a twinkle
      And blots all out.

See the rings pursue each other;
    All below grows black as night,
      Just as if mother
      Had blown out the light!

Patience, children, just a minute—
    See the spreading circles die;
      The stream and all in it
      Will clear by-and-by.

Conclusion

Stevenson's *A Child's Garden of Verses* reminds one that it takes the foreign to create a sense of community. We watch this principle at work as Stevenson's imagination, looking beyond the structure of the garden wall, brings what is outside back in to create a gathering of children. As the previous discussion suggests, Stevenson's mind needs to be both inside and outside a system; it requires both the wild and the domestic; it demands both the gentle and the aggressive; listens to a multiplicity of voices; likes to take another's part, but most of all it understands that one is never complete unless one recognizes that what is beyond oneself — what is alien to oneself — is part of and necessary to the community of the self: an awareness, of course, which the child achieves naturally. As I have pointed out, although the missionary culture occasionally paid lip service to this truth, it could never bring itself genuinely to accept what Stevenson embraced. Nor could the missionary culture relax into the child's voice. The way in which Stevenson plays with the missionary ethic in *A Child's Garden of Verses* helps one to understand how his bold but tolerant imagination enabled him later to cope with the novelty and the difficulties of his life in the South Seas.

Notes

1. At the Huntington Library, see HM 2404 ('Notebook Kept during Illness'). There, between verses, Stevenson has pencilled in such notes as 'I wonder if we might not have the chloral mixture in smaller doses to be taken more frequently in case of persistence? so that one could, in case of necessity, take a dose every 30 minutes.' A few lines later he asks, 'I think I might have a bit of pudding?' Before writing a draft of 'Farewell', he comments, 'You know the remarks of no doctor mean anything in my case; any case is a sport, I may die tonight or live till 60.'

2. In Hyères, during the summer of 1883, Stevenson almost reverted to his childhood when he thought of sending for Alison Cunningham, his childhood nurse, to help look after him.

3. For this fact about Kate Greenaway's influence, see, among other critics who mention the fact, Elizabeth Waterston. 'Going for Eternity: *A Child's Garden of Verses*'. *Canadian Children's Literature*. 93-96.4 (1999): 5-10. It is interesting to note that after Stevenson visited the leper colony in Hawaii, he arranged to have Kate Greenaway's poems sent to the Reverend Sister Maryanne for the girls of whom she had charge. See letter of 6 June 1889 to Edward L. Burlingame (*Letters* 6: 316).

4. The Stevenson family were parishioners of St. Stephen's Presbyterian Church in Edinburgh.

5. I am indebted to Roger Swearingen's study of Stevenson's prose reading for much of this information concerning Stevenson's early reading. See *The Early Literary Career of Robert Louis Stevenson 1850-1881: A Bibliographical Study, Volume One*. 1970. Bound and available at the Beinecke Rare Book and Manuscript Library, Yale U.

6. In a 23 or 24 March 1889 letter to the Reverend Francis Williams Damon, one of the missionaries of the American Board of Missions, Stevenson wrote, 'From my childhood I have been thrown much in contact with Mission workers, and count among them several of my friends' (*Letters* 6: 270).

7. Part of the missionary agenda was a campaign against slavery. The missionary periodicals often named the Arabs as being the main culprits. According to Margaret Stevenson's pocket diaries, when she told the young Stevenson about the way Americans used their slaves, he replied, with a good missionary phrase, 'I think God might send them a punishment' (21 March 1854: Beinecke ms. 7304).

8. The fragmentary lines are in an early copybook at the Beinecke Rare Book and Manuscript Library, Yale U.

9. It is interesting to note that several of the children and nephews and nieces of Stevenson's grandfather, the Reverend Lewis Balfour — a Scotch Presbyterian minister at Colinton since 1823 — entered the Indian civil service.

10. For an example of 'Black and White', see CWML G4S9 at The LMS Archives. SOAS, U of London. By the turn of the nineteenth century this impulse to connect with young folks abroad had occasioned Sunday School pageants that displayed Samoan village scenes, panoramas of the South Seas, and plays like the one entitled 'League of the World's Children' featuring South Sea, African, and Chinese children as well as Red Indians.

11. For examples of these letters to Adelaide Boodle, see letters 2447 (14 August 1892) and 2453 (4 September 1892) in Vol. 7 of Booth and Mehew. Eds. *The Letters of Robert Louis Stevenson*.

12. In all fairness, it should be acknowledged that after the turn of the century, there were missionaries who rebelled against this attitude. In a LMS pamphlet by Vera E. Walker and C. M. Preston entitled *Island Play Hours (South Seas and Papua)* published by the LMS (n.d.) and available at the LMS Archives at SOAS, U of London, the authors emphasize that 'If children are to help the work of missions it must be because of understanding and genuine sympathy with the people of foreign lands, and without a sense of British superiority in all things! Nothing creates this right attitude in boys and girls so much as a realization that in games and toys and handicrafts and all things that normal children care for, we have much in common with our brothers and sisters, and that in some things they beat us' (3).

13. Henry James once spoke of Stevenson as being 'a shameless Bohemian haunted with duty'. See *Henry James and Robert Louis Stevenson: A Record of Friendship and Criticism*. Ed. Janet Adam Smith. London: 1948. 257.

14. In the LMS Archives, there are pamphlets on how to produce Sunday School exhibitions and pageants. There are also copies of plays published especially by the LMS for Sunday School productions. One of these pamphlets is entitled: *Isles of the Seas: Exhibition and Pageant*. The scenes are of the South Seas: Samoan Village Scene, Panorama of the South Seas, Illuminated Map, and Marine Section containing some fine models of native canoes. One of the plays is entitled *Chalmer's Tableaux*. The characters are: James Chalmers, Mrs. Chalmers, Tomkins, Kirikeu, Bolvagi, Manuequ, Beata, Woman in Dancing Rig, Emai (the Sorcerer), Goropo, and a Crowd of Native Men and Women. Another of the plays is *League of the World's Children* by T. Wemyss Reid. The characters are: Mother, Father, Jack, Mary, and Red Indian, South Sea, African, and Chinese children.

15. These thoughts were shared in a conversation with Irving Massey.

Bibliography

Altick, Richard. *The Shows of London*. Cambridge, MA: Harvard UP, 1978.

Anderson, Benedict. *Imagined Communities*. Rev. ed. London: Verso, 1983.

Armstrong, Nancy. *Fiction in the Age of Photography: The Legacy of British Realism*. Cambridge, MA: Harvard UP, 1999.

Balfour, Graham. *The Life of Robert Louis Stevenson*. 2 vols. New York: Scribner's, 1904.

Barthes, Roland. *Camera Lucida: Reflections on Photography*. Trans. Richard Howard. New York: Hill and Wang, 1981.

Bartlett, Frederick C. *Remembering: A Study in Experimental and Social Psychology*. Cambridge: Cambridge UP, 1904.

Bell, Ian. *Dreams of Exile: Robert Louis Stevenson: A Biography*. New York: Holt, 1992.

'Bertie and his Missionary Garden.' *The Missionary News* 1 January 1885: 12.

Bingham, Hiram. A. M. *A Residence of Twenty-One Years in the Sandwich Islands; or the Civil; Religious, and Political History of those Islands comprising a particular view of the Missionary Operation connected with the introduction and progress of Christianity and Civilization among the Hawaiian People*. Canandaigua, NY: Goodwin, 1855.

Brown, George. *An Autobiography: A Narrative of Forty-eight Years Residence and Travel in Samoa, New Britain, New Ireland, New Guinea, and the Solomon Islands*. London: Hodder, 1908.

Buzacott, Rev. A. and Rev. J. P. Sunderland. *Mission Life in the Islands of the Pacific Being a Narrative of the Life and Labours of the Rev. A. Buzacott, Missionary of Rarotonga*. London: John Snow, 1866.

Calder, Jenni. *Robert Louis Stevenson: A Life Study*. New York: Oxford UP, 1980.

Catalogue of the Missionary Museum, Austin Friars; including Specimens in Natural History, Various Idols of Heathen Nations, Dresses, Manufactures, Domestic Utensils, Instruments of War etc. etc. etc. London: W. Phillips, 1826.

Catalogue of the Missionary Museum, Bloomfield Street, Finsbury; including Specimens in Natural History, Various Idols of Heathen Nations, Dresses, Manufactures, Domestic Utensils, Instruments of War etc. etc. etc. [1845?].

Chalmers, James. 'An Adventurous Journey in the Gulf of Papua'. *The Chronicle of the London Missionary Society* March, 1893: 52-57.

—— 'Cook Islands 1875 June-July. Rarotonga. Visit to out stations'. Ms. 163 LMS Archives. SOAS, U of London.

—— 'Explorations in South-Eastern New Guinea'. *Proceedings of the Royal Geographical Society and Monthly Record of Geography* ns 9 (February, 1887): 600-608. Reprinted by London: Clowes: 1-16. (Read at evening meeting 17 January 1887.)

—— Ms. 162 LMS Archives. SOAS, U of London.

—— *Pioneer Life and Work in New Guinea 1877-1894*. London: Religious Tract Society, 1895.

'A Child May Be Useful'. *Gleanings for the Young*. British and Foreign Bible Society. 1881: 16.

'A Chinese Dinner'. *The Illustrated Missionary News* 1 January 1885: 12.

The Chronicle of the London Missionary Society ns 2 (1893): 88-90.

Churchward, William B. *My Consulate in Samoa: A Record of Four Years' Sojourn in the Navigators Islands, with personal experiences of King Malietoa Laupepa, his country, and his men*. London: Richard Bentley, 1887.

Clarke, William Edward. 23 June 1891 LMS Archives. SOAS, U of London.

—— Letters to Rev. R. Wardlaw Thompson, Foreign Secretary of the LMS. 4 December 1888; 21 April 1889. Box 40 LMS Archives. SOAS, U of London.

—— 'Reminiscences of Robert Louis Stevenson'. Odds-Box LMS Archives. SOAS, U of London.

Claxton, Arthur E. 'Island Life at the Antipodes'. *The Chronicle of the London Missionary Society* October, 1872: 432.

—— 'A Samoan Boys' School'. *The Missionary Magazine and Chronicle* 1889: 317-18.

—— 'Stevenson as I Knew Him'. LMS Pamphlet, 1908. LMS Archives. SOAS, U of London.

'Column for the Young'. *The Missionary News* 14 July 1866: 94.

Cumming, C. F. Gordon. *A Lady's Cruise in a French Man-of-War*. Edinburgh: Blackwood, 1882.

Davies, S. H. and J. Marriott. Ms. 180 LMS Archives. SOAS, U of London.

Davis, J. Barnard. 'A Few Notes upon the Hair and Some other Peculiarities of Oceanic Races'. *Journal of Anthropological Institute* 2 (1873): 96-101.

'Discovery of Two New Rivers in British New Guinea'. *Proceedings of the Royal Geographical Society*. ns 9 (1887): 600-608.

'Do Not Forget the Heathen'. *The Juvenile Missionary Magazine* 19.221 (October, 1861): 240.

The Earl and the Doctor. South Sea Bubbles. London: Bentley, 1872.

Edmond, Rod. *Representing the South Pacific: Colonial Discourse from Cook to Gaugin*. Cambridge: Cambridge UP, 1997.

Edwards, Elizabeth, ed. *Anthropology and Photography: 1860-1920*. New Haven: Yale UP, 1992.

Elias, Frank. *Boy's Adventure in the South Seas or with Williams in Erromanga*. London: Religious Tract Society, n.d.

Ellis. William. *Polynesian Researches, during a residence of nearly six years in the South Sea Islands; including description of the natural history and scenery of the islands -- with remarks on the history, mythology, traditions, governments, arts, manners, and customs of the inhabitants*. 2 vols. London: Fisher, 1829.

'The Exeter Hall Meeting'. *The Missionary Repository for Youth* 4 (1842): 70.

'For the Young'. *The Missionary News* 1 August 1867: 98.

'For the Young'. *The Missionary News* 1 October 1867: 122.

'The Fourth of July in Micronesia'. *Missionary Herald* 82 (1886): 523.

From Saranac to the Marquesas and Beyond. Some Letters Written by Mrs. M. I. Stevenson to Miss Jane Whyte Balfour During 1881-1888. Ed. Marie Clothilde Balfour. New York: Scribner's, 1903.

Furnas, J. C. *Voyage to Windward: The Life of Robert Louis Stevenson*. New York: Sloane, 1951.

Geertz, Clifford. *The Interpretation of Cultures*. New York: Basic Books, 1973.

Gill, William Wyatt. *From Darkness to Light in Polynesia with Illustrative Clan Songs.* London: The Religious Tract Society, 1894.

—— *Historical Sketches of Savage Life in Polynesia with Illustrative Clan Songs.* Wellington: Didsbury, 1880.

—— *Life in the Southern Isles or Scenes and Incidents in the South Pacific and New Guinea.* London: The Religious Tract Society, [1876].

Gilson, R. P. *Samoa 1830 to 1900: The Politics of a Multi-Cultural Community.* Melbourne: Oxford UP, 1970.

Gleanings for the Young ns 5.6 (June, 1893).

Gunson, Neil. *Messengers of Grace: Evangelical Missionaries in the South Seas 1797-1860.* Oxford: Oxford UP, 1978.

Harris, G. A. Ms. 169 LMS Archives. SOAS, U of London.

—— 'Mangaia Jan. 13, 1891'. Box 40 LMS Archives. SOAS, U of London.

'Hearty Wish'. *The Juvenile Missionary Magazine* ns 1.50 (July, 1866): 8.

Hedley, Charles. *The Atoll of Funafuti, Ellice Group: Its Zoology, Botany, Ethnology, and General Structure.* Sydney, 1896.

Herbert, Christopher. *Culture and Anomie: Ethnographic Imagination in the Nineteenth Century.* Chicago: U of Chicago P, 1991.

Hickson, Sydney. *A Naturalist in North Celebes: A Narrative of Travels in Minahassa, the Sangir and Talaut Islands, with Notices of the Fauna, Flora and Ethnology of the Districts Visited.* London: John Murray, 1889.

Hillier, Robert Irwin. *The South Seas Fiction of Robert Louis Stevenson.* New York: Lang, 1989.

'An Indian Child Dying'. *The Missionary News* 15 February 1865: 34.

'An Infant's Prayer in Africa'. *The Juvenile Missionary Magazine* 2.9 (February, 1845): 52.

J.M.B. *He and She from O'er the Sea: Missionary Recitations and Hymns.* London: LMS n.d.

Jolly, Roslyn. 'Robert Louis Stevenson and Samoan History: Crossing the Roman Wall'. *Crossing Cultures: Essays on Literature and Culture of the Asia-Pacific.* Ed. Bruce Bennett, Jeff Doyle and Nandan Satendra, London: Skoob, 1996.

—— ed. *South Sea Tales by Robert Louis Stevenson.* Oxford: Oxford UP, 1996.

—— 'Stevenson's "Sterling Domestic Fiction", "The Beach of Falesá"'. *The Review of English Studies* ns 50.200 (1999): 463-82.

The Juvenile Missionary Magazine 1 October 1844: 152.

Kingsley, Mary Henrietta. *Travels in West Africa: Congo Français, Corisco and Cameroons.* 3rd ed. London: Frank Cass, 1965.

Kingston, William Henry Giles. *The Cruise of the Dainty or Rovings in the Pacific.* London: Society for Promoting Christian Knowledge, 1880.

Koskinen, Aarne A. *Missionary Influence as a Political Factor in the Pacific Islands.* Helsinki, 1953.

La Farge, John. *Reminiscences of the South Seas.* London: Richards, 1914.

Lamb, Jonathan, Vanessa Smith and Nicholas Thomas, eds. *Exploration and Exchange: A South Seas Anthology 1680-1900.* Chicago: U of Chicago P, 2000.

Lamont, E. H. *Wild Life among the Pacific Islanders.* London: Hurst, 1867.

Lawson, Barbara. *Collected Curios: Missionary Tales from the South Seas.* Montreal: McGill U Libraries, 1994.

Letters from Samoa. 1891-1895. Mrs. M. I. Stevenson. Ed. Marie Clothilde Balfour. New York: Scribner's, 1906.

The Letters of Robert Louis Stevenson. 8 vols. Eds. Bradford A. Booth and Ernest Mehew. Vols. 4-8. New Haven: Yale UP, 1994, 1995.

London Missionary Society Archives. Box 42. SOAS, U of London.

—— Correspondence. SOAS, U of London.

Lovett, Richard. *James Chalmers: His Autobiography and Letters.* London: The Religious Tract Society, 1902.

Marriott, John. 'Aug. 11 - Oct. 23, 1883: Samoa -- from Apia to Tokelau, Ellice and Gilbert Islands in the John Williams'. Box 12 ms. 80 LMS Archives. SOAS, U of London.

Massey, Irving. 'Introduction'. *Particularism.* Spec. issue of *Criticism* 32.3 (1990): 275-93.

Masson, Rosaline, ed. *I Can Remember Robert Louis Stevenson.* Enlarged ed. London: Chambers, 1925.

McKenzie, Kenneth S. 'Robert Louis Stevenson and Samoa, 1889-1894'. Diss. Dalhousie U, 1974.

Menikoff, Barry. *Robert Louis Stevenson and 'The Beach of Falesá': A Study in Victorian Publishing.* Stanford: Stanford UP, 1984.

'The Misery of the Heathen'. *Children's Missionary Hymn-Book.* London: John Snow, 1842.

Missionary Magazine and Chronicle 33 (April, 1855): 70.

'Missionary Meeting at the Samoas'. *The Missionary Magazine and Chronicle* 3 December 1840: 178.

'Missionary Methods in the Pacific'. *The Chronicle of the London Missionary Society* May, 1890: 149.

'Mission Work in the Pacific'. *The Chronicle of the London Missionary Society* March, 1890: 77.

Moors, H. J. *With Stevenson in Samoa.* London: T. Fisher Unwin, 1911.

Moss, Frederick J. *Through Atolls and Islands of the Great South Sea.* London: Sampson Low, 1889.

Murray, A. W. *The Martyrs of Polynesia: Memorials of Missionaries, Native Evangelists, and Native Converts, Who Have Died by the Hand of Violence, from 1796 to 1871.* London: Elliot Stock, 1885.

Neider, Charles, ed. *Our Samoan Adventure: Fanny and Robert Louis Stevenson. With a Three-year Diary by Mrs. Stevenson.* New York: Harper, 1955.

Newell, James. E. Box 9 LMS Archives. SOAS, U of London.

—— CWM Personal-Special, Box 6 LMS Archives. SOAS, U of London.

The Optical Magic Lantern Journal 2 (1 August 1890).

Osbourne, Lloyd. 'Diary for 1889'. Beinecke ms. 72-78 Vault. Beinecke Rare Book and Manuscript Library, Yale U.

—— *An Intimate Portrait of R..L.S.* New York: Scribner's, 1924.

—— Letters. Beinecke ms. 5267. Beinecke Rare Book and Manuscript Library, Yale U.

'Play and Work'. *The Juvenile Missionary Magazine* ns 1.4 (April, 1867).

Powell, T.and G. Pratt. 'Some Folk Songs and Myths from Samoa' (read before the Royal Society of N.S.W. 1890).

Prout, Ebenezer. *Memoirs of the Life of the Reverend John Williams, Missionary to Polynesia.* London: John Snow, 1846.

Ratzel, Friedrich. *The History of Mankind.* Trans. A. J. Butler. Introd. E. B. Tylor. 3 vols. Vols. 1-2. London: Macmillan, 1896-97.

Read, Charles H. 'On the Origin and Sacred Character of Certain Ornaments of the S. E. Pacific'. London: Harrison, 1891. Reprinted in *Journal of the Anthropological Institute* 21.

Rev. of *The Missionary Reward or, the Success of the Gospel in the Pacific*, by George Pritchard. *The Quarterly Review* 94.187: 180-82.

'Round About Apia — Samoa'. *The Chronicle of the London Missionary Society* September, 1890: 279.

Ryan, James R. *Picturing Empire: Photography and the Visualization of the British Empire*. Chicago: U of Chicago P, 1997.

St. Johnston, Alfred. *Camping among Cannibals*. London: Macmillan, 1883.

Sandison, Alan. 'Robert Louis Stevenson: A Modernist in the South Seas'. *The Durham University Journal* 52.1 (January, 1991): 45-51.

'Sketches for Girls'. *The Illustrated Missionary News* 1 December 1880: 139.

Smith, Vanessa. *Literary Culture and the Pacific: Nineteenth-Century Textual Encounters*. Cambridge: Cambridge UP, 1998.

'South Sea Island Evangelised'. *Juvenile Missionary Magazine of the United Presbyterian Church* 7 (1851): 144.

Stair, John B. *Old Samoa or Flotsam and Jetsam from the Pacific Ocean*. London: The Religious Tract Society, 1897.

Stevenson, Fanny. *The Cruise of the 'Janet Nichol'. Mrs. Robert Louis Stevenson's Diary of a South Sea Cruise*. New York: Scribner's, 1914.

—— Letters. Beinecke ms. 638. The Beinecke Rare Book and Manuscript Library, Yale U.

—— Mss. letters. Beinecke ms. 3670. Beinecke Rare Book and Manuscript Library, Yale U.

—— and Robert Louis Stevenson. *Our Samoan Adventure*. Ed. Charles Neider. New York: Harper, 1955.

Stevenson, Margaret. *From Saranac to the Marquesas and Beyond*. Ed. Marie Clothilde Balfour. New York: Scribner's, 1903.

—— *Letters from Samoa 1891-1895*. Ed. Marie Clothilde Balfour. New York: Scribner's, 1906.

—— Pocket Diaries. Beinecke ms. 7304. The Beinecke Rare Book and Manuscript Library, Yale U.

Stevenson, Robert Louis. *The Beach of Falesá*. Ed. Barry Menikoff. Stanford: Stanford UP, 1984.

—— *A Child's Garden of Verses*. New York: Airmont, 1969.

—— 'Child's Play'. *Virginibus Puerisque and Other Papers*. London: Chatto & Windus, 1905. 151-66.

—— 'The Circumnavigation of Tutuila'. HM 2413. The Huntington Library. San Marino, CA.

—— *The Complete Shorter Fiction*. Ed. Peter Stoneley. New York: Carroll, 1991.

—— 'Copy of Journal in Tutuila'. Ms. 9893. National Library of Scotland. Edinburgh, Scotland.

—— and Lloyd Osbourne. *The Ebb-Tide*. Ed. David Daiches. London: J. M. Dent, 1994.

—— and Lloyd Osbourne. *The Ebb-Tide: A Trio and Quartette*. Ed. Roslyn Jolly. *Robert Louis Stevenson: South Sea Tales*. Oxford: Oxford UP, 1996.

—— *A Footnote to History: Eight Years of Trouble in Samoa*. London: Dawson, 1967.

—— 'The Foreigner at Home'. *Memories and Portraits*. New York: Scribner's, 1897.

—— 'In the Lightroom'. HM 2394. The Huntington Library. San Marino, CA.

—— *In the South Seas*. Ed. Neil Rennie. London: Penguin, 1998.

—— 'The Isle of Voices'. *South Sea Tales*. Ed. Roslyn Jolly. Oxford: Oxford UP, 1996.

—— *The Letters of Robert Louis Stevenson*. Eds. Bradford A. Booth and Ernest Mehew. Vols. 4-8. New Haven: Yale UP, 1994, 1995.

—— 'A Malaga in Samoa'. Beinecke ms. 6556. The Beinecke Rare Book and Manuscript Library, Yale U.

—— *The Master of Ballantrae; Weir of Hermiston*. Introd. M. R. Ridley. London: Dent, 1976.

—— 'Notes on Hawaii'. HM 20534. The Huntington Library. San Marino, CA.

—— 'Notes on the Movements of Young Children'. *The Vailima Edition of the Works of Robert Louis Stevenson*. Vol. 7 New York: Collier, 1912, 350-55.

—— 'Notes on Dr. [George] Turner's Voyage in 1876 [with data on several different islands, especially in the Tokelau, Ellice, and Gilbert groups] [c. 1890] [Samoa]'. HM 2398. The Huntington Library. San Marino, CA.

—— 'Photographs Taken by Lloyd Osbourne During Trip on the Schooner Equator, List of' Beinecke ms. 6716. The Beinecke Rare Book and Manuscript Library, Yale U.

—— 'A Plea for Gas Lamps'. *Virginibus Puerisque and Other Papers*. London: Chatto & Windus, 1905.

—— 'Random Memories'. *Across the Plains with Other Memories and Essays*. New York: Scribner's, 1896.

—— *Records of a Family of Engineers*. *The Letters and Miscellanies of Robert Louis Stevenson: Memoir of Fleeming Jenkin; Records of a Family of Engineers*. New York: Scribner's, 1905. 191-365.

—— 'A Samoan Scrapbook'. Beinecke ms. 6825. The Beinecke Rare Book and Manuscript Library, Yale U.

—— 'Something in It'. *South Sea Tales*. Ed. Roslyn Jolly. Oxford UP, 1996. 255-57.

—— *Strange Case of Dr. Jekyll and Mr. Hyde*. Toronto: Bantam, 1985.

—— *Treasure Island*. London: Heinemann, 1924.

—— and Lloyd Osbourne. *The Wrecker*. New York: Scribner's, 1913.

Strong, Isobel. Ms. letter to Charles Warren Stoddard. 20 April 1889. Honolulu. HM 37985. The Huntington Library. San Marino, CA.

Sutton, Martin. *Strangers in Paradise*. Sydney: Angus & Robertson, 1995.

'Tahitian Children'. *The Juvenile Missionary Magazine*. 8.87 (August, 1851): 172-73.

Thomas, Nicholas. *Entangled Objects: Exchange, Material Culture, and Colonialism in the Pacific*. Cambridge, MA: Harvard UP, 1991.

Thomson, John. 'Photography and Exploration'. *Proceedings of the Royal Geographical Society*. ns 13 (1891): 669-73.

Thurn, E. F. C.M.G. 'Anthropological Use of the Camera'. *Journal of the Anthropological Institute*. 22 (1893): 184-203.

Traprock, Walter E. *The Cruise of the Kawa: Wanderings in the South Seas*. New York: Putnam's, 1921.

Turner, George. Diary 1876. Ms. 168 LMS Archives. SOAS, U of London.

—— *Nineteen Years in Polynesia: Missionary Life, Travels, and Researches in the Islands of the Pacific*. London: John Snow, 1861.

—— *Samoa a Hundred Years Ago and Long Before together with notes on the cults and customs of twenty-three other islands in the Pacific.* London: Macmillan, 1884.

Turner, William Y. M.D. 'The Ethnology of the Motu'. LMS Archives. Reprinted from *Journal of the Anthropological Institute.* May, 1887: 1-29.

Tylor, Edward B. *Anthropology: An Introduction to the Study of Man and Civilization.* 1881. Ann Arbor: The U of Michigan P, 1960.

Whitmee, James. Correspondence. Box 42 LMS Archives. SOAS, U of London.

Williams, John. *A Narrative of Missionary Enterprises in the South Sea Islands; with remarks upon the natural history of the islands, origins, languages, traditions, and usages of the inhabitants.* London: John Snow, 1837.

Wilson, James. *A Missionary Voyage to the Southern Pacific Ocean. 1796-1798.* Craz/Austria: Akademische Druck u. Verlagasanstalt, 1996.

Wood, C. F. *A Yachting Cruise in the South Seas.* London: Henry S. King, 1875.

Index

(Robert Louis Stevenson is referenced as RLS throughout the index, except for his own main entry)

Adams, Henry 53
alienation, and memory 82-3
American Congregational Society 15
American Missionary Society 13
Anderson, Benedict, *Imagined Communities* 7
Andrews, Thomas 128
Anthropological Society, London 112
Apemama 3, 4, 112, 126
    dancers 113 (photo)
Apia 4, 6, 17, 19, 21, 23, 26, 33, 128, 135, 139-40, 141, 145, 155
    Sunday School 27 (photo)
Armstrong, Nancy 117-18
artifacts, collection, by LMS 73-8
assimilation, and clothing 49-50
Atkin, J. Rev. 78
Augustine, St. on memory 88-9, 96 n. 7
authority, and clothing 50

Baker, Shirley Waldemar 155, 174
Balfour, Graham (cousin, RLS) 139, 141, 144, 154
Balfour, Jane Whyte 53
Bartlett, Frederic C. 87
Baxter, Charles 54, 89, 114, 116, 125
beachcombers 18, 45 n. 6
Berlin Act (1899), Samoa 136, 144-5, 150
Bingham, Hiram Rev. 76
Blacklock, William 141, 154, 165,
167
Blake, William, *Songs of Experience* 193
Boer War, RLS on 142-3
Boodle, Adelaide 25, 91
Bournemouth 2, 180
Breach, Annie E. 123
British Western Pacific High Commissioner 144
Brown, George Rev. 31-3, 35, 40, 47 n. 14
    photograph 32
Buckland, Jack 113
Burlingame, Edward L. 118, 139, 165
Butaritari 3, 4, 31, 126

Calder, Jenni 5, 10 n.5, 181
Cameron, Duncan 5
Carroll, Lewis, 'How doth the little crocodile' 193-4
Catholics 14, 28, 45 n.3
    LMS, rivalry 15
    Samoa 16
Cedercrantz, Conrad 140, 141, 145, 146, 150, 151, 152, 156, 162
Chalmers, James Rev. 6, 31, 33-5, 39, 47 n. 14, 51, 60, 76, 101
    death 35
    Pioneer Life...New Guinea 16, 33, 34
Chambers, W.L. 26, 27 (photo)
Chappell, George S., *The Cruise of the Kawa...* 64, 67
children

and duty 193-5
movement 195-6
single voice 197-9
*The Chronicle of the London
    Missionary Society* 17, 20,
    74, 102
Clarke, W.E. Rev. 19, 20-1, 24, 28,
    31, 52, 54, 104, 105, 114,
    140, 155, 161, 163
Claxton, Arthur E. Rev. 55, 138
    dynamite plot 159-60
    libelling, by RLS 138, 155, 161-
        70
    Samoan Land Commission 158-
        9, 160
clothing
    and assimilation 49-50
    and authority 50
    as boundary markers 55
    and death 68-70
    and fantasy 50
    and identity 49
    natives, missionaries' attitudes to
        50-1
    RLS 49-50, 52-6, 62-3, 69-70
Colley, George, Sir 142
Colvin, Sidney 21, 26, 54, 58, 64,
    140, 141, 145-6, 147, 149,
    151, 152, 153, 165, 169
Contagious Disease Act 23-4
Conrad, Joseph 40
Contemporary Review 142
Cook Islands 12
cricket, Samoan playing 120 (photo)
Cusack-Smith, Thomas B., Sir 148,
    151, 152, 163

Daiches, David 172 n.3
Damien, Francis Rev. 46 n.11, 126,
    177 n.25
darkness metaphor, RLS 99-133
Darwin, Charles, *Voyage of the
    Beagle* 74
Davies, Samuel H. Rev. 5, 99
Davis, John 128

death, and clothing 68-70
Dickens, Charles 181
diorama 115-16
Dordillon, Fr 30-1
Doudney, A.H. 139, 158, 160
duty, and children 193-5

Edinburgh Women's Association
    182
Elias, Frank, *Boy's Adventure in the
    South Seas* 184
Ellice Islands 15, 91, 104
Ellis, William 12, 74, 76
    Polynesian Researches 13, 75,
        132 n.2
Erromango 13

Fakarava 3
Fangaloa 19, 20
fantasy, and clothing 50
fiction, South Seas 35-44
Findlay, A.G., *Directory...South
    Pacific Ocean* 3
foreignness
    and missionary culture 187-8
    and reciprocity 192-3
Furnas, J.C. 142

Galton, Francis 119
Geertz, Clifford 7
German Plantation Company 24
Germans, in Samoa 136, 138
Gilbert Islands 3, 15, 31, 110, 124
    dancing girls 125 (photo)
Gill, William W. 77, 80, 90
    *From Darkness to Light in
        Polynesia* 76, 132 n.2
    Life in the Southern Isles 75
Gilson, R.P. 155, 172 n.5
Gladstone, W.E. 142-3
Gordon, Charles, Gen. 143
Gosse, Edmund 135, 171
Greenaway, Kate 181
Gunson, Neil 13
Gurr, Edwin W. 162

Haggard, Bazett M. 140, 149
Half-Caste Club 60-1, 62
   illustration 61
Harper, I.P. 165
Harris, G.A. Rev. 19, 101
Hawaii 5, 13
Hedley, Charles 74
Henley, W.E. 143, 180, 188
Hepworth, T.C., *The Book of the*
     lantern... 126
Herbert, Christopher 78, 96 n. 2
Hervey Islands 17, 19, 101, 102
Hillier, Robert Irwin 40-1
Hills, John William Rev. 23, 46 n.
   11
Hiva-oa 5
Honolulu 23
   RLS in 3, 23, 138
Hume, David 88
Hyde, Rev. Charles M. 46 n.11, 177
   n.25

Ide, Henry Clay 30, 141
identity
   and clothing 49
   and memory 87-9
Illustrated London News 118
Imperato, Ferrante, Cabinet of
     Curiosities 84, 85 (illus)

James, Henry 105, 129, 151, 155
Jolly, Roslyn 40, 44
Juvenile Missionary Magazine 11,
    185, 186

Kalakaua, David (King of Hawaii)
    138, 139
Kingsley, Mary H. 129
Klein, John C. 138, 172 n.2
Kyllacky, Lady 91

La Farge, John, *Reminiscences of the*
    South Pacific 74, 161-2
Lamb, Jonathan (co-editor),
    Explorations and Exchange...

   7, 17
Lang, Andrew 91, 117
Large, A.E. Miss 26, 27 (photo)
Laupepa (King of Samoa) 136, 154,
    156, 159, 173 n. 8
lava-lava 58, 69
Lawson, Barbara 84
light
   imagery, RLS 106-12, 129-31
   intimidating use of 104-5
   metaphor, missionaries 99-100,
     106
   see also magic lantern
Livingstone, David 101
LMS (London Missionary Society)
    1, 12
   Catholics, rivalry 15
   memory, preservation 73-8
   Museum 78-81
   illustration 79
   native artifacts, collection 73-8
   Reports 102
   Samoa 15, 16, 17, 19-21
   'territory' 15-16
London Missionary Chronicle 52
Low, W.H. 109
Lysaght, S.R. 62, 72 n.11

McClure, Samuel S. 3, 4
McKay, Wallis, 'Niga and His
    Creed' 86
magazines, children's 182-3
magic lantern
   missionaries' use 100-4
   RLS 126-7
Maka, Robert 31, 34, 127
malaga 19, 123
Malie 154, 157
Malua Training Institution 20, 25,
    29, 30, 170
Manchester Courier 151
Mangaia 102
Manua 105
maraes 75
Marquesas 3, 5, 12, 14, 15, 26, 37,

90, 107, 124, 137

Marriott, J. Rev. 51, 100, 132, 165, 169, 170

Marshall Islands 3, 15

Massey, Irving 7

Mataafa (King of Samoa) 22, 60, 136, 141, 146, 150, 151, 152-3, 154, 156, 157, 158, 163, 167, 169, 173 n. 8

Melville, Herman, *Typee* 3

memory
    and alienation 82-3
    Augustine on 88-9, 96 n. 7
    decontextualization 84-7
    and identity 87-9
    mutability 92-5
    preservation, LMS 73-8
    RLS, experience of 89-95

Menikoff, Barry 14, 43, 47 n.17

Meredith, George 22

missionaries 12-13
    competition 14-17, 37
    foreignness, notion of 192-3
    light metaphor 99-100, 106
    magic lantern 100-4
    and natives' clothing 50-1
    and politics 155-7
    RLS
        criticism 21-5
        praise 26-31
    in South Seas fiction 35-9
    teaching institutions 20-1
    traders, rivalry 18-19, 36
    see also LMS

missionary culture 2
    and foreignness 187-8
    RLS 182-4

Missionary Herald 51

The Missionary News 182, 185

Moipu (Chief of Atuono) 123

Moors, H.J. 28, 53, 86, 135, 140, 160, 161, 163, 164, 165, 167, 176 n.24

Mormons 14
    Samoa 16

Murray, A.W., *The Martyrs of Polynesia* 15, 99

New Britain 33

New Caledonia 3, 91

New Guinea 15, 33, 35, 45 n.5, 47 n.14, 51, 76, 80, 88
    map 16

New Hebrides 3, 12, 15, 184

The New Zealand Herald 148, 151

Newell, James E. Rev. 20, 45-6 n.8, 52, 56, 64, 76, 77, 90, 96 n.6

Noumea 3

Nuka-hiva 54

Osbourne, Lloyd (stepson, RLS) 3, 24, 38, 54, 64, 69, 91, 113, 114, 115, 122-3, 124-5, 138
    as Marquesan warrior (photos) 65, 66

Papeete Bay 14

Partington, J. Edge, *Ethnographic Album of the Pacific* 74, 80, 88

Paumotus archipelago 14, 26, 109

Philological Society of London 77

Philosophical Society 77

photography
    at Vailima 127-9
    RLS 63-8, 112-25

Pilsach, Senfft von, Baron 145, 146, 147, 148, 151, 152, 159, 160

politics, and missionaries 155-7

Polynesian Society 76

Pomare II (Chief of Tahiti) 12

Port Moresby 77

Powell, T. Rev. 76

Pratt, G. Rev. 21
    Some Folk-Songs and Myths from Samoa 76

Presbyterian Church of NSW, General Assembly 18

Pritchard, G. Rev. 174 n.13, 186

Punch 148

The Quarterly Review 21

Rarotonga 79
  depopulation 74
Read, Charles H. 80-1
reciprocity, and foreignness 192-3
Reid, George, Sir 91
Reed, Julia 5
Reid, Mayne, Capt.
  The Boy Hunters 181
  The Bush-Boys 181
  The Young Voyageurs 181
Robertson, H.A. Rev. 84
Royal Anthropological Institute 77
Royal Geographical Society 6, 77
Rurutu 75
Ryle, Gilbert 7

Sabbatarians 24
St James's Gazette 148
Samoa 3, 6, 13
  Berlin Act (1899) 136, 144-5
  Catholics 16
  Chief Justice 144-5, 172 n. 5
  colonial powers 135-6
  Germans in 136, 138
  LMS 16, 17, 19-21
  Mormons 16
  politics, RLS 138-53
  Wesleyans 15, 17
Samoan District Committee 17, 165
Samoan Land Commission 138, 175
  n. 17
  and Rev. Claxton 158-9, 160
San Francisco 2
Sandison, Alan 47 n.19
Saranac Lake
  RLS at 2-3
  Stevenson Museum 70
Schultze, Wilhelmine Vanessa 165,
  166, 170
Scotland, South Seas, comparison 5,
  9 n. 4, 193
Scots, South Seas 5
Scribner's Magazine 141, 142

sea, and RLS 3
Sewall, Harold M. 152, 157, 162,
  166, 167, 168, 170
Siva 24, 46 n. 9
Smith, Thomas 131
Smith, Vanessa 12, 127
  (co-editor), *Explorations and
    Exchange...* 7, 17
SOAS (School of Oriental & African
  Studies) 1
Society Islands 12, 15
South Seas
  fiction 35-44
  missionaries 12-13
  RLS in 2-4
  Scotland, comparison 4, 9 n. 4,
    193
  Scots 5
Speculative Society of Edinburgh
  142
Stair, John Rev. 77, 104
Stevenson, Fanny (wife, RLS) 3, 9 n.
  1, 55, 60, 64, 72 n.16, 91,
  112, 144, 166
  The Cruise of the 'Janet Nichol'
    46 n.9, 116-17
  photographs 119, 122
Stevenson, Margaret (mother, RLS)
  3, 5, 26-7, 28, 53, 54, 62, 69,
  85, 102, 105, 129, 166, 182
  works
    *From Saranac to the
      Marquesas...* 14, 27,
      53, 54, 106, 112, 115,
      123
    Letters from Samoa 55, 60,
      107, 127, 128
Stevenson Museum, Saranac Lake
  70
Stevenson, Robert Louis
  barefoot 56 (photo)
  on the Boer War 142-3
  Claxton, Rev., libelling of 138,
    155, 161-70
  clothing 49-50, 52-6, 62-3, 69-70

formal 57-8, 60
darkness, metaphor 99-133
dressing up 62-3
and Empire 5-6, 29-30, 136-7
health 3
in Honolulu 3, 23, 138
illustration 56
light imagery 106-12, 129-31
magic lantern 126-7
memory, experience of 89-95
missionaries
    criticism 21-5
    praise 26-31
missionary culture 182-4
and particularity 6-8
photography 63-8, 112-17
    and writing 117-18
political imagination 137-8
red sash, symbolism 58
Samoa
    consulship, possibility 151-3
    politics 138-53
Saranac, Lake 2-3
and the sea 3
self-portrait 57
shoes 56-7
South Seas
    fiction 35-44
    reception 4-5
on Sudanese campaign 143-4
on traders 18
Vailima 58
    staff, photograph 59
works
    The Beach of Falesá 36-7,
        38, 41-3, 44, 57, 62,
        93, 94, 110, 111, 118,
        192
    'The Bottle Imp' 157
    Catriona 4
    'A Chapter on Dreams' 132
        n.8
    A Child's Garden of Verses 2,
        8, 111, 112, 130, 179-
        81, 184-9, 190-2, 193,

        194-200
    'Child's Play' 196
    The Complete Shorter Fiction
        137
    'Confessions of a Unionist'
        142
    'The Cow' (poem) 189
    'The Day After Tomorrow'
        142
    Dr Jekyll and Mr Hyde 2,
        109, 110, 130
    The Ebb-Tide 38, 39-40, 49,
        93, 118, 139, 147
    essays 2
    A Footnote to History 4, 93,
        135, 136, 137, 139-40,
        150, 151, 152, 153,
        157, 159, 164, 165, 190
    In the South Seas 4, 5, 6, 7,
        14, 21, 25, 26, 28, 30,
        31, 74, 90, 93-4, 107-
        8, 109, 111, 112, 118,
        122, 123, 124, 126,
        127, 130, 137
    An Inland Voyage 2, 93
    'The Isle of Voices' 38, 41,
        137, 168
    Kidnapped 2
    'The Lantern Bearers' 106
    Letters 5, 7, 13, 22, 24-5, 28,
        33, 35, 40, 54, 90, 92,
        106, 113, 114, 116,
        126, 139, 140, 142,
        146, 149, 151, 152,
        161, 163, 165, 180
    'Looking-Glass River'
        (poem) 199
    The Master of Ballantrae 4,
        62, 89, 109
    'On a New Form of
        Intermittent Light for
        Lighthouses' 131
    Our Samoan Adventure 107
    'A Plea for Gas Lamps' 106
    'Protest on Behalf of Boer

Independence' 143
Records of a Family of Engineers 131, 153
St. Ives 89
'Something in It' 38, 40-1, 91, 93
'The Swing' (poem) 191
'Travel' (poem) 184
travel writings 2
Treasure Island 2, 109
Underwood 180
Weir of Hermiston 4, 89, 142, 171
The Wrecker 93, 107, 109, 142, 147
writing habits 107
Stevenson, Thomas 91
Stewart, Robert 5
Stoddard, Charles, W. 86
Strong, Isobel (Osbourne) 3, 9 n.1, 60, 72 n.10, 128, 139
Strong, Joe 3, 114, 115, 116, 120 (photo), 126, 139
Sudan, campaign, RLS on 143-4
Swank, Herman 64, 67 (photo)
Sydney Morning Herald 151
Symonds, John Addington 143

Tahiti 3, 5, 12, 26, 37, 75
Tana 51
Tattersall, Alfred John 128
Tautira 3, 14
teaching institutions, missionaries 20-1
Tembinoka 5, 94, 111, 118, 124
Thiersens, J.C. 53
Thomas, Nicholas 84, 86 (co-editor), *Explorations and Exchange...* 7, 17
Thompson, Ralph W. Rev. 155, 156, 157, 158, 161, 170
Thurston, John, Sir 148, 152, 155, 163
The Times 138, 140, 143, 146, 148, 150, 153, 154, 156, 157

Tokelaus 146
Tonga 12
Torres Straits 15
traders
    missionaries, rivalry 18-19, 36
    RLS on 18
Tupou, George I (King of Tonga) 155
Turner, George Rev. 45 n.7, 51, 76, 112, 129
Turner, William Y. Rev. 77, 117

United States Consular Court 144
Upolu 3, 4, 13, 17, 135, 144, 145

Vailima (RLS household) 4, 6, 19, 91, 135
    livery 59 (photo), 60, 62
    photography at 63, 127-9
Vaipuhiahi, illustration 108
Vavau Islands 75
Victoria (Queen Victoria) 5-6, 10 n.6, 60, 104

Wachtmeister, Hans, Count 141
Wellington Evening Post 151
Wesleyan Missionary Society 23
Wesleyans 14
Samoa 15, 16, 17
Whitmee, S.J. Rev. 17, 76, 78, 132 n.4, 156, 157, 165, 170
Williams, John 12, 13, 74, 75, 76-7, 82, 91, 100-1, 174 n.10
    death 13
    watercolour 83
    works
        A Narrative of Missionary Enterprises 13, 58
Women's Missionary Association 18, 29
Wood, C.F., *Yachting Cruise in the South Seas* 68, 69
Writers' Museum, Edinburgh 64, 70

Zoological Society of London 77